Introduction to Dynamic Macroeconomic General Equilibrium Models

José L. Torres
Department of Economics
University of Málaga

VERNON PRESS

www.vernonpress.com
Vernon Press is an imprint of Vernon Art & Science Inc.

In the Americas:
Vernon Press
1000 N West Street,
Suite 1200, Wilmington,
Delaware 19801
United States

In the rest of the world:
Vernon Press
C/Sancti Espiritu 17,
Malaga, 29006
Spain

Library of Congress Control Number: 2014932232

Revised Edition, ISBN: 978-1-62273-024-7

Contents

PART IV The government

PART VI Imperfect competition

To Anelí and Carla

Preface

Dynamic General Equilibrium (DGE) models have become the fundamental tool in current macroeconomic analysis. Static models and partial equilibrium macroeconomic models could be useful in some applications but they are of limited value to study how the economy as a whole responds to a particular shock. The widespread use of DGE models in modern macroeconomic analysis reflects their usefulness as a "macroeconomic laboratory" that allow us to analyze how economic agents respond to changes in their environment, in a dynamic general equilibrium micro-founded theoretical setting in which all endogenous economic variables are determined simultaneously. Notwithstanding the approach's important shortcomings, DGE models are now in common use everywhere, from academic research to Central Banks and other public and private economic institutions. Though these models are probably too aggregated and include an awful lot of assumptions about the real world that are clearly too simplistic, they can be very useful to help understand some of the dynamics driving the economy.

This book offers an introductory step-by-step course to Dynamic Stochastic General Equilibrium (DSGE) modelling. Modern macroeconomic analysis is increasingly concerned with the construction, calibration and-or estimation, and simulation of DSGE models. DSGE models start from what we call the micro-foundations of macro-economics, with a heart based on the rational expectation forward-looking economic behavior of agents. The book is intended for graduate students as an introductory course to DSGE modelling and for those economists who would like a hands-on approach to learning the basics of modern dynamic macroeconomic modelling. While theoretical developments are not too complex to understand for the beginner in this topic, practical applications to the data is usually a more difficult task. Taking models to the data is now fortunately easier thanks to the development of specific DSGE modelling computer software. Once the theoretical model is on hands and the functions are parameterized, the next step is its application to the data. The usual procedure consists in the calibration of the parameters of the model using previous information or matching some key ratios or moments provided by the data, or more recently, from the estimation of the parameters using maximum likelihood or Bayesian techniques. Taking model to the data is a major barrier of entry that has to be paid by those who want to incorporate this state-of-the-art tool into their economic analysis. DSGE models cannot be solved analytically, except some very simple and unrealistic examples of limited interest. This is not a book about solution methods neither about estimation techniques.

The book starts with the simplest canonical neoclassical DSGE model and then gradually extends the basic framework incorporating a variety of additional features, such as consumption habit formation, non-Ricardian agents, investment adjustment costs, investment-specific technological change, taxes, public spending, public capital, human capital, household production, and monopolistic competition. All these additional features are introduced in the standard DSGE model separately in order to clearly identify the effects of each additional feature whereas keeping the model as simple as possible.

At the end of each chapter associated Dynare code is included with the model to be implemented in Matlab or Octave. Dynare is a very useful and powerful tool to deal with DSGE modelling. With the supply of minimal information regarding the calibration of the parameter and the equilibrium equations of the model, Dynare can solve a DSGE model, compute the steady state and carry out stochastic simulations of shocks in a very simple way. Dynare codes can also be downloaded from the book's homepage:

http://www.vernonpress.com/title.php?id=18

Finally, I would like to thank Dimitris Pontikakis, Gonzalo F-de-Córdoba, Jesús Rodríguez, Noelia Fernández and graduate students at the University of Málaga and University Pablo de Olavide (Seville), for their helpful comments and corrections of earlier versions of this book.

José L. Torres
Faraján (Málaga), January 2014

Part I

Introduction to DSGE modelling

Chapter 1

Introduction

The Dynamic Stochastic General Equilibrium (DSGE) approach is a cornerstone of modern macroeconomic analysis. The development of DSGE models in macroeconomics is mainly a response to two long-lasting challenges: The need to address the Lucas critique (Lucas, 1976) and the desire to build micro-founded macroeconomic models. Three main terms define this theoretical approach: Dynamic (D), Stochastic (S), and General Equilibrium (GE).

One of the objectives of economic analysis is to understand how an economy works and to carry out experiments to study the effects of a particular change or disturbance on the economy. This kind of analysis presents enormous difficulties due to the complexity of the phenomena we want to explain. In other fields such as physics or chemistry, which in some ways can be thought as analogous to economics, researchers have experimental laboratories in which to replicate the conditions that exist in the real world and thus, perform experiments using scale models. In fact, this has long been the goal of economic analysis; to build scale models of the real world with which to perform a number of experiments and to know in advance the effects of certain disturbances or changes in economic policies at the macroeconomic level.[1]

However, when we compare economics to either physics or chemistry we should keep in mind that although the analytical tools can be similar, there is an important difference: the human factor. In the economy, the effects of a particular disturbance will be determined by the decisions taken by economic agents and how they re-

[1] Most Central Banks and some other public and private institutions have recently developed Dynamic Stochastic General Equilibrium (DSGE) models as the basic tool for macroeconomic analysis and monetary and fiscal policy studies. Representative examples are the model of Sveriges Riksbank (RAMSES model) developed by Adolfson, Laseen, Lindé and Villani (2007); the New Area-Wide Model (NAWM) developed at the European Central Bank by Christofell, Coenen and Warne (2008); the model developed at the Federal Reserve Board by Edge, Kiley and Laforte (2008); the SIGMA model developed by Erceg, Guerrieri and Gust (2006); the MEDEA model developed by Burriel, Fernández-Villaverde and Rubio-Ramírez (2010); the REMS model by Boscá, Diaz, Domenech, Ferri, Perez and Puch (2010), among many other examples.

act to the disturbance. This difference between the economy and other experimental sciences is a major obstacle to the construction of macroeconomic laboratories in which to perform scale experiments that can subsequently be transferred to the real world.

Currently, macroeconomic analysis has a widely accepted theoretical scheme, the DSGE framework, which avails a scale model economy and, therefore, a laboratory in which to carry out experiments. This theoretical framework, initially developed by Ramsey in the late 1920s (Ramsey, 1927, 1928), has been widely adopted today as one of the main tools for macroeconomic modelling. DSGE models represent a scale model of the real world that can be considered as too aggregated and too simple, but very useful to study how the economy responds to different shocks or to quantify the effects of monetary and fiscal policy. The success of neoclassical DSGE models as the basic framework for macroeconomic analysis is based on the following three main characteristics that render that theoretical setting a valid representation of reality.

- First, the outcome of the model depends on the decisions taken by the economic agents. Instead of modelling markets, as has been done traditionally, the general equilibrium neoclassical model focuses on the behavior of three main types of economic agents: households, firms and the government, but it may include additional economic agents such as a central bank or the foreign sector. The basic idea is to determine the basic rules of behavior of the different economic agents and then observe how they react to changes in the environment. The equilibrium results from the combination of economic decisions taken by all economic agents.

- Second, it is a general equilibrium model. For a macroeconomic model to be a valid replica of an economy, such a model must consider the multiple and complex relationships between the different economic variables. In reality, all macroeconomic variables are related to each other, either directly or indirectly, so we must abandon that pipe dream of "ceteris paribus", which does nothing but hinder our understanding of how the economy works.

- Finally, it is a dynamic model in which time plays a fundamental role. This ingredient is very important, because when a disturbance hits the economy, macroeconomic variables do not return to the equilibrium instantaneously, but they change very slowly over time, producing complex reactions in the economy as a whole. Furthermore, in our model economy we need to consider investment decisions, which are of great importance for the economy but only makes sense in a dynamic context.

Macroeconomic DSGE Modelling

The general strategy used by current applied macroeconomics for both disturbance and policy analysis and forecasting, is the construction of formal structures through equations that reflect the interrelationships between the different economic variables. These simplified structures is what we call a model. The essential question here is not that these theoretical constructions are realistic descriptions of the economy, but that they are able to explain the dynamics observed in the economy.

After a long period characterized by a deep rift between macroeconomics and microeconomics, current developments in macroeconomics are based on the microeconomic analysis of economic agents decisions. It is not intended that macroeconomics goes down to the decisions of individual consumers or firms, but it is important that macroeconomic theoretical frameworks be consistent with the underlying behavior of millions of consumers and millions of firms that inhabit an economy, and in this sense we speak about the microfoundations of modern macroeconomics. These microfoundations have created a rigorous formal theoretical setting that we call modern macroeconomics, the workhorse of which is the neoclassical growth model based on Ramsey.

Modern macroeconomics uses formal and rigorous models in order to provide explanations of different problems observed in real economies, with the aim to offer solutions or policy recommendations to prevent these problems or alleviate their consequences on social welfare. Current macroeconomics is formalized through mathematical models and subject to the traditional scientific method of measurement, theory and validation. Measurement, which is a description of the facts, is a necessary step of any economic analysis, but the description of an observed phenomenon does not itself constitute an explanation of it. For that a second step is necessary: the development of a theory. Although data can be tortured using a large variety of statistical and econometric techniques, they will not confess. Data will only speak through theoretical models. The third step is the hardest. The theoretical models are based on abstract assumptions which represent a simplification of reality, but the important thing is that they can be useful to offer a valid explanation of an economic fact. Therefore, it is not possible to reject a model *ex ante* because it is based on assumptions that we believe not too realistic. Rather, the validation must be based on the usefulness of these models to explain reality, and whether they are more useful than other models (Canova, 2007).

Our macroeconomic laboratory consists of a DSGE model (and a computer with appropriate software). This model economy is a necessary simplification of reality. The reason we trust them is easy to understand. Think of a street plan. A street plan is a simplification of a city, but it is an extremely useful tool to move in it. A street plan includes a number of non-real assumptions: The scale is different to the real one, is a two-dimensional representation of a three-dimensional space, is totally flat, etc. The lack of realism of a street plan does not hinder its effectiveness. What makes street plans useful is the proper matching of symbolic elements on the plan with the actual layout of the elements to which the plan refers. In the same way, the degree of realism offered by an economic model is not a goal to be pursued by macroeconomists, but rather the model's usefulness in explaining macroeconomic reality.

Overall, the structure of a macroeconomic model is similar to those models used to explain the behavior of a physical system, except for one important difference: the behavior of the economy depends on decisions taken by humans. In a physical system, the particles are neutral with respect to the laws driving their dynamics and interactions. In the economy, particles (economic agents) have theories about how the system they belong to works, and they make decisions that affect the dynamics of the system.

The basic structure of a macroeconomic model can be defined in terms of the following system of equations:

$$X_t = E_t\left[F(X_{t+1}, Z_t, u_t)\right] \tag{1.1}$$

where X_t is a vector of endogenous variables, Z_t a vector of exogenous variables, E_t is the expectation operator, and u_t is a vector of random disturbances with proper density functions. The function $F(\cdot)$ is what we call economic theory. The solution to this system of stochastic equations would be a sequence of probability distributions. This system of equations contains a key element: the value of the endogenous variables in a given period of time depends on its future expected value.

The use of theoretical models to describe and understand the behavior of an economy is important for a variety of reasons:

1. First, theoretical models are important to understand the complex relationships between macroeconomic variables which cannot be observed just by looking directly at the data. Data only speaks through models.

2. Theoretical models introduce a metric to talk about the economy in commonly understandable terms and to define non-observable variables, such as the marginal productivity of capital, or state variables, such as total factor productivity.

3. Theoretical models can be used to make simulations for policy analysis and counterfactual experiments.

4. Finally, forecasting is only possible by using a theoretical model (structural forecasting approach).

As discussed above, macroeconomic analysis depends on the availability of a laboratory in which an artificial economy can be simulated in an attempt to replicate certain phenomena we observe in reality. This artificial economy is based on the construction of a theoretical macroeconomic model. The main theoretical framework we use in current macroeconomic analysis is the neoclassical dynamic general equilibrium growth model. The basis of this model is not new, as it was developed by Ramsey in the late 1920s. This model is easy to understand: it is an economy in which there are three (although they may be other economic agents) types of economic agents: households, firms, and the government (only the first two in the simplest version). Households take decisions in terms of how much to consume (save) and how much time is devoted to work (leisure). Firms decide how much they will produce. Equilibrium of the economy will be defined by a situation in which all decisions taken by all economic agents are compatible and feasible.

With this theoretical framework at hand it is possible to obtain numerical solutions for the steady state and for the dynamics of the variables by calibrating or estimating the model for a given economy. National Accounts will provide the necessary information to calibrate or estimate the parameters of the model. Therefore, there must be a direct correspondence between National Accounts and the DSGE model. If this is the case, we already have our macroeconomic laboratory.

DSGE software

DSGE modelling requires the use of numerical solution methods. This means that once a particular DSGE model has been built up, to make it quantitatively operative, we need software and hardware. Taking theoretical models to the computer is a compulsory step for DSGE modelling. Whereas in the past this was a very difficult task, currently we can find a large number of publicly available software tools for DSGE modelling written in different computer languages, such as Matlab, R, Gauss, Mathematica, C, etc. Most of these tools can be found in DSGE-NET, which is an International Network for DSGE modelling, monetary and fiscal policy,[2] or in the QM&RBC (Quantitative Macroeconomics and Real Business Cycle) page by Christian Zimmermann.[3] General software platforms for DSGE modelling are, for instance, Dynare, gEcon and IRIS.

Dynare is a pre-processor that uses a very simple language that allows the conversion of a DSGE model in a program that can be implemented in various programming languages (Matlab or Octave) to solve, estimate and simulate the model.[4] The source syntax is very friendly and simple. We only need to provide the set of endogenous variables, the set of exogenous variables, the parameters, the value of the parameters and the equations of the model. This software platform can use data to estimate the parameters of DSGE model, using both maximum likelihood or Bayesian techniques. Dynare has been developed at CEPREMAP, by a team directed by Michel Julliard, Stéphane Adjemian and Sébastien Villemot. This is the tool used in this book.

Another software tool for solving DSGE models is gEcon.[5] This tool has been developed in R by the Department for Strategic Analyses at the Chancellery of the Prime Minister of the Republic of Poland by Grzegorz Klima, Karol Podemski and Kaja Retkiewicz-Wij-

[2]http://www.dsge.net

[3]http://dge.repec.org

[4]http://www.dynare.org

[5]http://gecon.r-forge.r-project.org

tiwiak. The main characteristic of gEcon is that the model can be solved directly by writing the optimization problems for the economic agents. That is, it is not necessary to derive first order conditions and equilibrium equations. gEcon implements an algorithm for automatic derivation of first order conditions, steady state and linearization matrices.

Finally, IRIS is a toolbox in Matlab for macroeconomic modelling and forecasting, developed by the IRIS Solutions Team since 2001, headed by Jaromír Beneš.[6] IRIS can solve, simulate, and estimate (using maximum likelihood methods) a DSGE model. Forecasting using the structural model is also allowed.

Book organization

All chapters in this book follow a similar structure. In each chapter a particular DSGE model is developed, introducing a relevant topic in the basic DSGE model. Equilibrium conditions are obtained and parameters calibrated. Then, we study the effects of a shock and compute impulse-response functions of the macroeconomic variables. This exercise is done using Dynare for Matlab. Each chapter includes an appendix with the corresponding Dynare code.

Chapter 2 presents the basic dynamic general equilibrium model, considering the behavior of two economic agents: Households and firms. Here we show the basic structure of the model used in current macroeconomics. The structure of this model is very simple (although even simpler versions are possible). Households make decisions about how much to consume (how much to save) and how many hours they will devote to work (or to leisure), given the price of the production factors, in order to maximize lifetime utility. Firms decide how much labor and capital will be hired to maximize profits. Once equilibrium of the model economy is obtained and the parameters calibrated, this framework can be used to perform a variety of simulation exercises. In our setting, the simulation exercise will study how the economy responds to an aggregate productivity shock, that is, the prototype RBC analysis.

Chapter 3 introduces consumption habit formation as an extension to the basic DSGE model developed in the previous chapter. In the standard neoclassical DSGE model, utility function is instantaneous time-separable. This means that current utility only de-

[6] http://www.iris-toolbox.com

pends on current consumption and does not depend on the level of consumption in previous periods. However, empirical evidence shows the existence of habit formation which implies that utility function is not time-separable. This can explain one observed deviation from the permanent income-life cycle hypothesis: the excess smoothness of consumption with respect to changes in income.

Chapter 4 develops a DSGE model in which a portion of the population cannot make optimal decisions regarding their consumption path because they cannot borrow, that is, they cannot bring future income to the current period. This is the case when there are liquidity constraints and imperfect financial markets. The purpose of introducing liquidity constraints is to explain another observed deviation from the permanent income-life cycle hypothesis: The excess sensitivity of consumption to current income. The model assumes that the economy is composed of two types of agents: Ricardian agents, who have no liquidity constraints and can take optimal decisions regarding consumption-saving path, and non-Ricardian agents, who are subject to liquidity constraints, and consumption of each period is restricted by their income in that period. The aggregate behavior of the economy is given by the weighted sum of the behavior of each group of agents.

Chapter 5 takes into account the existence of adjustment costs in the investment process, taking as reference the Tobin's Q theory. Variations in the physical capital stock of the economy are subject to adjustment costs that could be important in explaining investment decisions. These costs may be associated to the existing capital stock and/or to investment. The DSGE model developed in this chapter considers the existence of adjustment costs associated with investment. The simulation exercise will show how investment decisions react to a Total Factor Productivity shock when investment adjustment costs are present.

Chapter 6 studies the role of investment-specific technological progress. Standard DSGE model considers a single source of technological progress: Total Factor Productivity changes or neutral technological progress. However, physical capital assets are not homogeneous over time and new vintages of capital assets are an important source of technological progress. New capital assets incorporate an improved technology compared to previously existing assets. This type of technological progress is associated to the investment process. The model includes two types of technological change: total factor productivity (TFP) or neutral technological change and investment-specific technological (ISTC) change.

Chapter 7 introduces a new economic agent in the basic DSGE model: The government. The government can be introduced in the standard DSGE model is a large variety of ways. This chapter considers the role of the government as a tax-levying entity. In particular, the model incorporates three types of taxes: consumption tax, labor income tax, and capital income tax. For simplicity, it is assumed that the government returns fiscal revenues as lump-sum transfers. A number of exercises are conducted using this theoretical framework: computation of Laffer curves, changes in taxes, and a productivity shock.

Chapter 8 continues with the role of the public sector, but incorporating to the previous model the existence of public spending. In this model the households' utility depends not only on their consumption of private goods, but also depends on the consumption of goods provided by the government (public consumption). The key element of this analysis is to determine how public consumption affects agents utility relative to private consumption. We use this model to study the effects of a change in public consumption.

Chapter 9 considers the role of the public sector from another point of view: as a provider of public inputs. In this context, the production function of the economy does not only depend on the quantity of private production factors but also on the amount of public capital. A proportion of fiscal revenues is investment in physical public capital. In this setting we study the effects of a change in public investment.

Chapter 10 focuses on the role of human capital to study business cycle properties of education. The chapter develops a DSGE model in which skill acquisition activities are endogenous. Discretionary available time can be used for three activities: leisure, work and education. Households decide how much time to devote to education and skill acquisition. Investment in education is then transformed into human capital stock. This model is used to study how skill acquisition activities are affected by the business cycle.

Chapter 11 introduces home production in the standard DSGE model. In this setting available time is divided into three parts: leisure, work and time spent on home activities. Households want to consume two types of goods: market goods and goods produced at home. This is a two-sector model where market production can used either for consumption or investment, while domestic production of goods can only be consumed. In this context we will study the effects of productivity shocks in both sectors and the nature of the interaction between working time and time devoted to home production.

Finally, Chapter 12 considers the existence of imperfect goods markets, developing a DSGE model in a context of monopolistic competition. The model considers the existence of two production sectors: an intermediate goods sector and a final goods sector. In the intermediate goods sector there are a number of monopolistic firms, each producing a differentiated good. Each firm has the power to determine the price of the good it produces. Perfect competition in the final good sector is assumed, so there is a firm that aggregates intermediate goods into a final production good. As a consequence the prices of production factors do not correspond to their marginal productivity.

Bibliography

Adolfson, M., Laséen, S., Lindé, J. and Villani, M. (2007): RAMSES, a new general equilibrium model for monetary policy analysis, *Economic Review*, 2, Riskbank.

Boscá, J. Díaz, A., Doménech, R., Ferri, J, Pérez, E. and Puch, L. (2010): A rational expectations model for simulation and policy evaluation of the Spanish economy. *SERIEs*, 1(1-2), 135-169.

Burriel, P., Fernández-Villaverde, J. and Rubio-Ramírez, J. (2010): MEDEA: a DSGE model for the Spanish economy. *SERIEs*, 1(1-2), 175-249.

Christoffel, K., Coenen, G. and Warne, A. (2008). The new area-wide model of the euro area - a micro-founded open-economy model for forecasting and policy analysis, *European Central Bank Working Paper Series* n. 944.

Canova F. (2007): *Methods for Applied Macroeconomic Research*. Princeton University Press.

Edge, R., Kiley, M. and Laforte, J.P. (2008): Natural rate measures in an estimated DSGE model of the U.S. economy. *Journal of Economic Dynamics and Control*, 32(8), 2512-2535.

Erceg, C., Guerrieri, L. and Gust, C. (2006): SIGMA: A new open economy model for policy analysis. *International Journal of Central Banking*, 2(1), 1-50.

Lucas, R. (1976): Econometric Policy Evaluation: A Critique. In Brunner, K., Meltzer, A. (Eds.), *The Phillips Curve and Labor Markets*. Carnegie-Rochester Conference Series on Public Policy 1. New York, 19–46.

Ramsey, F. (1927): A contribution to the theory of taxation. *Economic Journal*, 37(145), 47-61.

Ramsey, F. (1928): A mathematical theory of saving. *Economic Journal*, 38(152), 543-559.

Chapter 2

The Canonical Dynamic Macroeconomic General Equilibrium model

Introduction

This chapter describes the main characteristics of the canonical Dynamic General Equilibrium (DGE) model used in current macroeconomic analysis. The basis of this model was initially developed by Ramsey in the late 1920s (Ramsey, 1927, 1928). More recently, Cass (1965), Koopmans (1965), and Brock and Mirman (1972) made further contributions in the same direction. However, the Dynamic Stochastic General Equilibrium (DSGE) revolution in macroeconomics started in the 1980s, thanks to the possibilities offered by ever-increasing computing power. The last phase of this macroeconomic revolution started with the seminal work by Kydland and Prescott (1982), who established DSGE models as the central working tool in modern macroeconomic analysis. Although the initial developments focused on growth, this theoretical framework emerged as the keystone of macroeconomic analysis when it was applied to the business cycle with the birth of the so-called Real Business Cycle (RBC) analysis.

Starting from a simple initial canonical theoretical framework, the scale of DSGE models has grown over time, particularly during the late 1990s and the early 2000s, with the incorporation of a large number of New Keynesian features.[1] Recently, there has been an important increase in the size of DSGE models with the introduction of many nominal and real rigidities. This has led to the emergence of so-called New Keynesian economics in contrast to New Classical economics. New Keynesian models have the same foundations as New Classical general equilibrium models, but incorpo-

[1] However, as pointed out by Diebold (1998) the scale of DSGE models should be as small as possible for two reasons. Firstly, the demise of large-scale macroeconomic models has shown that bigger models are not necessarily better. Secondly, the parameters of DSGE models need to be jointly estimated, which places a limit on their complexity.

rate different types of rigidities in the economy. This new school of economic thought was introduced by Rotemberg and Woodford (1997). Whereas New Classical DSGE models are constructed on the basis of a perfect competition environment, New Keynesian models include additional elements to the basic classical framework, such as imperfect competition, the existence of adjustment costs in the investment process, liquidity constraints, or rigidities in the determination of prices and wages. This makes New Keynesian models far more complex than New Classical models, despite them having the same basis: the microfoundation of the behavior of economic agents.

The basic structure of the prototypical DSGE model is relatively simple. This chapter describes the behavior of the two types of agents that exist in a closed economy without government: consumers, households, or families on the one hand, and firms on the other. This basic structure can be enriched by adding, for example, the government, the foreign sector, or a central bank. The key aspect of DSGE models is that they are based on the microeconomic behavior of forward-looking rational expectations agents. That is what we call the microfoundations of macroeconomics. The idea is to reduce our economy to the interaction of just one (representative) consumer and one (representative) firm. If this average consumer represents all the consumers in the economy, the aggregate variables are obtained by simply multiplying the decisions of this average consumer by the number of consumers. The same procedure holds in the case of firms. In reality there are a huge number of consumers or households (millions of agents) and we can simply assume that they are identical in preferences, thus making aggregation possible. This allows us to talk about the representative household. There are also a large number of firms (millions of agents) and we assume that they have identical technology. Similarly, this allows us to speak about the representative firm.

As the analysis is dynamic and thus time plays a role, an important element in the construction of DSGE models is the definition of lifetime of the different economic agents. By lifetime we mean the period of time that the agent takes as the reference for making economic decisions. Let's assume that firms and the government both have infinite life. Obviously, we know that in reality firms and governments have finite life, i.e., current firms and governments will disappear at a given moment in the near future. A glance at history shows that no government or firm established 2000 years ago still exists. What is really meant is that firms and governments both use the infinite time as the reference period for taking economic decisions. No government thinks it will cease to exist at some point in the future, and no entrepreneur takes decisions based on the idea that the firm will go bankrupt sometime in the future.

The assumption about consumer lifetime is a little more difficult. Although we can assume that consumer life is finite or infinite, in the present framework we also assume that consumers have infinite life.[2] If this causes problems, we can think about families or households rather than consumers. And yes, we can assume that the life of a family is infinite. Just remember that you are alive because for thousands of years all of your ancestral families lived at least until childbearing age. This means that all your relatives were all alive and that your family, as represented by you, is still alive. In any case, if we want to study the life cycle of an agent as finite, the so-called Overlapping Generations (OLG) models are more suitable.

The result of the interaction of different agents is what we call General Equilibrium. Each agent takes economic decisions based on the maximization of an objective function. We call this function utility or felicity in the case of households and profits in the case of firms. As we assume the existence of a perfect competition environment, the outcome is what we call Competitive General Equilibrium.

In this chapter we first study the dynamic general equilibrium model in a deterministic context. Later, we define the model in a stochastic environment. In practice we can add different types of disturbances to the deterministic structure of the model. The most common disturbance is a total factor productivity or neutral technological shock. However, other shocks can be added, such as technological change specific to investment, shocks in preferences, consumption shocks, labor supply shocks, etc.

The rest of the chapter is structured as follows. Section 2 begins by studying the behavior of households, consisting in the maximization of their utility function subject to the budget constraint. We assume that this utility function depends positively on consumption and leisure, where leisure is defined as the discretionary time

[2]The infinity of time refers to the termination or transversality condition. If we assume a finite number of periods, the stock of capital in the last period should be equal to zero (for maximization). However, this would give us a path of capital stock not so realistic. In contrast, the temporal path of capital would be more realistic if time is considered as infinite.

available minus working time. From the intertemporal maximization of this objective function we obtain a set of equations describing the behavior of consumers in terms of their consumption-saving decisions and the labor supply (leisure-work decisions). Section 3 studies the behavior of firms, under the assumption of a competitive environment in which, by definition, all firms are identical. This means that all the firms' decisions are restricted to the same technology and so we can again use the concept of representative agent, i.e., we study the behavior of a representative firm. The problem of the firm is to find optimal values for the production factors, physical capital and labor, in order to maximize profits, taking the price of the production inputs as given. Section 4 presents the equilibrium of the model, which is defined in two alternative environments: a competitive market and a centrally planned economy. As agents' decisions are not subject to distortions in this basic framework, both environments lead to the same results. The steady state of the model economy is calculated in Section 5. Section 6 presents a stochastic version of the model by simply adding some shocks to the deterministic structure. The resolution of the stochastic model appears in Appendix B. Section 7 shows the equations of the model and the calibration of the parameters. Section 8 shows the impulse response functions of the model variables following a total factor productivity shock. Some conclusions are presented at the end of the chapter.

Households

Let's start by studying the behavior of households, families or consumers. The economy is populated by millions of households and each one takes economic decisions. To analyze these individual economic decisions we use the concept of a representative agent and assume that all agents have identical preferences. This allows us to analyze the behavior of one of them and then add. In addition, we have to make a set of assumptions about how these preferences are.

The next assumption is that the representative agent is an optimizer, i.e., he/she maximizes a given objective function. The objective function for consumers is what we call the instantaneous utility function. In general, we can consider that an individual's happiness is composed of three elements: health, money, and love (not necessarily in this order). As we are talking about the economy, we will focus on money. This concept of money is an abstraction of all the economic factors involved in an individual's happiness that will be the arguments of its utility function. In general, these arguments are the consumption of goods and services, real balance holdings, and leisure.

The first object to be defined is the utility function. Let us assume that utility or happiness depends on two elements: consumption, C, and leisure, O. Consumption refers to the amount of goods and services consumed by an individual, while leisure is the time available for the individual not spent in working. The household will take decisions about the variables under its control to maximize utility. The maximization of the objective function is carried out subject to a resource restriction, which we call the budget constraint. In summary, to define consumer behavior we only need to specify two objects: the utility function and the budget constraint.

The utility function can be written as:

$$U(C,O) \tag{2.1}$$

where $U(\cdot)$ is a mathematical function representing individual utility and that must satisfy the following conditions:

$$U_C > 0, \qquad U_O > 0 \tag{2.2}$$

that is, the first derivative with respect to both consumption and leisure is positive. This means that both variables have a positive effect on the level of happiness of the individual. The higher the level of consumption or leisure, the higher the level of utility or felicity. In other words, we are simply assuming that people want to consume a lot (they want to earn large amounts of money) with little work (much more leisure). In contrast, the second derivative is negative, such that:

$$U_{CC} < 0, \qquad U_{OO} < 0 \tag{2.3}$$

which means that the utility function is concave in both arguments. That is, higher consumption implies greater utility, but at a decreasing rate. The assumption of concavity in the utility function is a fundamental element in our analysis and is based on human nature. Note that this property is important for survival. The only animals that may have a non-concave utility function are aquarium fishes, which keep consuming food until they die of indigestion.

A further assumption is that the utility function is additively separable in time and is assumed just for convenience, as it makes the problem more mathematically tractable. This is the reason why we speak about the instantaneous utility function. This implies that the consumer's utility over a period of time simply depends on consumption and leisure during this period. Therefore, in a dynamic setting, we can add one period's utility to another period's utility.

The second object to be defined is the budget constraint. In order to specify the household budget constraint we must first introduce property rights. In particular, we have to specify who is the productive factors' owner. In our economy there are two production factors: labor, L_t, and physical capital, K_t. There is no question in the case of labor. Labor comes from the available endowment of time of each individual. In fact, time cannot be saved or accumulated and this is the reason why labor decisions will be static. In addition to labor, we assume that households are also the owners of capital stock as they will transform savings into investment and investment into capital. Thus, household income comes from renting both productive factors to the production sector of the economy at given rental prices. The households can do two things with these earnings: income can be expended in consumption or can go into savings.

The budget constraint can be defined as:

$$P_t(C_t + S_t) \leq W_t L_t + R_t K_t \tag{2.4}$$

where P_t is the price of final output, S_t is savings, W_t is the wage defined in terms of consumption units, and R_t is the capital rate or return, that is, the user cost of capital which is also a relative price defined in terms of consumption units. The human rent is given by $W_t L_t$, that is, the wage multiplied by the fraction of discretionary time devoted to working activities. Non-human rent, $R_t K_t$, comes from the rent of capital. P_t is the price of the final output which is measured in units of consumption and, to simplify matters, is normalized to one, $P_t = 1$.[3] The right side of the above expression de-

[3]Note that both wages and the rental rate of capital are defined in real terms, that is, in units of consumption. In fact, the budget constraint can also be written as:

$$C_t + S_t \leq \frac{W_t}{P_t} L_t + \frac{R_t}{P_t} K_t$$

scribes the resources available, whereas the left side describes the uses.

At this point, we need an additional equation: the process of accumulation of physical capital over time. We will use the simple inventory accumulation equation:

$$K_{t+1} = (1-\delta)K_t + I_t \tag{2.5}$$

where I_t is (gross) investment and $\delta > 0$ is the depreciation rate of physical capital. As this parameter is assumed to be positive, i.e., part of gross investment that takes place in a period is devoted to the replacement of capital that depreciates between periods. In reality, capital stock is composed of a variety of different types of assets, which have different characteristics and, therefore, have different rates of depreciation. Some capital assets have very low depreciation rates, such as buildings, and other types with very high depreciation rates, such as software or computers. So, the value of δ depends on the proportion of each type of capital asset over the aggregate capital stock.

To keep things simple, we assume that there is a competitive sector that transforms savings directly into investment without any cost. Thus:

$$S_t = I_t \tag{2.6}$$

Having defined the utility function, the budget constraint, the capital accumulation process and the technology transforming saving into investment, the next step is to define the household's dynamic maximization problem. The aim of households is to maximize the sum of discounted utilities over their lifetime (be happy not only today but for ever). Given the assumption about the time-separable utility function, the intertemporal maximization problem of the individual would be given by:[4]

$$\max_{(C_t,O_t)} E_t \sum_{t=0}^{\infty} \beta^t U(C_t, O_t) \tag{2.7}$$

$$s.t. \quad C_t + I_t = W_t L_t + R_t K_t \tag{2.8}$$

[4] Note that the household's utility function is in fact:

$$U(C_0, C_1, ..., C_\infty, O_0, O_1, ..., O_\infty)$$

with $K_0 > 0$ and where $E_t(\cdot)$ is the mathematical expectation operator of future variables at time t, subject to all available information at that time and where β is the intertemporal discount factor, $\beta \in (0,1)$, being:

$$\beta = \frac{1}{1+\theta} \tag{2.9}$$

where θ is the intertemporal subjective rate of preference ($\theta > 0$). This parameter indicates how much an individual values his/her future utility compared to his/her current utility. The greater the value of this parameter the lower the valuation of future utility in relation to current utility. This parameter can be interpreted as to what extent the individual is concerned about the future. The discount factor is based on a characteristic associated with human nature, i.e., we discount the future or, in other words, we value the present more than the future. A value of θ close to zero means that the individual is very concerned about the future (he/she rarely discounts the future). The opposite would be true for a large value of θ. In real life, we would expect this parameter to differ between individuals. At an aggregate level, we would also expect different values for the intertemporal subjective rate of preferences among economies.

The household maximization problem can be written as follows:

$$\max_{(C_0,C_1,...,C_\infty,O_0,O_1,...,O_\infty)} U(C_0,O_0)+\beta E_0 U(C_1,O_1)+\beta^2 E_0 U(C_2,O_2)$$
$$+\beta^3 E_0 U(C_3,O_3)+...+\beta^\infty E_0 U(C_\infty,O_\infty) \tag{2.10}$$

The weight of the future utility function, for a value of $\beta = 0.97$ (as an example), is plotted in Figure 2.1. This is a decreasing function as the weight of future utility is lower as we move away in time. When the number of periods is large enough, the weight reaches zero, as we assume that $\beta < 0$.

To solve the above problem, we first define the functional form of the utility function, that is, we use a specific utility function. We can solve the model using an unspecified utility function and thus arrive at general equilibrium conditions. However, as the model needs to be calibrated and solved numerically, the specification of a particular utility function is a compulsory step. In practice, several functional forms for the consumers' utility function can be used. Specifically, we assume a logarithmic utility function in both consumption and leisure as the following:

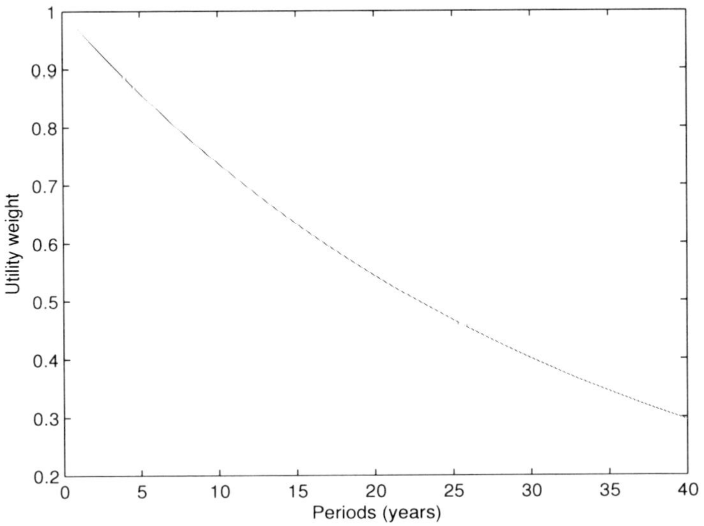

Figure 2.1: Utility weight with $\beta = 0.97$

$$U(C_t, O_t) = \gamma \log C_t + (1-\gamma)\log(N_t \overline{H} - L_t) \tag{2.11}$$

where $\gamma \in (0,1)$, is the proportion of consumption, N_t is the total population (in general, it refers to a population between 16 and 65 years old, that is, the working-age population), and $\overline{H}$ is the total discretionary available time in hours, a constant which is approximately 4,992 hours per year (16 hours per day × 6 days per week × 52 weeks per year, as it is assumed that we need 8 hours of sleep per day and there are only six working days by week). Leisure is defined as the total available discretionary time less working time. Total available discretionary time is normalized to $N_t \overline{H} = 1$, so:

$$O_t + L_t = 1 \tag{2.12}$$

The consumer's maximization problem can be defined then as:

$$\max_{(C_t, I_t, O_t)} \mathscr{L} = E_t \sum_{t=0}^{\infty} \beta^t \left[\gamma \log C_t + (1-\gamma)\log(1-L_t)\right] \tag{2.13}$$

subject to the budget constraint:

$$C_t + I_t = W_t L_t + R_t K_t \tag{2.14}$$

where I_t is derived from the capital accumulation equation:

$$I_t = K_{t+1} - (1-\delta) K_t \tag{2.15}$$

and therefore, the budget constraint can be written as:

$$C_t + K_{t+1} - (1-\delta) K_t = W_t L_t + R_t K_t \tag{2.16}$$

The consumer problem can be solved, for instance, through dynamic Lagrangian calculation:

$$\max_{(C_t,K_t,L_t)} \mathcal{L} = E_t \sum_{t=0}^{\infty} \beta^t \left\{ \begin{array}{c} \gamma \log C_t + (1-\gamma) \log(1-L_t) \\ -\lambda_t \left[C_t + K_{t+1} - K_t - W_t L_t - (R_t - \delta) K_t \right] \end{array} \right\} \tag{2.17}$$

where λ_t is the Lagrange parameter. From this problem we obtain the optimum path for consumption and the labor supply for each period, given the relative prices of the productive factors, i.e., wages and the rental rate of capital.[5]

When maximizing the above problem we must note that the budget restriction is defined for each period and therefore the restric-

[5]Although the household maximization problem as defined in the text is theoretically correct, in computational terms the time subscripts for the capital stock accumulation process would be different. To obtain a quantitatively consistent model, investment must be transformed to capital stock in the same period, as this amount cannot disappear from the economy and then return in the next period. To avoid this problem, we simply set the capital accumulation equation as:

$$K_t = (1-\delta) K_{t-1} + I_t$$

while the budget constraint is defined as:

$$C_t + I_t = W_t L_t + R_t K_{t-1}$$

In this case, the auxiliar Lagrangian function for the consumer maximization problem can be defined as:

$$\max_{(C_t,K_t,L_t)} \mathcal{L} = \sum_{t=0}^{\infty} \beta^t \left\{ \begin{array}{c} \gamma \log C_t + (1-\gamma) \log(N_t \overline{H} - L_t) \\ -\lambda_t \left[C_t + K_t - K_{t-1} - W_t L_t - (R_t - \delta) K_{t-1} \right] \end{array} \right\}$$

tion faced by the consumer at time t is the following:

$$\begin{aligned}&\ldots - \beta^{t-1}\lambda_{t-1}\left[C_{t-1} + K_t - K_{t-1} - W_{t-1}L_{t-1} - (R_{t-1} - \delta)K_{t-1}\right]\\&- \beta^t\lambda_t\left[C_t + K_{t+1} - K_t - W_tL_t - (R_t - \delta)K_t\right]\ldots\end{aligned}$$

since in the budget constraint the capital stock for a given period appears in time t and in time $t+1$.

The first-order conditions (FOCs) of the problem are:

$$\frac{\partial \mathcal{L}}{\partial C} : \beta^t\left[\frac{\gamma}{C_t} - \lambda_t\right] = 0 \tag{2.18}$$

$$\frac{\partial \mathcal{L}}{\partial L} : \beta^t\left[\frac{1-\gamma}{1-L_t} - \lambda_t W_t\right] = 0 \tag{2.19}$$

$$\frac{\partial \mathcal{L}}{\partial K} : \beta^t\lambda_t\left[R_t + 1 - \delta\right] - \beta^{t-1}\lambda_{t-1} = 0 \tag{2.20}$$

For the individual decisions we have to calculate the value of the Lagrange parameter, which represents the shadow price of consumption (the valuation in utility terms of the last unit of consumption). To do this, we solve the first FOC and substitute into the second FOC. This leads to a condition that equates the marginal rate of substitution between consumption and leisure to the opportunity cost of an additional unit of leisure:

$$\frac{1-\gamma}{\gamma}\frac{C_t}{1-L_t} = W_t \tag{2.21}$$

On the other hand, from the third FOC we obtain the Lagrange parameter in time t and in time $t-1$. From the first FOC we obtain $\lambda_t = \gamma/C_t$, and thus, $\lambda_{t-1} = \gamma/C_{t-1}$. Substituting, we obtain the condition that equals the marginal rate of consumption with the marginal rate of investment:

$$\frac{C_t}{C_{t-1}} = \beta\left[R_t + 1 - \delta\right] \tag{2.22}$$

The above equilibrium condition determines the individual decisions about savings, or equivalently, investment. Thus, when making decisions about savings, the individual compares the utility that would provide today an additional unit of consumption with the weighted utility that would provide such unit if saved and consumed in a future period.

In summary, the household's maximization problem leads to a system of two equations: A dynamic equation representing the optimal path of consumption or investment decisions, and a static equation defining labor supply. This system of equations includes four endogenous variables (C_t, L_t, W_t, R_t). To obtain a solution we need to know the values for the prices of the production factor.

Alternative functional forms for the utility function

The functional form of the utility function chosen in expression (2.11) is arbitrary. In practice, the literature provides many alternative parametric specifications of the utility function of individuals, both in relation to its functional form and the arguments to be included. One of the most widely used functional forms is the CRRA (Constant Relative Risk Aversion) type utility function, which has the following form:

$$U(X_t) = \frac{X_t^{1-\sigma} - 1}{1-\sigma} \tag{2.23}$$

where $\sigma > 0$, represents the degree of risk aversion, i.e., the degree of curvature of the utility function. This functional form can be used for both consumption and leisure. Thus, we can define a functional form in which the utility function of the individuals is as follows:

$$U(C_t, L_t) = \log C_t - \omega \frac{L_t^{1-\sigma} - 1}{1-\sigma} \tag{2.24}$$

with $\omega > 0$, that is, the utility function can be a combination of both the logarithmic function and the CRRA function.

An alternative specification that is also widely used in the literature is to assume that consumption and leisure have a Cobb-Douglas type function nested within a CRRA function, for example:

$$U(C_t, L_t) = \frac{\left[C_t^{\omega}(1-L_t)^{1-\omega}\right]^{1-\sigma}}{1-\sigma} \tag{2.25}$$

The firms

The second economic agents we consider in our economy are firms, representing the productive sector of the economy. Firms produce the goods and services the households will consume or save. To do this, the firms need to transform production factors into final output. We consider two production factors: physical capital and labor. As we assume that the owners of the production factors are the households, the firms need to rent both capital and labor. The rental prices of these factors of production are determined by the technology and the preferences.

We assume that firms maximize profits, subject to the technological constraint. As we also assume the existence of a perfect competitive environment, this means that corporate profits will be zero since the cost of the production factors will be equal to the value of their productivity. In this setting, the firm will determine the quantity of productive factors which maximize profits subject to the technological constraint. The aggregate production function (the technological constraint) is assumed to have the following form:

$$Y_t = A_t F(K_t, L_t) \tag{2.26}$$

where Y_t is the aggregate output of the economy and A_t is total factor productivity (TFP). Similar to the household's utility function, this technological function must satisfy the following properties: strictly increasing, strictly concave, and twice differentiable:

$$F_K > 0, F_L > 0 \tag{2.27}$$

$$F_{KK} < 0, F_{LL} < 0 \tag{2.28}$$

Condition (2.27) indicates that the first derivatives are positive in relation to each of the inputs, that is, it is an increasing function. The higher the level of capital the higher the level of production. The same applies to the other production factor: labor. In contrast, condition (2.28) tells us that the second derivative of the production function is negative, indicating that the marginal productivity of the capital and labor factors of production is decreasing.

The production function has another element apart from inputs: A_t,. This represents the state of neutral technology and is called Total Factor Productivity (TFP). In principle, TFP is unobservable, but can be calculated as a residual.[6] TFP can be interpreted as the level

[6]The economic concept of TFP is similar to the cosmological constant concept in Einstein's theory of relativity. Although it is uncertain whether such a constant exists, it represents some previously unknown force that is needed to explain the behavior of the Universe. Without this constant, the Theory of Relativity does not

of general knowledge about the productive arts available to an economy; that is, it would represent a broad concept of technology. In economic terms, it would reflect the aggregate productivity of the economy in the use of all inputs. That is, TFP represents the aggregate level of efficiency in production and although it is not defined in theoretical terms, it would be determined by a variety of factors such as technological knowledge, organizational structure, human capital, and institutional factors.

Let us assume that the production function of our economy has constant returns to scale. That is, if we double the amount of productive factors, the production of the economy also doubles. This means that the production function is linearly homogeneous in relation to production factors. So we would have:

$$F(\zeta K_t, \zeta L_t) = \zeta Y_t \tag{2.29}$$

Moreover, the production function satisfies the so-called Inada conditions, which are given by:

$$\lim_{K \longrightarrow 0} F_K = \infty, \lim_{K \longrightarrow \infty} F_K = 0 \tag{2.30}$$

$$\lim_{L \longrightarrow 0} F_L = \infty, \lim_{L \longrightarrow \infty} F_L = 0 \tag{2.31}$$

Additionally we assume that:

$$A_t F(0, L_t) = 0 \tag{2.32}$$

$$A_t F(K_t, 0) = 0 \tag{2.33}$$

The above two conditions state that both production factors are needed to produce final output. The idea is simple: trucks do not drive themselves and drivers need trucks to transport goods.

Profit is defined as the difference between total income (output, as its price is normalized to one) and total cost (labor and capital rental costs), such as:

$$\Pi_t = Y_t - W_t L_t - R_t K_t \tag{2.34}$$

The assumption about the property rights of productive factors is

work. Something similar is the case with TFP, about which there is no theory, but is essential in explaining the output growth of an economy as an element additional to the accumulation of productive factors.

fundamental in defining the maximization problem for the firms. There is no confusion in the case of labor, as it is always owned by the households. However, the owner of the capital stock can be either the household or the firm. If we assume that firms are the owners of the capital stock, they will take the investment decisions in order to maximize profits. In this setting, the problem would be dynamic, as firms take decisions to not only maximize current profits but also future profits. This means that the firm would maximize the present value of the profits. The discount rate would be the real interest rate. Therefore, similar to the consumer problem, the firm's maximization problem can be defined as:

$$\max_{(L_t,K_t)} E_t \sum_{t=0}^{\infty} \left(\frac{1}{1+R_t}\right)^t \Pi_t \tag{2.35}$$

subject to the technological constraint:

$$Y_t = A_t F(K_t, L_t) \tag{2.36}$$

where Π_t are profits now defined as:

$$\Pi_t = Y_t - W_t L_t - R_t I_t \tag{2.37}$$

However, the result would be the same as it would be if the problem were static, given that under the assumption that households are the owners of the production factors, the firms do not take decisions on investment and decide the amount of inputs to be hired period-by-period. Therefore, we can directly define the firm's maximization problem in a static form. In this context, the problem to be solved is how firms maximize profits:

$$\max \Pi_t = Y_t - W_t L_t - R_t K_t \tag{2.38}$$

$$s.t. \quad Y_t = A_t F(K_t, L_t) \tag{2.39}$$

Assuming constant returns to scale and competitive markets we obtain that in the optimum $\Pi_t = 0$. As we can see, the problem regarding maximizing the firm's profits as considered in standard DSGE models is static, whereas firms make their decisions in a dynamic context, where investment decisions are crucial to their behavior. In fact, if we solve the problem of profit maximization in a dynamic context the result we obtain is exactly the same, given the assumptions we are making, that firms hire production inputs period-by-period.

First order condition (FOCs) of the profit maximization problem are:

$$\frac{\partial \Pi}{\partial K} : A_t F_K(K_t, L_t) - R_t = 0 \tag{2.40}$$

$$\frac{\partial \Pi}{\partial L} : A_t F_L(K_t, L_t) - W_t = 0 \tag{2.41}$$

From the above FOCs we find that the relative price of productive factors equals their marginal productivity. The return on capital is equal to the marginal productivity of capital and wages are equal to the marginal productivity of labor.

We now define a specific functional form for the production function. In the literature, the most widely used functional form is to assume that the production function is a Cobb-Douglas function (Cobb and Douglas, 1928), so that:

$$A_t F(K_t, L_t) = A_t K_t^{\alpha} L_t^{1-\alpha} \tag{2.42}$$

where α is the output elasticity in relation to capital. This parameter can also be interpreted as the share of capital income over total income. Accordingly, $1-\alpha$ will be the share of labor income over total income.[7] Using the Cobb-Douglas production function, the maximization problem for the firm can be stated as:

$$\max \Pi_t = A_t K_t^{\alpha} L_t^{1-\alpha} - W_t L_t - R_t K_t \tag{2.43}$$

FOCs are given by:

$$\frac{\partial \Pi}{\partial K} : \alpha A_t K_t^{\alpha-1} L_t^{1-\alpha} - R_t = 0 \tag{2.44}$$

$$\frac{\partial \Pi}{\partial L} : (1-\alpha) A_t K_t^{\alpha} L_t^{-\alpha} - W_t = 0 \tag{2.45}$$

[7]Although we define production at time t as a function of the amount of production factors at that moment in time, for computational purposes we use the following specification:

$$F(K_t, L_t) = A_t K_{t-1}^{\alpha} L_t^{1-\alpha}$$

where capital input refers to the stock of capital in the previous period. The idea is that saving (investment) can be transformed into capital stock in the same period, but do not enter the production function until the next period.

These FOCs can also be written as:

$$R_t = \frac{\alpha A_t K_t^{\alpha} L_t^{1-\alpha}}{K_t} = \alpha \frac{Y_t}{K_t} \tag{2.46}$$

$$W_t = \frac{(1-\alpha) A_t K_t^{\alpha} L_t^{1-\alpha}}{L_t} = (1-\alpha)\frac{Y_t}{L_t} \tag{2.47}$$

that is, the price of the productive factors is a constant proportion of the total output/factor quantity ratio.

We can also check that marginal productivities are decreasing:

$$F_{KK} = (\alpha - 1)\alpha A_t K_t^{\alpha-2} L_t^{1-\alpha} < 0 \tag{2.48}$$

$$F_{LL} = -\alpha(1-\alpha) A_t K_t^{\alpha} L_t^{-\alpha-1} < 0 \tag{2.49}$$

On the other hand, we can show that profits are in fact zero in this competitive environment. We only have to replace the price of the production factors in the profit function. The profit function is given by:

$$\Pi_t = A_t K_t^{\alpha} L_t^{1-\alpha} - R_t K_t - W_t L_t \tag{2.50}$$

Substituting the value of the rental cost of capital and wages we obtain:

$$\Pi_t = A_t K_t^{\alpha} L_t^{1-\alpha} - \alpha A_t K_t^{\alpha} L_t^{1-\alpha} - (1-\alpha) A_t K_t^{\alpha} L_t^{1-\alpha} = 0 \tag{2.51}$$

where we find that the profits are in fact zero, since the price of inputs is equal to their marginal productivity.

Finally, combining the FOCs we find that the capital-labor ratio (capital stock per capita) is given by:

$$\frac{\alpha A_t K_t^{\alpha-1} L_t^{1-\alpha}}{(1-\alpha) A_t K_t^{\alpha} L_t^{-\alpha}} = \frac{R_t}{W_t} \tag{2.52}$$

or

$$\frac{\alpha A_t Y_t L_t}{(1-\alpha) A_t Y_t K_t} = \frac{R_t}{W_t} \tag{2.53}$$

Solving, we obtain:

$$\frac{\alpha}{(1-\alpha)} = \frac{R_t K_t}{W_t L_t} \tag{2.54}$$

indicating that the proportion of capital income relative to labor income is a constant, which is one of the most important features of the Cobb-Douglas type production function.

Alternative functional forms of the production function

Although most of the DSGE models use a Cobb-Douglas type technology, there are alternative specifications that consider other elasticities of substitution between production factors different from unity. An alternative production function also widely used in the literature is the so-called CES (Constant Elasticity of Substitution) function, which has the following form:

$$F(K_t, L_t) = \left[\alpha K_t^{\rho} + (1-\alpha) L_t^{\rho}\right]^{\frac{1}{\rho}} \tag{2.55}$$

where $\rho \in (-\infty, 1)$ is a parameter that determines the elasticity of substitution between the two inputs. The elasticity of substitution between the production factors is defined as $\varepsilon = 1/(1-\rho)$. If $\rho = 0$, then the above production function (2.55) becomes a Cobb-Douglas function (2.42).[8]

Model Equilibrium

Having described the behavior of each economic agent in our economy, we now study their interaction to determine the macroeconomic equilibrium by putting the two agents together. Each type of agent takes its own decisions over the control variables. Households decide how much to consume, C_t, how much to invest (save), $I_t = S_t$, and how much to work, L_t, with the objective of maximizing their happiness, taking as given the prices of the inputs. Firms produce a given amount of final goods, Y_t, which depends on decisions regarding how much capital, K_t and labor L_t, they will hire, given the prices of the production factors.

[8] Taking logarithms in (2.55) yields:

$$\ln(Y_t) = \frac{1}{\rho} \ln\left[\alpha K_t^{\rho} + (1-\alpha) L_t^{\rho}\right]$$

Applying the L'Hôpital Rule, we obtain:

$$\lim_{\rho \to \infty} \ln(Y_t) = \alpha \ln K_t + (1-\alpha) \ln L_t$$

and using the exponential function we reach the production function given by (2.42).

Therefore, the balance path of the economy is composed of the following three sets of elements:

i) A pricing system for W and R.

ii) A set of values assigned to Y, C, I, L and K.

iii) A feasibility constraint of the economy, given by:

$$Y_t = C_t + I_t \tag{2.56}$$

As we can see, the definition of equilibrium implies that all markets (goods and service market, capital market, and labor market) are in equilibrium. This is what we simply call general equilibrium. A more formal definition of equilibrium is the following:

Definition 1 *The competitive equilibrium for our economy is a sequence of consumption, leisure, and investment by consumers* $\{C_t, L_t, I_t\}_{t=0}^{\infty}$ *and a sequence of capital and labor hours used by firms* $\{K_t, L_t\}_{t=0}^{\infty}$*, such that given a sequence of prices* $\{W_t, R_t\}_{t=0}^{\infty}$*: i) The consumers optimization problem is satisfied; ii) Profit maximization FOCs for the firms hold; and iii) The feasibility condition of the economy holds.*

The model defined above will lead to a Pareto optimal solution, ensuring that social welfare is maximized. Any deviation from this equilibrium implies welfare losses for the agents in the model. Thus, the previous theoretical specification meets the two Welfare Theorems.

Definition 2 *Welfare Theorems: If there are no distortions such as taxes (distortionary) or externalities, then: i) First Welfare Theorem: Any competitive equilibrium is Pareto optimal; and ii) Second Welfare Theorem: For each Pareto optimum a price system exists which makes it a competitive equilibrium.*

Model equilibrium can be derived in two alternative settings: First, we can assume the existence of a freedom setting in which each agent makes decisions to maximize their objective function in a competitive environment. This is what is called the competitive or decentralized problem and it is intended to represent a market economy in which agents make decisions based on the relative prices. The other option is to jointly maximize the welfare of all the agents in the economy. This is what is called the Central Planner or Benevolent Dictator problem (no prices are needed).

In our basic theoretical framework the two alternative solutions are the same, since there are no distortions and therefore the decisions of the individual agents are such that they also ensure the maximization of the social welfare function. With distortions, the Central Planner solution generates a higher level of welfare than the decentralized problem, because the externalities or market failures are incorporated in the equilibrium, whereas the competitive solution would be inefficient.

Model Equilibrium (Competitive Equilibrium)

First we consider the existence of a competitive environment or decentralized economy, in which each agent makes his/her own decisions to maximize their respective objective functions. The decentralized problem would be given by the maximization of the following problem:

$$\max_{(C_t,I_t,O_t)} \mathcal{L} = \sum_{t=0}^{\infty} \beta^t \left[\gamma \log C_t + (1-\gamma)\log(1-L_t)\right] \tag{2.57}$$

subject to the budget constraint:

$$C_t + I_t = W_t L_t + R_t K_t \tag{2.58}$$

where investment is derived from the inventory capital accumulation equation:

$$I_t = K_{t+1} - (1-\delta)K_t \tag{2.59}$$

In this case, given the price of the production factors, the consumers choose how much to consume (and also how much they will save, which will determine the process of capital accumulation) and how much time they will devote to work. That is, there is a price vector that will constitute the essential information that is used by individuals to make their decisions.

To solve this problem we construct the following Lagrangian (we assume perfect foresight):

$$\max_{(C_t,K_t,O_t)} \mathcal{L} = \sum_{t=0}^{\infty} \beta^t \begin{pmatrix} \left[\gamma \log C_t + (1-\gamma)\log(1-L_t)\right] \\ -\lambda_t \left[C_t + K_{t+1} - W_t L_t - (R_t + 1 - \delta)K_t\right] \end{pmatrix}$$

The FOCs are given by:

$$\frac{\partial \mathcal{L}}{\partial C}:\gamma\frac{1}{C_t}-\lambda_t-0 \tag{2.60}$$

$$\frac{\partial \mathcal{L}}{\partial L}:-\frac{1-\gamma}{1-L_t}+\lambda_t W_t=0 \tag{2.61}$$

$$\frac{\partial \mathcal{L}}{\partial K}:\beta^t\lambda_t(R_t+1-\delta)-\beta^{t-1}\lambda_{t-1}=0 \tag{2.62}$$

$$\frac{\partial \mathcal{L}}{\partial \lambda}:C_t+K_{t+1}-(R_t+1-\delta)K_t-W_tL_t=0 \tag{2.63}$$

Substituting the FOC (2.60) in the FOC (2.61), we obtain the condition that equates the marginal rate of substitution between consumption and leisure to the opportunity cost of an additional unit of leisure:

$$\frac{1-\gamma}{\gamma}\frac{C_t}{1-L_t}=W_t \tag{2.64}$$

Substituting the FOC (2.60) in the FOC (2.62), we obtain the condition that equates the marginal rate of consumption with that of investment:

$$\frac{C_t}{C_{t-1}}=\beta[R_t+1-\delta] \tag{2.65}$$

On the other hand, the firm's maximization problem is simply defined by:

$$\max\Pi_t=A_tK_t^{\alpha}L_t^{1-\alpha}-W_tL_t-R_tK_t \tag{2.66}$$

From the FOCs of the profit maximization problem we find that R_t and W_t are equal to their marginal products:

$$R_t=\alpha A_tK_t^{\alpha-1}L_t^{1-\alpha} \tag{2.67}$$

$$W_t=(1-\alpha)A_tK_t^{\alpha}L_t^{-\alpha} \tag{2.68}$$

The following is obtained by substituting the FOCs for the firm in the equilibrium conditions for the consumer's maximization problem:

$$\frac{1-\gamma}{\gamma}\frac{C_t}{1-L_t}=(1-\alpha)A_tK_t^{\alpha}L_t^{-\alpha} \tag{2.69}$$

$$\frac{C_t}{C_{t-1}}=\beta\left[\alpha A_tK_t^{\alpha-1}L_t^{1-\alpha}+1-\delta\right] \tag{2.70}$$

The last FOC of the consumer problem ensures that the consumer budget constraint holds:

$$\frac{\partial \mathcal{L}}{\partial \lambda} = C_t + K_{t+1} - K_t - (R_t - \delta)K_t - W_t L_t = 0 \qquad (2.71)$$

By substituting the relative price of productive factors in the above expression we obtain:

$$C_t + K_{t+1} - K_t - (\alpha A_t K_t^{\alpha-1} L_t^{1-\alpha} - \delta)K_t - (1-\alpha)A_t K_t^{\alpha} L_t^{-\alpha} L_t = 0$$

$$C_t + K_{t+1} - K_t - \alpha A_t K_t^{\alpha} L_t^{1-\alpha} + \delta K_t - A_t K_t^{\alpha} L_t^{1-\alpha} + \alpha A_t K_t^{\alpha} L_t^{1-\alpha} = 0$$

and operating we reach the following expression:

$$C_t + K_{t+1} - (1-\delta)K_t - A_t K_t^{\alpha} L_t^{1-\alpha} = 0 \qquad (2.72)$$

which simply shows the accumulation process for the capital stock over time, in which the next period's capital stock is equal to today's capital stock plus total output minus consumption minus depreciation.

Therefore, the competitive solution is determined by two difference equations:

$$C_t = \beta\left[\alpha A_t K_t^{\alpha-1} L_t^{1-\alpha} + 1 - \delta\right] C_{t-1} \qquad (2.73)$$

$$K_{t+1} = (1-\delta)K_t + A_t K_t^{\alpha} L_t^{1-\alpha} - C_t \qquad (2.74)$$

plus a static equation that relates labor to the real wage:

$$\frac{1-\gamma}{\gamma} \frac{C_t}{1-L_t} = (1-\alpha)A_t K_t^{\alpha} L_t^{-\alpha} \qquad (2.75)$$

In fact, the competitive equilibrium of our economy can be reduced to a system of two equations: a static equation from which we would obtain the level of employment in the economy, and a dynamic second-degree equation which would give us the capital stock of the economy by substituting the dynamic equation for consumption in the dynamic equation for capital stock. From expression (2.72):

$$C_t = K_{t+1} - (1-\delta)K_t - A_t K_t^{\alpha} L_t^{1-\alpha} \qquad (2.76)$$

and substituting in expression (2.73) yields:

$$K_{t+1} - (1-\delta)K_t - A_t K_t^{\alpha} L_t^{1-\alpha} = \beta\left[\alpha A_t K_t^{\alpha-1} L_t^{1-\alpha} + 1 - \delta\right] K_t - (1-\delta)K_{t-1} - A_{t-1} K_{t-1}^{\alpha} L_{t-1}^{1-\alpha} \tag{2.77}$$

In summary, competitive equilibrium consists in computing sequences of the variables $\{C_t, I_t, K_t, L_t, R_t, W_t, Y_t\}_{t=0}^{\infty}$ such that the balance path conditions are satisfied. Thus, our economy is characterized by seven endogenous variables and so we need a system with seven equations for the equilibrium to be computed. The set of equations characterizing our economy are the following:

$$\frac{(1-\gamma)}{\gamma} \frac{C_t}{1-L_t} = W_t \tag{2.78}$$

$$\frac{C_{t+1}}{C_t} = \beta\left[R_{t+1} + 1 - \delta\right] \tag{2.79}$$

$$R_t = \frac{\alpha A_t K_t^{\alpha} L_t^{1-\alpha}}{K_t} = \alpha \frac{Y_t}{K_t} \tag{2.80}$$

$$W_t = \frac{(1-\alpha) A_t K_t^{\alpha} L_t^{1-\alpha}}{L_t} = (1-\alpha)\frac{Y_t}{L_t} \tag{2.81}$$

$$Y_t = A_t K_t^{\alpha} L_t^{1-\alpha} \tag{2.82}$$

$$K_{t+1} = (1-\delta)K_t + I_t \tag{2.83}$$

$$C_t + I_t = Y_t \tag{2.84}$$

Model Equilibrium (Central Planning)

An alternative setting to a competitive market environment is to consider a centrally planned economy. To do this, we can assume the existence of an agent, who we call the benevolent dictator or the central planner, who makes decisions regarding the joint maximization of social welfare. That is, the two agents of our economy do not make decisions about the optimal paths of consumption, investment, and labor such that firms maximize profits and consumers maximize their utility. No freedom exists and the only agent who makes economic decisions is the benevolent dictator. As a direct consequence, prices have no role in this economy.

The centralized planning problem for the whole economy can be defined as:

$$\max_{(C_t,I_t,L_t)} \mathcal{L} = \sum_{t=0}^{\infty} \beta^t \left[\gamma \log C_t + (1-\gamma)\log(1-L_t)\right] \tag{2.85}$$

subject to:

$$C_t + I_t = A_t K_t^{\alpha} L_t^{1-\alpha} \tag{2.86}$$

As we can now see, the economy feasibility condition appears instead of the consumer budget constraint. The prices of production factors no longer have a role and what is produced in the economy equals the income received by households in order to be either consumed or saved.

The Lagrangian corresponding to this problem would be:

$$\max_{(C_t,K_t,O_t)} \mathcal{L} = \sum_{t=0}^{\infty} \beta^t \begin{pmatrix} \left[\gamma \log C_t + (1-\gamma)\log(1-L_t)\right] - \\ \lambda_t \left[C_t + K_{t+1} - (1-\delta)K_t - A_t K_t^{\alpha} L_t^{1-\alpha}\right] \end{pmatrix} \tag{2.87}$$

The FOCs are given by:

$$\frac{\partial \mathcal{L}}{\partial C} : \gamma \frac{1}{C_t} - \lambda_t = 0 \tag{2.88}$$

$$\frac{\partial \mathcal{L}}{\partial L} : -\frac{1-\gamma}{1-L_t} + \lambda_t (1-\alpha) A_t K_t^{\alpha} L_t^{-\alpha} = 0 \tag{2.89}$$

$$\frac{\partial \mathcal{L}}{\partial K} : \beta^t \lambda_t (\alpha A_t K_t^{\alpha-1} L_t^{1-\alpha} + 1 - \delta) - \beta^{t-1} \lambda_{t-1} = 0 \tag{2.90}$$

$$\frac{\partial \mathcal{L}}{\partial \lambda} : C_t + K_{t+1} - (1-\delta)K_t - A_t K_t^{\alpha} L_t^{1-\alpha} = 0 \tag{2.91}$$

Operating we will arrive to the following two expressions:

$$\frac{1-\gamma}{\gamma} \frac{C_t}{1-L_t} = (1-\alpha) A_t K_t^{\alpha} L_t^{-\alpha} \tag{2.92}$$

$$\frac{C_t}{C_{t-1}} = \beta \left[\alpha A_t K_t^{\alpha-1} L_t^{1-\alpha} + 1 - \delta\right] \tag{2.93}$$

Therefore, the equilibrium of the economy can be defined in terms of two difference equations:

$$C_t = \beta \left[\alpha A_t K_t^{\alpha-1} L_t^{1-\alpha} + 1 - \delta\right] C_{t-1} \tag{2.94}$$

$$K_{t+1} = (1-\delta)K_t + A_t K_t^{\alpha} L_t^{1-\alpha} - C_t \tag{2.95}$$

plus one additional static equation for labor:

$$\frac{1-\gamma}{\gamma}\frac{C_t}{1-L_t} = (1-\alpha)A_t K_t^{\alpha} L_t^{-\alpha} \tag{2.96}$$

As can be observed, the solution under a centrally planned economy environment is exactly the same as under a competitive environment. This is because there are no distortions in our model economy that alters the agents' decisions regarding the efficient outcome. The only difference between the two settings is that whereas in the decentralized economy there is a market for production factors which determines their price, in a centralized economy there is no such market for production factors and therefore no price for inputs exist.

In summary, centralized equilibrium consists in computing sequences of the variables $\{C_t, I_t, K_t, L_t, Y_t\}_{t=0}^{\infty}$ such that the balance path conditions are satisfied. Thus, our economy is now characterized by five endogenous variables, so we need a system with five equations for equilibrium to be computed. The set of equations characterizing our centralized economy are the following:

$$\frac{(1-\gamma)}{\gamma}\frac{C_t}{1-L_t} = (1-\alpha)A_t K_t^{\alpha} L_t^{-\alpha} \tag{2.97}$$

$$\frac{C_{t+1}}{C_t} = \beta\left[\alpha A_t K_t^{\alpha-1} L_t^{1-\alpha} + 1 - \delta\right] \tag{2.98}$$

$$Y_t = A_t K_t^{\alpha} L_t^{1-\alpha} \tag{2.99}$$

$$K_{t+1} = (1-\delta)K_t + I_t \tag{2.100}$$

$$C_t + I_t = Y_t \tag{2.101}$$

The Steady State

Once the equilibrium path of the economy has been defined, the next step consists in the computation of the steady state. In fact, the model presented above is stationary in the sense that there is a set of values for the endogenous variables that in equilibrium remain constant over time. The steady state refers to a situation in which the variables are held constant from period to period (as no growth is assumed in our environment). This means, for example, that we would have an equilibrium value for consumption such as $... = C_{t-1} = C_t = C_{t+1} = ... = \overline{C}$. To calculate the steady state, we first eliminate the time subscripts of the variables. Thus, the equations of the model can be written as:

$$\frac{(1-\gamma)}{\gamma}\frac{\overline{C}}{1-\overline{L}} = \overline{W} \tag{2.102}$$

$$1 = \beta\left[\overline{R} + 1 - \delta\right] \tag{2.103}$$

$$\overline{R} = \alpha\frac{\overline{Y}}{\overline{K}} \tag{2.104}$$

$$\overline{W} = (1-\alpha)\frac{\overline{Y}}{\overline{L}} \tag{2.105}$$

$$\overline{Y} = \overline{A}\overline{K}^{\alpha}\overline{L}^{1-\alpha} \tag{2.106}$$

$$\overline{I} = \delta\overline{K} \tag{2.107}$$

$$\overline{C} + \overline{I} = \overline{Y} \tag{2.108}$$

The steady-state rental rate of capital can be directly obtained from equation (2.103):

$$\overline{R} = \frac{1}{\beta} + \delta - 1 \tag{2.109}$$

This expression is interesting in the sense that the steady-state real interest rate of the economy will depend on the discount factor, which is a characteristic of individuals.

The first thing we do is express all the variables in terms of the equilibrium output level. Using expression (2.104), we can write expression (2.103) as:

$$1 = \beta\left[\alpha\frac{\overline{Y}}{\overline{K}} + 1 - \delta\right]$$

Solving for $\overline{K}$ results:

$$\overline{K} = \frac{\alpha\beta}{1-\beta+\beta\delta}\overline{Y} \tag{2.110}$$

Second, using (2.107), and given (2.110), the steady-state value for investment is given by:

$$\overline{I} = \frac{\alpha\beta\delta}{1-\beta+\beta\delta}\overline{Y} \tag{2.111}$$

Third, using expressions (2.108) and (2.111) we reach the steady-state value of consumption:

$$\overline{C} = \frac{1-\beta+(1-\alpha)\beta\delta}{1-\beta+\beta\delta}\overline{Y} \tag{2.112}$$

Next, using (2.102) and (2.105) we obtain:

$$\overline{L} = \frac{\gamma(1-\alpha)(1-\beta+\beta\delta)}{(1-\gamma)\left(1-\beta+(1-\alpha)\beta\delta\right)+\gamma(1-\alpha)\left(1-\beta+\beta\delta\right)} \tag{2.113}$$

Finally, substituting (2.110) and (2.113) in (2.106) we reach the steady-state value of output:

$$\overline{Y} = \overline{A}^{\frac{1}{1-\alpha}}\left[\frac{\alpha\beta}{1-\beta+\beta\delta}\right]^{\frac{\alpha}{1-\alpha}} \left[1+\frac{\gamma(1-\alpha)(1-\beta+\beta\delta)}{(1-\gamma)\left(1-\beta+(1-\alpha)\beta\delta\right)}\right] \tag{2.114}$$

given $\overline{A}$. By just using (2.114) in (2.110), (2.111), and (2.112) we can recover the steady-state values for capital, investment, and consumption, respectively. Having obtained the steady state of the economy, we can calculate the deviation of each variable in relation to its steady-state value. Appendix B shows how to derive the log-linearized version of the model.

The Dynamic Stochastic General Equilibrium model

In the previous section we solved a deterministic version of a DSGE model. This means that we have assumed that all disturbances that could affect the economy are zero for any point in time. However, in practice, the economy is subject to a variety of shocks to the different macroeconomic variables and hence we have to incorporate these shocks in our analysis.

The conversion of our model economy from deterministic to stochastic means that there cannot be a solution except in very specific cases (for example, when the utility function is logarithmic and capital fully depreciates between periods). For this reason the use of computational methods are needed for the numerical resolution of the model. In practice, there are alternative methods for solving DSGE models: The method of Blanchard and Kahn (1980), the method of Uhlig (1999), Sims' method (2001), and the method of Klein (2000). In Appendix B we show the application of the method of Blanchard and Kahn (1980) to our basic model economy.

The conversion from a deterministic to a stochastic environment is easy. Without altering the basic structure of the model described above, we can directly introduce, for instance, five types of disturbances: an aggregate productivity shock, an aggregate shock to the utility function, a consumption shock, a labor shock, and an investment shock. An exogenous variable, A_t, which was assumed to be exogenously fixed, appears in the deterministic version of the model. The easiest way to transform the previous model to a stochastic environment is to assume that this variable is not a constant, but follows a given stochastic process. In fact, this was the assumption which led to the birth of the RBC literature.

We assume that the productivity shock follows a first-order autoregressive process, such that:

$$\ln A_t = (1-\rho_A)\ln \overline{A} + \rho_A \ln A_{t-1} + \varepsilon_t^A, \qquad \varepsilon_t^A \sim N(0,\sigma_A^2) \qquad (2.115)$$

where $|\rho_A| < 1$ for the process to be stationary and where $\overline{A}$ is the steady-state value for A_t. Alternatively, the consumer problem utility function can be written as:

$$\max_{(C_t,K_t,L_t)} \mathcal{L} = \sum_{t=0}^{\infty} \beta^t B_t \left[\gamma D_t \log C_t + (1-\gamma) H_t \log(1-L_t)\right] \qquad (2.116)$$

where B_t is a disturbance that generally reflects a preference shock that affects the consumer's intertemporal substitution, D_t represents a disturbance in consumption, and H_t represents a disturbance to the labor decision. Let's assume that the process followed by these three disturbances is the following:

$$\begin{bmatrix} \ln B_t \\ \ln D_t \\ \ln H_t \end{bmatrix} = \begin{bmatrix} \rho_B & \upsilon_{BD} & \upsilon_{BH} \\ \upsilon_{DB} & \rho_D & \upsilon_{DH} \\ \upsilon_{HB} & \upsilon_{HD} & \rho_H \end{bmatrix} \begin{bmatrix} \ln B_{t-1} \\ \ln D_{t-1} \\ \ln H_{t-1} \end{bmatrix} + \begin{bmatrix} \varepsilon_t^B \\ \varepsilon_t^D \\ \varepsilon_t^H \end{bmatrix} \tag{2.117}$$

where $\left|\rho_i \pm \upsilon_{ij}\right| < 1,\ i \neq j,\ i,j = B, D, H$, in order to ensure stationarity, where $E(\varepsilon_t^i) = 0$ and $E(\varepsilon_t^i \varepsilon_t^i) = \sigma_i^2,\ \forall i$.

To keep things as simple as possible, we only consider the existence of the productivity shock, i.e., the productivity shock studied in the classical RBC literature. However, as we incorporate new elements in the basic structure of the model, we can also study the effects of other types of disturbances on the dynamics of the economy.

Equations of the model and calibration

Once the equilibrium conditions of the model have been obtained, to proceed further we need to parametrize the model economy, that is, numerical values must be assigned to the parameters. This is an important issue as otherwise numeral resolution methods cannot be applied. At this step, we have two alternatives: To estimate the parameters using some econometric technique or to calibrate the parameters. Calibration involves calculating the value of the parameters in some way: for example, by giving an arbitrary value, by obtaining the values directly from the data using some identities from the model equilibrium, by directly using the equilibrium conditions, or even by simply using the values supplied by the empirical literature. Until recently, most studies have chosen calibration techniques. In contrast, the estimation approach, via maximum likelihood or Bayesian methods, is rather more complex and consists in adjusting the model to the observed data in order to determine the parameter values. The latter method has recently been gaining ground. The recent development of specific software packages for the estimation of DSGE models, such as DYNARE or IRIS, dramatically facilitate this cumbersome task.

Nevertheless, the estimation of DSGE models has proven to be problematic. First, the number of control variables exceeds the number of state variables. This results in the so-called stochastic singularity problem. Basically, this problem is solved in two ways: either by adding measurement errors to the data (this is the strategy followed, for instance, by Sargent (1989), Altug (1989), and Ireland (2004)), or by increasing the number of disturbances in the model (most authors appear to follow this latter strategy). Furthermore, some of the maximum likelihood estimates incur problems in relation to the expected value of some parameters. For instance, some estimates yield very low values for the intertemporal discount rate, β. In our analysis we use the first method, that is, the calibration approach. Once the values of the parameters have been set we then calculate and simulate the model numerically. To do this, we use the Dynare software tool for MatLab, which allows us to numerically compute the model in a programming setting that has very simple and basic requirements.

Equilibrium equations

In the case of a central planner economy, the equilibrium of the stochastic version of the model is represented by a set of six equations, which correspond to the set of six endogenous macroeconomic variables of the economy, Y_t, C_t, I_t, K_t, L_t and the variable A_t representing Total Factor Productivity, which is assumed to follow a particular stochastic process. This set of equilibrium equations is the following:

$$\frac{1-\gamma}{\gamma}\frac{C_t}{1-L_t} = (1-\alpha)Y_t/L_t \tag{2.118}$$

$$\frac{C_t}{C_{t-1}} = \beta[\alpha Y_t/K_t + 1 - \delta] \tag{2.119}$$

$$Y_t = C_t + I_t \tag{2.120}$$

$$Y_t = A_t K_t^{\alpha} L_t^{1-\alpha} \tag{2.121}$$

$$K_{t+1} = (1-\delta)K_t + I_t \tag{2.122}$$

$$\ln A_t = (1-\rho_A)\ln \overline{A} + \rho_A \ln A_{t-1} + \varepsilon_t \tag{2.123}$$

In the case of a market economy, equilibrium is defined by eight equations: the above six equations plus two additional equations representing the production factor prices: wages and the rental rate of capital. These two additional equations can be written as follows:

$$W_t = (1-\alpha)Y_t/L_t \tag{2.124}$$

$$R_t = \alpha Y_t / K_t \tag{2.125}$$

Calibration

For the model to be completely computationally operational, a value must be assigned to the parameters. We specifically use the calibration procedure to do this. The following six parameters form the set to be calibrated:

$$\Omega = \{\alpha, \beta, \delta, \gamma, \rho_A, \sigma_A\}$$

α: This is the technological parameter defining the productivity of capital. As we assume a Cobb-Douglas production function, this parameter represents the proportion of capital income to the total income of the economy, given the assumption of constant returns to scale, $\alpha \in (0,1)$. Under this assumption, this parameter determines how national income is distributed among the production factors, depending on the contribution of each factor to the final output. In fact, this is the parameter determining the productivity of labor and capital. Note that the Cobb-Douglas production function implies that the proportion of each production factor income to total income remains constant over time. The value of this parameter can be obtained from National Accounts data, such as 1 minus the share of labor income over the total income of the economy. For most developed economies the value for this parameter is in the range 0.25 to 0.35.

β: This parameter represents how agents value future utility in relation to present utility, depending on the subjective intertemporal preference rate of individuals. This parameter is called the discount factor and usually takes a value slightly less than unity, indicating how the agents discount the future. If the value was equal to 1, this would mean that the agents equally valued future utility that utility at the present, i.e., no discount about the future. The further this value from unity, the greater the discount that makes the future, i.e., the lower the weight given to future utility relative to current utility. The literature typically provides values of around 0.97 in the case of annual data and around 0.99 in the case of quarterly data. One way to calculate this preferences parameter is by using the steady-state conditions of the model. In fact, from the FOC (2.119) we can obtain a calibrated value for this parameter depending on the depreciation rate of capital and the marginal productivity of capital, as measured by the real interest rate. The result of calculating this expression in the steady state is:

$$\beta = \frac{1}{\overline{R}+1-\delta} \tag{2.126}$$

δ: This parameter represents the physical depreciation rate of capital stock. Estimates of this parameter may be found in different databases, such as EU-Klems. In the case of quarterly data, the literature uses values in the range 0.02 to 0.03. In the case of annual data values range from about 0.04 to 0.1.

γ: This parameter represents the individual's preferences regarding consumption - leisure decisions, $\gamma \in (0,1)$. Its value represents the proportion of consumer spending to total income. In fact, it can be easily shown that in a world with no physical capital or investment, this parameter is simply the ratio of hours worked to the total available hours (between 0.3 and 0.5). A possible estimate of this parameter can be obtained by FOCs of the model. In fact, in steady state, from the condition (2.118), the value of this parameter would be:

$$\gamma = \frac{\overline{C}}{\overline{C}+\overline{W}(1-\overline{L})} \tag{2.127}$$

ρ_A: This is the autoregressive parameter for the TFP process. The value of this parameter reflect the persistence over time of productivity shocks. In the literature, the most commonly used parameter value is greater then 0.9. Nevertheless, it is possible to obtain an estimation of TFP as a residual (the so-called Solow residual), and from that we can estimate this parameter.

σ_A: is the standard deviation of the error term associated with the stochastic process that follows total factor productivity. Like the autoregressive parameter, this parameter can also be estimated econometrically from the production function residuals.

Table 2.1 shows the values of the calibrated parameters used in our analysis, assuming annual frequency. These values are fairly similar to the ones used in the literature in a large variety of exercises.

Aggregate productivity shock

At this point, we can perform a variety of numerical experiments and empirical applications in order to explain the dynamics of the

Table 2.1: Calibrated parameters

Parameter	Definition	Value
α	Technological parameter	0.350
β	Discount factor	0.970
γ	Preference parameter	0.400
δ	Depreciation rate	0.060
ρ_A	TFP autoregressive parameter	0.950
σ_A	TFP standard deviation	0.010

macroeconomic variables considered in our model economy. Given the simplicity of our theoretical framework only a few economic problems can be solved, but despite its limitations, this framework can be useful in understanding some aspects of the economy. Furthermore, we can check the goodness-of-fit of the model by simply comparing some moments from the simulated variables of the model with those observed in the data.

One worthwhile exercise is to study how the model responds to different shocks, calculating the deviations of the variables in relation to their steady-state values. It can also be of interest to study how the system returns to its initial steady state or moves to a new steady state, depending on whether the shock has transitory or permanent effects. As an exercise we consider the case of an exogenous positive neutral shock to the economy: an increase in TFP. That is, we analyze the effects of a change in total factor productivity, which represents the standard exercise conducted in the so-called real business cycle (RBC) literature.

As noted above, we assume that the productivity shock follows a first-order autoregressive process, such that:

$$\ln A_t = (1-\rho_A)\ln \overline{A} + \rho_A \ln A_{t-1} + \varepsilon_t^A; \qquad \varepsilon_t^A \sim N(0,\sigma_A^2) \tag{2.128}$$

where $\rho_A = 0.95$, $\sigma_A = 0.01$ and $\overline{A} = 1$. By computing numerically the model, we can calculate the deviations of the variables to its steady-state values from the moment the shock occurs onwards until the economy reaches the new steady state. A standard procedure to present this analysis is by plotting the so-called impulse response functions for each variable, which show the dynamics of the economy following a perturbation. In Appendix A of this chapter we present the Dynare program corresponding to this exercise. As we

Table 2.2: Steady State

Variable	Value	Ratio to $\overline{Y}$
$\overline{Y}$	0.74469	1.000
$\overline{C}$	0.57270	0.769
$\overline{I}$	0.17199	0.231
$\overline{K}$	2.86649	3.849
$\overline{L}$	0.36039	-
$\overline{R}$	0.09092	-
$\overline{W}$	1.34312	-
$\overline{A}$	1.00000	-

can see, the model is composed of a total of eight equations, defined by the system (2.118)-(2.125) for a total of 8 endogenous variables in which TFP stochastic process is included. The model contains an exogenous variable: the productivity shocks.

Table 2.2 shows the steady-state values of the variables. The steady-state value of the production level is 0.744. This value is determined by the fact that we have assumed that the discretional time endowment of the economy is equal to unity and that the steady-state TFP is also equal to one. Moreover, we find that the value of steady-state employment is 0.36, i.e., 36% of the total discretional time endowment is devoted to work. Given that the total output is the sum of consumption plus investment, we find that in equilibrium about 77% of income is consumed while the remaining 23% is saved. Finally, the capital stock is nearly 4 times the production, which is consistent with the available statistical data on the capital stock of developed economies.

Figure 2.2 shows the effects of the shock on the variables of the model over 40 periods after the disturbance occurs. The plots show the deviation in percentage points from steady-state values. We assume that initially the TFP increases by one standard deviation on impact. Given the persistence of the process assumed to follow the TFP, this shock not only has an effect at the time its hits the economy, but also afterwards, depending on the autoregressive parameter value. Additional persistence is caused by the physical capital stock accumulation process.

First, we find that the level of production increases on impact, rising above its steady-state value as more output is produced for given production inputs. Subsequently, the positive deviation begins to decrease but shows significant persistence over time. In fact, after 20 periods the production level is still 0.5% above its steady-state value. This persistence in output following the shock is due to two factors: the persistence of shock itself and the persistence introduced by the process of accumulation of physical capital. Therefore, as expected, a positive productivity shock (a change that increases the overall productivity of the economy) has a positive effect on the level of production.

Secondly, consumption also instantaneously increases in relation to its steady-state value, but by a small proportion. Subsequently, the deviation continues to increase until it reaches a maximum (around period 10), and gradually decreases thereafter. We can see that the consumer response to this shock is bell-shaped. This consumer behavior is explained by the performance of output and investment. Investment instantaneously increases as a result of the productivity shock (the shock increases the return to capital), but afterwards investment rapidly declines towards its steady-state value. Capital stock also shows a bell-shaped impulse-response function. Initially, the increase in investment also causes an increase in capital stock (net investment is positive). However, as investment decreases, the capital stock reaches a maximum after which it begins to decrease, but always above its steady-state value. The effect on employment is very limited. The hours worked also increases as the return to work increases, although by a very small percentage (about 0.2%) and then decreases, even at values slightly below its steady state.

Finally, regarding production factor prices, there is an increase in wages as a result of the gains in productivity. Labor marginal productivity also displays a bell-shaped impulse-response function. Finally, the real interest rate initially undergoes a slight positive change, given the increase in the marginal productivity of capital, but later decreases very slightly to below its steady-state value as a result of the process of capital accumulation.

The above exercise is commonly found in the RBC literature. It was initially developed by Kydland and Prescott (1982) and Long and Plosser (1983), in which the cycles are generated by real exogenous shocks to the production function. The mechanism underlying these models is as follows. The real disturbance on the production function makes agents optimally alter their consumption-leisure decisions. The productivity shock changes the marginal productivity of production factors, affecting both consumption-saving and labor-leisure decisions. The accumulation of capital introduces an additional element of persistence, even in the case that the disturbance is not serially correlated. In this context, the model is able to simulate a set of effects which are broadly similar to those observed during cycles. The resulting exercise is highly illustrative of the functioning of a simple DSGE model and the dynamic relationships between the different variables. However, we should note that the model presented is highly stylized and involves a large number of assumptions that may prove too restrictive to replicate the dynamics of the variables of an economy.

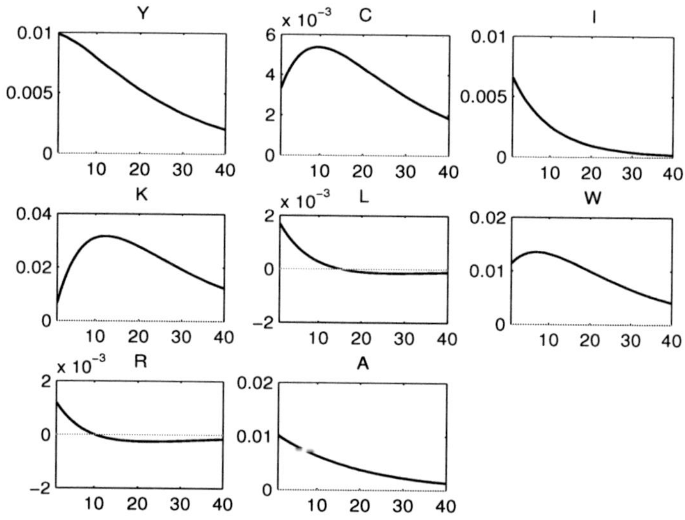

Figure 2.2: Impulse-response functions to a TFP shock

Conclusions

This chapter presented a basic version of the standard Dynamic Stochastic General Equilibrium (DSGE) model, which has currently become the main tool of macroeconomic analysis. This approach has been widely accepted as representing the standard macroeconomic laboratory. This theoretical framework is a very simplified version of the models that both central banks and other public and private organizations are currently using to understand the behavior of the economy and to conduct monetary and fiscal policy analysis, although they all have the same basis. In our simplified version, the structure of the model economy is given by the optimizing behavior of two economic agents: Households and firms. Consumers' decisions determine the optimal paths of consumption, investment (saving), and labor supply, given a set of prices. Firms choose the quantity of inputs that will be used to produce final output, given the technology.

The great popularity of this kind of model is due to the fact that it is a highly stylized, micro-founded theoretical framework in which the macroeconomic variables are endogenously determined, given the decisions of forward-looking rational expectations agents. Despite some important limitations and shortcomings, DSGE models are the best and most powerful tools we have at hand.

The model presented in this chapter is very simple and some important assumptions can be relaxed. Settings other than a competitive environment can be considered, additional agents (the government, a central bank, the foreign sector, the financial sector, etc.) can be included, and other sources of disturbances can be studied. Furthermore, a large number of exercises, simulations, and goodness-of-fit tests can be carried out.

Appendix A: Dynare code

The Dynare code corresponding to the model developed in this chapter, named *model2.mod*, is the following:

```
//Model 2:  Basic DSGE model
//Dynare code
//File:  model2.mod
//José L. Torres.  University of Málaga (Spain)
//Endogenous variables
var Y, C, I, K, L, W, R, A;
//Exogenous variables
varexo e;
// Parameters
parameters alpha, beta, delta, gamma, rho;
// Calibration
```

```
alpha = 0.35;
beta  = 0.97;
delta = 0.06;
gamma = 0.40;
rho   = 0.95;
// Equations of the model
model;
C = (gamma/(1-gamma))*(1-L)*(1-alpha)*Y/L;
1 = beta*((C/C(+1))*(R(+1)+(1-delta)));
Y = A*(K(-1)^alpha)*(L^(1-alpha));
K = (Y-C)+(1-delta)*K(-1);
I = Y-C;
W = (1-alpha)*A*(K(-1)^alpha)*(L^(-alpha));
R = alpha*A*(K(-1)^(alpha-1))*(L^(1-alpha));
log(A) = rho*log(A(-1))+ e;
end;
// Initial values
initval;
Y = 1;
C = 0.8;
L = 0.3;
K = 3.5;
I = 0.2;
W = (1-alpha)*Y/L;
R = alpha*Y/K;
A = 1;
e = 0;
end;
// Steady State computation
steady;
// Blanchard-Kahn conditions
check;
// Shock analysis:  TFP shock
shocks;
var e; stderr 0.01;
end;
// Stochastic simulation
stoch_simul;
```

Appendix B: Stochastic model solution

In this appendix we solve the stochastic version of the model. To do this, we start by linearizing the model around its steady state. Despite the simplicity of the structure of the proposed DSGE model, it is highly nonlinear, reflecting very complex relationships between different economic variables. This hampers their practical application. To solve this problem, we resort to performing a linear approximation to the equations of the model, which would allow us to direct application to the data.

The log-linearization of the model consists in expressing the variables as log-linear deviations with respect to their steady state values. The log-linear deviation of a variable u around its steady state, $\overline{u}$, is denoted as $\widehat{u}$, where $\widehat{u}_t = \ln u_t - \ln \overline{u}$. That is

$$u_t = \overline{u}e^{\widehat{u}_t} \approx \overline{u}(1 + \widehat{u}_t)$$

In constructing the log-linear deviations we follow two basic rules (Uhlig, 1999). First, for the case of two variables u_t and z_t, we have:

$$u_t z_t \approx \overline{u}(1 + \widehat{u}_t)\overline{z}(1 + \widehat{z}_t) \approx \overline{uz}(1 + \widehat{u}_t + \widehat{z}_t)$$

that is, we assume that the product of the two deviations, i.e., $\widehat{u}_t\widehat{z}_t$, is approximately equal to zero, as they are small numbers. Second, we assume the following approximation:

$$u_t^a \approx \overline{u}^a(1 + \widehat{u}_t)^a \approx \overline{u}^a(1 + a\widehat{u}_t)$$

Taking into account the above definitions, we can proceed to the log-linearization of our model. We start from the production function:

$$Y_t = A_t K_t^{\alpha} L_t^{1-\alpha}$$

In steady state, the production function can be written as:

$$\overline{Y} = \overline{AK}^{\alpha}\overline{L}^{1-\alpha}$$

Therefore, using the above basic rules, we can write:

$$\overline{Y}(1 + \widehat{y}_t) = \overline{AK}^{\alpha}\overline{L}^{1-\alpha}(1 + \widehat{a}_t + \alpha\widehat{k}_t + (1-\alpha)\widehat{l}_t)$$

Substituting, we obtain the log-linear equation for the production function:

$$\widehat{y}_t = \widehat{a}_t + \alpha\widehat{k}_t + (1-\alpha)\widehat{l}_t \tag{A.1}$$

This procedure must be applied to the other equations of the model. For instance, the second equation we consider is:

$$C_t = Y_t - I_t$$

By calculating the deviation with respect to the steady state we obtain:

$$\widehat{c}_t = \frac{\overline{Y}}{\overline{C}}\widehat{y}_t - \frac{\overline{I}}{\overline{C}}\widehat{i}_t$$

Substituting the steady state values in the feasibility condition of the economy, we obtain:

$$\left[1-\beta+(1-\alpha)\beta\delta\right]\widehat{c}_t = (1-\beta+\beta\delta)\widehat{y}_t - \alpha\beta\delta\widehat{i}_t \tag{A.2}$$

The log-linear version of the capital stock accumulation equation is given by:

$$\widehat{k}_{t+1} = (1-\delta)\widehat{k}_t + \delta\widehat{i}_t \tag{A.3}$$

Next equation of the model is the following:

$$\frac{1-\gamma}{\gamma}\frac{C_t}{1-L_t} = (1-\alpha)\frac{Y_t}{L_t}$$

and after the necessary transformation we obtain:

$$(1-\gamma)\overline{CL} = \gamma(1-\alpha)\overline{Y}(1-\overline{L})$$

Again, substituting the steady state values previously computed, we obtain the following expression:

$$\left[1+\frac{\gamma(1-\alpha)}{(1-\gamma)}\frac{1-\beta+\beta\delta}{1-\beta+(1-\alpha)\beta\delta}\right]\widehat{l}_t = \widehat{y}_t - \widehat{c}_t \tag{A.4}$$

The next equation is:

$$\frac{E_t C_{t+1}}{C_t} = E_t\beta\left[1+\left(\alpha\frac{Y_{t+1}}{K_{t+1}}-\delta\right)\right]$$

and applying the same procedure, we obtain the following expression:

$$E_t\widehat{c}_{t+1}-\widehat{c}_t=\left(1-\beta+\beta\delta\right)E_t\widehat{y}_{t+1}-\left(1-\beta+\beta\delta\right)E_t\widehat{k}_{t+1} \tag{A.5}$$

Finally, given our assumption that the TFP follows an AR(1) process, the log-deviation with respect to the steady state is given by:

$$\widehat{a}_t=\rho\widehat{a}_{t-1}+\varepsilon_t \tag{A.6}$$

Once we have the model in log-linear form, we can proceed with its resolution, although we have to bear in mind that this is an approximation of the original highly nonlinear model. The literature had proposed different alternative methods to solve a DSGE model. These methods are the proposed by Blanchard and Kahn (1980), Uhlig (1999), Sims (2001) and Klein (2000). Here, we use the procedure developed by Blanchard and Kahn (1980). We follow Ireland (2004) in applying Blanchard-Kahn method. We start by defining the following two vectors of deviations from the steady state:

$$x_t^0=\begin{bmatrix}\widehat{y}_t\\ \widehat{i}_t\\ \widehat{l}_t\end{bmatrix} \tag{A.7}$$

$$s_t^0=\begin{bmatrix}\widehat{k}_t\\ \widehat{c}_t\end{bmatrix} \tag{A.8}$$

where the first vector comprises deviations in production, investment, and employment from their steady state valuesand the second vector is formed by the deviations of the capital stock and consumption, the variables for which we have not only its current value but also future value.

First, we can write the following system:

$$Ax_t^0=Bs_t^0+C\widehat{a}_t \tag{A.9}$$

consisting of the following three equations:

$$\widehat{y}_t-(1-\alpha)\widehat{l}_t=\widehat{a}_t+\alpha\widehat{k}_t$$

$$(1-\beta+\beta\delta)\widehat{y}_t-\alpha\beta\delta\widehat{i}_t=\left[1-\beta+(1-\alpha)\beta\delta\right]\widehat{c}_t$$

$$\widehat{y}_t - \left[1 + \frac{\gamma(1-\alpha)}{(1-\gamma)} \frac{1-\beta+\beta\delta}{1-\beta+(1-\alpha)\beta\delta}\right] \widehat{i}_t = \widehat{c}_t$$

To simplify notation, we define the following three parameters:

$$\theta = 1-\beta+\beta\delta$$

$$\phi = 1-\beta+(1-\alpha)\beta\delta$$

$$\eta = 1 + \frac{\gamma(1-\alpha)}{(1-\gamma)} \frac{\theta}{\phi}$$

and where the constant matrices are given by:

$$A = \begin{bmatrix} 1 & 0 & \alpha-1 \\ \theta & \phi-\theta & 0 \\ 1 & 0 & -\eta \end{bmatrix}$$

$$B = \begin{bmatrix} \alpha & 0 \\ 0 & \phi \\ 0 & 1 \end{bmatrix}$$

$$C = \begin{bmatrix} 1 \\ 0 \\ 0 \end{bmatrix}$$

We also define the following system in terms of the expected future value of the variables in the model:

$$DE_t s_{t+1}^0 + FE_t x_{t+1}^0 = Gs_t^0 + Hx_t^0 \tag{A.10}$$

consisting in the following two equations:

$$\left(1-\beta+\beta\delta\right) E_t \widehat{k}_{t+1} + E_t \widehat{c}_{t+1} - \left(1-\beta+\beta\delta\right) E_t \widehat{y}_{t+1} = \widehat{c}_t$$

$$\widehat{k}_{t+1} = (1-\delta)\widehat{k}_t + \delta \widehat{i}_t$$

where the matrices as given by:

$$D = \begin{bmatrix} \theta & 1 \\ 1 & 0 \end{bmatrix}$$

$$F = \begin{bmatrix} -\theta & 0 & 0 \\ 0 & 0 & 0 \end{bmatrix}$$

$$G = \begin{bmatrix} 1 & 0 \\ 0 & 1-\delta \end{bmatrix}$$

$$H = \begin{bmatrix} 0 & 0 & 0 \\ 0 & \delta & 0 \end{bmatrix}$$

Finally, the matrix model is closed by incorporating the expected deviation of total factor productivity:

$$E_t \widehat{a}_{t+j} = \rho_A^j \widehat{a}_t$$

The system (A.9) can be written as:

$$x_t^0 = A^{-1} B s_t^0 + A^{-1} C \widehat{a}_t$$

Taking one period ahead, the above system should be:

$$E_t x_{t+1}^0 = A^{-1} B E_t s_{t+1}^0 + A^{-1} C \rho_A \widehat{a}_t$$

Substituting in the system (A.10) we find that:

$$(D + FA^{-1}B) E_t s_{t+1}^0 = (G + HA^{-1}B) s_t^0 + (HA^{-1}C - FA^{-1}C\rho_A)\widehat{a}_t$$

Solving for the matrices, the final system would be:

$$E_t s_{t+1}^0 = J s_t^0 + M \widehat{a}_t$$

where:

$$J = (D + FA^{-1}B)^{-1}(G + HA^{-1}B)$$

$$M = (D + FA^{-1}B)^{-1}(HA^{-1}C - FA^{-1}C\rho_A)$$

Using the Jordan decomposition, the matrix J can be decomposed such as:

$$J = O^{-1} N O$$

where:

$$N = \begin{bmatrix} N_{11} & 0 \\ 0 & N_{22} \end{bmatrix}$$

and where:

$$O = \begin{bmatrix} O_{11} & O_{12} \\ O_{21} & O_{22} \end{bmatrix}$$

Notice that the elements of the diagonal of N are the eigenvalues of the matrix J. In order the solution to be unique, the value of N_{11} must be inside the unit circle and the value of N_{22} outside the unit circle. This is the so-called the Blanchard-Kahn rank condition. If the rank condition does not hold, then the equilibrium is not unique. The columns of O^{-1} are the eigenvectors of the matrix J. Therefore, the system can be written as:

$$E_t s^0_{t+1} = \begin{bmatrix} O_{11} & O_{12} \\ O_{21} & O_{22} \end{bmatrix}^{-1} \begin{bmatrix} N_{11} & 0 \\ 0 & N_{22} \end{bmatrix} \begin{bmatrix} O_{11} & O_{12} \\ O_{21} & O_{22} \end{bmatrix} s^0_t + \begin{bmatrix} M_{11} \\ M_{21} \end{bmatrix} \widehat{a}_t$$

$$\begin{aligned} \begin{bmatrix} O_{11} & O_{12} \\ O_{21} & O_{22} \end{bmatrix} E_t s^0_{t+1} &= \begin{bmatrix} N_{11} & 0 \\ 0 & N_{22} \end{bmatrix} \begin{bmatrix} O_{11} & O_{12} \\ O_{21} & O_{22} \end{bmatrix} s^0_t \\ &+ \begin{bmatrix} O_{11} & O_{12} \\ O_{21} & O_{22} \end{bmatrix} \begin{bmatrix} M_{11} \\ M_{21} \end{bmatrix} \widehat{a}_t \end{aligned}$$

Alternatively, we write the following expectations:

$$E_t s^1_{1,t+1} = N_{11} s^1_{1,t} + Q_{11} \widehat{a}_t$$

$$E_t s^1_{2,t+1} = N_{22} s^1_{2,t} + Q_{21} \widehat{a}_t$$

where:

$$s^1_{1,t} = O_{11} \widehat{k}_t + O_{12} \widehat{c}_t$$

$$s^1_{2,t} = O_{21} \widehat{k}_t + O_{22} \widehat{c}_t$$

and where:

$$Q = \begin{bmatrix} Q_{11} \\ Q_{21} \end{bmatrix} = OM$$

Given that the value of N_{22} is outside the unit circle, we can solve $s^1_{2,t}$ ahead:

$$s^1_{2,t} = \frac{1}{N_{22}} E_t s^1_{2,t+1} - \frac{Q_{21}}{N_{22}} \widehat{a}_t$$

resulting:

$$\begin{aligned} s^1_{2,t} &= -\frac{Q_{21}}{N_{22}} \sum_{j=0}^{\infty} \left(\frac{1}{N_{22}}\right)^j E_t \widehat{a}_{t+j} \\ &= -\frac{Q_{21}}{N_{22}} \sum_{j=0}^{\infty} \left(\frac{\rho_A}{N_{22}}\right)^j \widehat{a}_t = \frac{Q_{21}}{\rho_A - N_{22}} \widehat{a}_t \end{aligned}$$

Solving for $\widehat{c}_t$ we obtain:

$$\frac{Q_{21}}{\rho_A - N_{22}} \widehat{a}_t = O_{21} \widehat{k}_t + O_{22} \widehat{c}_t$$

Thus, the log-deviation of consumption is:

$$\widehat{c}_t = -\frac{O_{21}}{O_{22}} \widehat{k}_t + \frac{Q_{21}}{O_{22}(\rho_A - N_{22})} \widehat{a}_t$$

or alternatively:

$$\widehat{c}_t = S_1 \widehat{k}_t + S_2 \widehat{a}_t$$

being

$$S_1 = -\frac{O_{21}}{O_{22}}$$

$$S_2 = \frac{Q_{21}}{O_{22}(\rho_A - N_{22})}$$

In the case of the vector $s^1_{1,t}$ we find that:

$$s^1_{1,t} = (O_{11} + O_{12} S_1) \widehat{k}_t + O_{12} S_2 \widehat{c}_t$$

and substituting we obtain:

$$E_t s^1_{1,t+1} = N_{11} s^1_{1,t} + Q_{11}\widehat{a}_t$$

$$E_t s^1_{1,t+1} = N_{11}\left[(O_{11} + O_{12}S_1)\widehat{k}_t + O_{12}S_2\widehat{c}_t\right] + Q_{11}\widehat{a}_t$$

$$(O_{11} + O_{12}S_1)\widehat{k}_{t+1} = N_{11}(O_{11} + O_{12}S_1)\widehat{k}_t + (Q_{11} + O_{12}S_2(1-\rho_A))\widehat{a}_t$$

or alternatively:

$$\widehat{k}_{t+1} = S_3\widehat{k}_t + S_4\widehat{a}_t$$

where:

$$S_3 = N_{11}$$

$$S_4 = \frac{Q_{11} + N_{11}O_{12}S_2 - O_{12}S_2\rho_A}{O_{11} + O_{12}S_1}$$

Finally, returning to the initial system:

$$x^0_t = A^{-1}Bs^0_t + A^{-1}C\widehat{a}_t$$

$$x^0_t = A^{-1}B\begin{bmatrix} \widehat{k}_t \\ \widehat{c}_t \end{bmatrix} + A^{-1}C\widehat{a}_t$$

$$x^0_t = A^{-1}B\begin{bmatrix} 1 \\ S_1 \end{bmatrix}\widehat{k}_t + \left[A^{-1}C + A^{-1}B\begin{bmatrix} 0 \\ S_2 \end{bmatrix}\right]\widehat{a}_t$$

or:

$$x^0_t = S_5 s^0_t + S_6\widehat{a}_t$$

where:

$$S_5 = A^{-1}B\begin{bmatrix} 1 \\ S_1 \end{bmatrix}$$

$$S_6 = A^{-1}C + A^{-1}B\begin{bmatrix} 0 \\ S_2 \end{bmatrix}$$

Having completed all these computations, the solution of the model can be obtained. Collecting terms, the solution of the model is given by:

$$\begin{bmatrix} \widehat{k}_{t+1} \\ \widehat{a}_{t+1} \end{bmatrix} = \begin{bmatrix} S_3 & S_4 \\ 0 & \rho_A \end{bmatrix} \begin{bmatrix} \widehat{k}_t \\ \widehat{a}_t \end{bmatrix} + \begin{bmatrix} 0 \\ 1 \end{bmatrix} \begin{bmatrix} \varepsilon_{1,t+1} \\ \varepsilon_{2,t+1} \end{bmatrix}$$

and

$$\begin{bmatrix} \widehat{y}_t \\ \widehat{i}_t \\ \widehat{l}_t \\ \widehat{c}_t \end{bmatrix} = \begin{bmatrix} S_5 & S_6 \\ S_1 & S_2 \end{bmatrix} \begin{bmatrix} \widehat{k}_t \\ \widehat{a}_t \end{bmatrix}$$

that is, the solution implies that the vector of log-deviation of control variables is a function of the vector of the state variables, and where the matrices S_5 and S_6 are function on the parameters of the model $(\alpha, \beta, \gamma, \delta, \rho_A, \sigma_A)$. Therefore, the resolution of the model involves the calibration or estimation of the above matrices, i.e., the structural parameters of the model, linking the dynamic of the control variables with the state variables, where the state variables follow an autoregressive vector of order 1. Given the process for the state variables, we can predict its future value, so using the latter system, we can obtain projections for the future value of control variables.

Given the calibrated parameter values, the specific solution for our model would be:

$$A = \begin{bmatrix} 1.0000 & 0.0000 & -0.6500 \\ 0.0882 & -0.0204 & 0.0000 \\ 1.0000 & 0.0000 & -1.5635 \end{bmatrix}$$

$$B = \begin{bmatrix} 0.35 & 0 \\ 0 & 0.0678 \\ 0 & 1 \end{bmatrix}$$

$$C = \begin{bmatrix} 1 \\ 0 \\ 0 \end{bmatrix}$$

$$D = \begin{bmatrix} 0.0882 & 1 \\ 1 & 0 \end{bmatrix}$$

$$F = \begin{bmatrix} -0.0882 & 0 & 0 \\ 0 & 0 & 0 \end{bmatrix}$$

$$G = \begin{bmatrix} 0 & 1 \\ 0.94 & 0 \end{bmatrix}$$

$$H = \begin{bmatrix} 0 & 0 & 0 \\ 0 & 0.06 & 0 \end{bmatrix}$$

Given the above matrices, we can proceed to define the following two matrices J and M:

$$J = \begin{bmatrix} 1.0956 & -0.3847 \\ -0.0365 & 0.9537 \end{bmatrix}$$

$$M = \begin{bmatrix} 0.4447 \\ 0.1201 \end{bmatrix}$$

Applying the Jordan decomposition to matrix J, we obtain:

$$O = \begin{bmatrix} 0.1320 & 0.7570 \\ -0.1320 & 0.2430 \end{bmatrix}$$

$$N = \begin{bmatrix} 0.8866 & 0 \\ 0 & 1.1627 \end{bmatrix}$$

being

$$Q = \begin{bmatrix} 0.1497 \\ -0.0295 \end{bmatrix}$$

Finally, we can compute:

$$S_1 = 0.5433$$

$$S_2 = 0.5709$$

$$S_3 = 0.8866$$

$$S_4 = 0.2251$$

$$S_5 = \begin{bmatrix} 0.2124 \\ -0.8893 \\ -0.2116 \end{bmatrix}$$

$$S_6 = \begin{bmatrix} 1.3054 \\ 3.7513 \\ 0.4698 \end{bmatrix}$$

Therefore, the solution of the model is given by the following two systems of equations:

$$\begin{bmatrix} \widehat{k}_{t+1} \\ \widehat{a}_{t+1} \end{bmatrix} = \begin{bmatrix} 0.8866 & 0.2251 \\ 0 & 0.9500 \end{bmatrix} \begin{bmatrix} \widehat{k}_t \\ \widehat{a}_t \end{bmatrix} + \begin{bmatrix} 0 \\ 1 \end{bmatrix} \begin{bmatrix} \varepsilon_{1,t+1} \\ \varepsilon_{2,t+1} \end{bmatrix}$$

and

$$\begin{bmatrix} \widehat{y}_t \\ \widehat{i}_t \\ \widehat{l}_t \\ \widehat{c}_t \end{bmatrix} = \begin{bmatrix} 0.2124 & 1.3054 \\ -0.8893 & 3.7513 \\ -0.2116 & 0.4698 \\ 0.5433 & 0.5709 \end{bmatrix} \begin{bmatrix} \widehat{k}_t \\ \widehat{a}_t \end{bmatrix}$$

Bibliography

Altug, S. (1989): Time-to-build and aggregate fluctuations: Some new evidence. *International Economic Review*, 30(4), 889-920.

Blanchard, O. and Kahn, C.M. (1980): The solution of linear difference models under rational expectations. *Econometrica*, 48(1), 305-311.

Brock, W. and Mirman, L. (1972): Optimal economic growth and uncertainty: The discounted case. *Journal of Economic Theory*, 4(3), 479-513.

Cass, D. (1965): Optimum growth in an aggregative model of capital accumulation. *Review of Economic Studies*, 32, 233-240.

Cobb, C. and Douglas, P. (1928): A Theory of Production. *American Economic Review*, 18 (Supplement), 139–165.

Diebold, F. (1998): Past, present and future of macroeconomic forecasting. *Journal of Economic Perspectives*, 12(2), 175-192.

Ireland, P. (2004): A method for taking models to the data. *Journal of Economic Dynamic and Control*, 28, 1205-1226.

Klein, P. (2000): Using the generalized Schur form to solve a multivariate linear rational expectations model. *Journal of Economic Dynamics and Control*, 24(1), 405-423.

Koopmans, T. (1965): On the concept of optimal economic growth, en *The Econometric Approach to Development Planning*, North-Holland, Amsterdam.

Kydland, F. and Prescott, E. (1982): Time to build and aggregate fluctuations. *Econometrica*, 50, 1350-1372.

Long, J. and Plosser, C. (1983): Real Business Cycles. *Journal of Political Economy*, 91(1), 39-69.

Ramsey, F. (1927): A contribution to the theory of taxation. *Economic Journal*, 37(145), 47-61.

Ramsey, F. (1928): A mathematical theory of saving. *Economic Journal*, 38(152), 543-559.

Rotemberg, J. and Woodford, M. (1997): An optimization-based econometric framework for the evaluation of monetary policy. *NBER Macroeconomics Annual*, 12, 297-346.

Sargent, T. (1989): Two models of measurements and the investment accelerator. *Journal of Political Economy*, 97(2), 251-287.

Sims, C. (2001): Solving linear rational expectations models. *Computational Economics*, 20, 1-20.

Uhlig, H. (1999): A toolkit for analyzing non-linear dynamic stochastic models easily, in R. Marimon and A. Scott (Eds.), *Computational Methods for the Study of Dynamic Economies*, Oxford University Press, New York.

Part II

Deviations from the Permanent Income-Life Cycle hypothesis

Chapter 3

Habit Formation

Introduction

In the previous chapter we have presented a simple DSGE model in which households objective was to maximize what we called the instantaneous utility function. In this simple theoretical framework, households utility at time t only depends on the level of consumption at time t and does not depend on the level of consumption of previous periods. The implicit assumption behind this particular functional form is that utility function is additively separable in time. This assumption is useful for mathematical tractability of the intertemporal consumer problem. However, empirical evidence shows the existence of the so-called habit formation or habit persistence in consumption by which the utility function is not instantaneous, and hence, preferences are non-separable over time.

Habit formation derives from the fact that when a behavior is repeated regularly, that behavior becomes automatic. In particular, consumption habit formation refers to the fact that consumer happiness is not only affected by current consumption but also by the level of consumption in previous periods. As pointed out by Campbell and Cochrane (1999) habit formation is a fundamental aspect of psychology: repetition of a stimulus decreases the perception of the stimulus and the response to it. This characteristic was first introduced in economics by Duesenberry (1949). Past consumption translates to a stock of habits or a standard of living, which households want to maintain over time. In the case of a negative shock on current income, the individual will try to get the same level of consumption than in the previous period by adjusting saving. If this negative shock is permanent, consumption must be adjusted downturn but habit persistence prevents the adjustment to be instantaneous. In other words, if an individual is accustomed to a high level of consumption and a sudden negative shock reduces her income, that individual will tend to maintain the same pattern of consumption, at least during some periods, by reducing saving until the reduction in consumption is inevitable.

The rationale for the introduction of consumer habits in the standard DSGE model is based on the observed deviations from the permanent income -life cycle hypothesis. Empirical evidence shows the existence of two types of deviations from the permanent income-life cycle hypothesis: excess sensitivity of consumption to current income and excess smoothness of consumption relative to non-anticipated changes in income. The existence of habit formation can explain the excess smoothness of consumption.

The structure of the rest of the chapter is as follows. Section 2 presents a brief review of some relevant concepts regarding consumption habit formation. Section 3 presents a simple DSGE model with habit formation, describing how the basic consumer problem must be changed to consider the existence of habits. Section 4 shows the equilibrium equations and the calibration of the parameters of the model. Section 5 studies the effects of a productivity shock. Finally, Section 6 presents some conclusions.

Habit formation

The basic DSGE model assumes that utility in a given period only depends on the consumption in that period, without being affected by the consumption made in previous periods. This is the so-called instantaneous utility function. This implies the assumption that the utility function is additively separable in time.

However, a feature found in consumption patterns is the so-called *habit formation* or *habit persistence*. Habits formation introduces a new element in the basic DSGE model, since its incorporation causes the utility function of consumers not to be additively separable in time. In the basic model it is assumed that the utility function of consumers is additively separable in time. This implies that the discounted sum of the value at each moment of time is equal to the total discounted utility granted over the life cycle. The consideration of habits formation implies that the utility function of consumers is not separable over time, as consumption decisions in previous periods affect current utility. Under the existence of consumer habits, an increase in current consumption decreases marginal utility of consumption at the present, but increases future marginal utility of consumption. The opposite is also true. Therefore, the consumer maximization problem to be solved is technically more complex as current consumption does not only determine current utility but also future utility.[1]

The existence of consumption habits is an element that may explain the excess smoothness of consumption relative to (non-anticipated) changes in the level of income, since in this case the preferences are not separable in time. Consumption habits can be understood as the cost of adjusting consumption when a shock affects income. This adjustment cost is measured in terms of utility or happiness. If consumption habits are very pronounced, given a change in income, consumption tends to change very slowly over time. Therefore, consumption habits may be responsible for the empirically observed excess smoothness of consumption to changes in income. Moreover, as shown by Boldrin, Christiano and Fisher (2001), habit persistence may also explain the other observed deviation with respect to the permanent income-life cycle hypothesis: the excess sensitivity of consumption to current income.

Consumption habits are introduced regularly in DSGE models in order to try to better explain the observed dynamics of the economy. Empirical evidence suggests that the response of consumption to a positive shock is hump-shaped, with the greatest response occurring a few periods after the date the disturbance occurs. This hump-shaped behavior (also observed in the standard basic model without habit persistence, although less pronounced) and a smoother instantaneous change in consumption at the hit of the shock can be obtained by considering the existence of habits formation.

Consumption habits may be internal or external. One possibility is to assume that habits are external to the individual, i.e., they do not depend on the individual's past decisions regarding his consumption but on the aggregate consumption of the economy. This specification is used by Duesenberry (1949), Pollak (1970) and Abel (1990). When habits are external, the stock of habits depends on the history of past aggregate consumption and not on the agent's own past consumption. This type of consumption habit is what is known in the literature as the "catching up with the Joneses" formulation.

The alternative is to consider internal consumption habits, which refer to a specification in which the stock of habits of the individual is determined in terms of their own past consumption. This specification of habit formation is used, for instance, by Constantinides (1990). However, as pointed out by Schmitt-Grohé and Uribe (2008), the dynamics of the model economy in both cases are very similar,

[1] For a review of the literature on habit formation, see for instance, Denton (1992).

especially when in equilibrium the representative agent's consumption coincides with aggregate per capita consumption.

Consumer habits have been particularly relevant to explaining the so-called “equity premium puzzle”, some observed business cycle fluctuations facts, the dynamics of inflation, or to develop a theory to explain the counter-cyclical behavior of price-cost margins. For instance, Constantinides (1990) shows that consumption habits can resolve the "equity premium puzzle", mainly due to the increasing divergence between the relative risk aversion of the representative agent and the elasticity of intertemporal substitution of consumption. Carroll, Overland and Weil (2000) use consumption patterns to explain the existence of a positive relationship between saving and growth. In this sense, the empirical literature shows that high economic growth also causes high saving, which contradicts standard models of economic growth, in which forward-looking agents save less in an economy with high growth because they know that in the future they will be richer. These authors show that under the existence of habits, it is obtained a result consistent with the empirical evidence. Boldrin, Christiano and Fisher (2001) show that habit persistence can explain a variety of empirical facts, such as the excess sensitivity of consumption to changes in income, persistence in output, and the negative correlation between interest rate and future output. Ravn, Schmitt-Grohé and Uribe (2006) introduce what they call "deep habits", in which consumption habits are not formed over a single aggregate good, but are determined on a good-by-good basis, depending on the particular characteristics of each of them.

The literature offers a variety of alternative specifications for the introduction of habit persistence in the household utility function. The most commonly used functional form is to introduce into the utility function the quasi-difference of consumption, i.e., as a function of the difference between current consumption and a proportion of consumption in previous periods. Thus the utility of the individual in a given period does not depend on the level of consumption of the period but the quasi-difference of consumption.

Let us assume that the representative consumer maximizes the following utility function:

$$U(C_t - X_t, O_t) \tag{3.1}$$

where C_t is consumption, X_t represents consumption habits and

O_t is leisure. Consumption habits at time t are assumed to be a proportion of the level of consumption at time $t-1$:

$$X_t = \phi C_{t-1} \tag{3.2}$$

where $\phi > 0$ is a coefficient of persistence in habits. The parameter ϕ represents the intensity of consumer habits and introduces non-separability of preferences over time. The direct implication of using this functional form is that an increase in current consumption decreases the marginal utility of consumption in the current period but increases utility in the following period. Another way of introducing consumption habits is considering that the utility depends on the quasi-ratio of consumption instead of the quasi-difference of consumption. This type of utility function was introduced by Duesenberry (1949).

More general specifications allow the level of habit is a function of all past consumption. For instance, we can assume that the utility function has the following form:

$$U(C_t - \phi X_{t-1}) \tag{3.3}$$

where

$$X_{t-1} = X(C_{t-1}, C_{t-2}, ...) \tag{3.4}$$

being X_{t-1} the habits stock at time t. In general, it is assumed that the habits stock follows an autoregressive process of order 1, AR(1), such as:

$$X_t = (1-\delta_X)X_{t-1} + \theta C_t \tag{3.5}$$

where the parameter δ_X is the depreciation rate of the habits stock and where the parameter θ reflects the sensibility of the habits stock relative to current consumption.

Abel (1990) uses a general utility function that can embed three alternative specifications of the utility function: the standard utility function additively separable in time; an utility function that depends on the level of individual consumption relative to aggregate consumption in the previous period, i.e., external habits; and an utility function that incorporates the individual's own habits, i.e., internal habits. The functional form of this general utility function is given by:

$$U(C_t, V_t) \tag{3.6}$$

where

$$V_t = \left[C_{t-1}^{\lambda}\tilde{C}_{t-1}^{1-\lambda}\right]^{\phi} \tag{3.7}$$

and where $\tilde{C}_{t-1}$ is the economy aggregate consumption at period $t-1$. If $\phi = 0$, then $V_t = 1$, the utility function is additively separable in time as utility at time t only depends on consumption at time t. If $\phi > 0$ and $\lambda = 0$, then V_t depends on the aggregate level of consumption in the previous period, that is, external habits. Finally, if $\phi > 0$ and $\lambda = 1$, this is the case of internal habits, where V_t depends on the own level of consumption of the agent in the previous period.

The model

The model presented here is similar to the standard DSGE model except for the consideration of consumer's habit persistence. We abandon the assumption of time-separable preferences and instead it is assumed that the utility function is time-non-separable and depends on the quasi-difference in consumption. Therefore, the only change from the basic model lies in the definition of the household's utility function.

Households

The economy is inhabited by an infinitely lived, representative household, who has preferences represented by the following utility function:

$$U(C_t - H_t, O_t) \tag{3.8}$$

where C_t is consumption, H_t reflects consumption habits and O_t is leisure. As consumption habits we assume that they are proportional to the level consumption in the previous period, such that:

$$H_t = \phi C_{t-1} \tag{3.9}$$

where $\phi > 0$ is the coefficient of persistence in consumption habits. This means that the utility function is not instantaneous anymore in terms of consumption, i.e., utility at time t does not only depend on consumption at time t, but also on the level of consumption in the previous period depending on the intensity of habit persistence, given by the value of ϕ. The economic interpretation of this term is that current utility is derived from current consumption relative to previous period consumption.

We assume that preferences have the following functional form:

$$U(C_t - H_t, O_t) = \gamma \log(C_t - \phi C_{t-1}) + (1-\gamma)\log(1 - L_t) \qquad (3.10)$$

where L_t is working time and total available discretionary time is normalized to 1 ($L_t + O_t = 1$) and $\gamma \in (0,1)$ is the elasticity of substitution between consumption and leisure.

The problem faced by the stand-in consumer is to maximize the value of her lifetime utility given by:

$$\max_{(C_t,K_t,L_t)} \mathcal{L} = E_0 \sum_{t=0}^{\infty} \beta^t \left[\gamma \log(C_t - \phi C_{t-1}) + (1-\gamma)\log(1-L_t)\right] \quad (3.11)$$

subject to the budget constraint:

$$C_t + S_t = W_t L_t + R_t K_t \qquad (3.12)$$

where S_t is saving, W_t is the wage, R_t is the rental rate of capital and K_t is the physical capital stock. The low of motion for physical capital stock is given by:

$$K_{t+1} = (1-\delta)K_t + I_t \qquad (3.13)$$

where I_t is (gross) investment and δ is the capital depreciation rate. By assuming that $S_t = I_t$ and substituting investment is the budget constraint we have:

$$C_t + K_{t+1} = W_t L_t + (R_t + 1 - \delta)K_t \qquad (3.14)$$

Therefore, the Lagrangian problem to be solved by households is to choose C_t, I_t, and L_t so as to maximize:

$$\max_{(C_t,K_t,L_t)} \mathcal{L} = E_0 \sum_{t=0}^{\infty} \beta^t \left\{ \begin{array}{c} \gamma \log(C_t - \phi C_{t-1}) + (1-\gamma)\log(1-L_t) \\ -\lambda_t \left[C_t + K_{t+1} - W_t L_t - (R_t + 1 - \delta)K_t\right] \end{array} \right\} \qquad (3.15)$$

Corresponding first-order conditions are given by the following expressions:

$$\frac{\partial \mathcal{L}}{\partial C}: \beta^t \left[\gamma \frac{1}{C_t - \phi C_{t-1}} - \lambda_t\right] - \beta^{t+1}\left[\gamma\phi \frac{1}{C_{t+1} - \phi C_t}\right] = 0 \tag{3.16}$$

$$\frac{\partial \mathcal{L}}{\partial L}: -(1-\gamma)\frac{1}{1-L_t} + \lambda_t W_t = 0 \tag{3.17}$$

$$\frac{\partial \mathcal{L}}{\partial K}: \beta^t \lambda_t [R_t + 1 - \delta] - \lambda_{t-1}\beta^{t-1} = 0 \tag{3.18}$$

where $\beta^t \lambda_t$ is the Lagrange multiplier associated to the budget constraint at time t. Note that consumption at time t also enters in the utility function at time $t+1$, and hence, the first order condition with respect to consumption is given by:

$$\frac{\partial U_t}{\partial C_t} = U_{C,t} + \beta U_{C,t+1} \tag{3.19}$$

Solving for the Lagrange multiplier, we get:

$$\lambda_t = \gamma \frac{1}{C_t - \phi C_{t-1}} - \beta\gamma\phi \frac{1}{C_{t+1} - \phi C_t}$$

Combining equations (3.16) and (3.17) we obtain the condition that equates the marginal disutility of additional hours of work with the marginal return on additional hours:

$$(1-\gamma)\frac{1}{1-L_t} = \left[\gamma \frac{1}{C_t - \phi C_{t-1}} - \beta\gamma\phi \frac{1}{C_{t+1} - \phi C_t}\right] W_t \tag{3.20}$$

Combining equation (3.16) with equation (3.18), and taking into account that:

$$\lambda_{t-1} = \gamma \frac{1}{C_{t-1} - \phi C_{t-2}} - \beta\gamma\phi \frac{1}{C_t - \phi C_{t-1}} \tag{3.21}$$

we obtain the following intertemporal equilibrium condition,

$$\frac{\left[\frac{1}{C_{t-1} - \phi C_{t-2}} - \beta\phi \frac{1}{C_t - \phi C_{t-1}}\right]}{\left[\frac{1}{C_t - \phi C_{t-1}} - \beta\phi \frac{1}{C_{t+1} - \phi C_t}\right]} = \beta [R_{t+1} + 1 - \delta] \tag{3.22}$$

representing the optimal consumption path over time, that is, the intertemporal equation that equates the marginal rate of consumption to the rate of return of investment. If $\phi = 0$, expression (3.22) reduces to the standard case. If $\phi > 0$, investment decisions does not only depend on the consumption of a period over another, but on the consumption in four different points in the time, reflecting the fact that the agent want to maintain their consumption level as stable as possible across time.

The firms

The problem of firms is to find optimal values for the utilization of labor and capital. The production of final output Y requires the services of labor L and K. The firms rent capital and employ labor in order to maximize profits at period t, taking factor prices as given. The technology is given by a constant returns to scale Cobb-Douglas production function,

$$Y_t = A_t K_t^{\alpha} L_t^{1-\alpha} \tag{3.23}$$

where A_t is a measure of total-factor, or sector-neutral, productivity and where $0 \leq \alpha \leq 1$.

The static maximization problem for the firms is:

$$\max_{(K_t, L_t)} \Pi_t = A_t K_t^{\alpha} L_t^{1-\alpha} - R_t K_t - W_t L_t \tag{3.24}$$

The first order conditions (FOCs) for the firms profit maximization are given by:

$$\frac{\partial \Pi_t}{\partial K_t} : R_t - \alpha A_t K_t^{\alpha-1} L_t^{1-\alpha} = 0 \tag{3.25}$$

$$\frac{\partial \Pi_t}{\partial L_t} : W_t - (1-\alpha) A_t K_t^{\alpha} L_t^{-\alpha} = 0 \tag{3.26}$$

From these FOCs we obtain the price for the production inputs:

$$R_t = \alpha A_t K_t^{\alpha-1} L_t^{1-\alpha} \tag{3.27}$$

$$W_t = (1-\alpha) A_t K_t^{\alpha} L_t^{-\alpha} \tag{3.28}$$

Equilibrium

Once optimal decisions from both households and firms have been derived, next we can proceed to compute the equilibrium of our model economy. This is done just by putting together both economic agents decisions. Households decide how much they want to consume, C_t, how much they want to invest (save), I_t, and how much hours are devoted to work, L_t, in order to maximize life-time utility function, taken the price of production factors as given. On the other side, the firms will produce a quantity of the final good, Y_t, depending on their decisions about how much capital, K_t and labor L_t, to be hired, taken as given their prices. A more formal definition of the equilibrium is the following:

Definition 3 *A competitive equilibrium for this economy is a sequence of consumption, leisure, and private investment* $\{C_t, 1-L_t, I_t\}_{t=0}^{\infty}$ *for the consumers, a sequence of capital and labor utilization for the firm* $\{K_t, L_t\}_{t=0}^{\infty}$, *such that, given a sequence of prices,* $\{W_t, R_t\}_{t=0}^{\infty}$:
i) The optimization problem of the consumer is satisfied.
ii) Given prices for capital and labor, the first-order conditions of the firm hold.
iii) The feasibility constraint of the economy is satisfied.

By combining the first order conditions for households and firms we obtain the equilibrium condition that equates the marginal rate of substitution between consumption and leisure to the opportunity cost of one additional unit of leisure. In other words, the condition that equates the disutility of working an additional hour with the marginal utility derived from the income obtained by such additional working hour is given by:

$$(1-\gamma)\frac{1}{1-L_t} = \left[\gamma\frac{1}{C_t-\phi C_{t-1}} - \beta\gamma\phi\frac{1}{C_{t+1}-\phi C_t}\right](1-\alpha)A_t K_t^{\alpha} L_t^{-\alpha} \tag{3.29}$$

while the intertemporal investment equilibrium condition would be,

$$\frac{\left[\frac{1}{C_{t-1}-\phi C_{t-2}} - \beta\phi\frac{1}{C_t-\phi C_{t-1}}\right]}{\left[\frac{1}{C_t-\phi C_{t-1}} - \beta\phi\frac{1}{C_{t+1}-\phi C_t}\right]} = \beta\left[\alpha A_{t+1}K_{t+1}^{\alpha-1}L_{t+1}^{1-\alpha} + 1 - \delta\right] \tag{3.30}$$

As can be observed in the above expressions, habit persistence affects both the equilibrium condition for labor supply and the intertemporal consumption-saving decision equilibrium condition. Finally, the economy must satisfy the following feasibility constraint:

$$C_t + I_t = Y_t \tag{3.31}$$

Equations of the model and calibration

The competitive equilibrium of the model economy is given by a set of eight equations, driving the dynamics of the seven macroeconomic endogenous variables, $Y_t, C_t, I_t, K_t, L_t, R_t, W_t$, plus the Total Factor Productivity, A_t, which it is assumed to follow an autorregressive process of order 1. This set of equations is the following:

$$(1-\gamma)\frac{1}{1-L_t} = \left[\gamma\frac{1}{C_t - \phi C_{t-1}} - \beta\gamma\phi\frac{1}{C_{t+1} - \phi C_t}\right] W_t \tag{3.32}$$

$$\frac{\left[\frac{1}{C_{t-1}-\phi C_{t-2}} - \beta\phi\frac{1}{C_t-\phi C_{t-1}}\right]}{\left[\frac{1}{C_t-\phi C_{t-1}} - \beta\phi\frac{1}{C_{t+1}-\phi C_t}\right]} = \beta\left[R_{t+1} + 1 - \delta\right] \tag{3.33}$$

$$Y_t = C_t + I_t \tag{3.34}$$

$$Y_t = A_t K_t^{\alpha} L_t^{1-\alpha} \tag{3.35}$$

$$K_{t+1} = (1-\delta)K_t + I_t \tag{3.36}$$

$$W_t = (1-\alpha)A_t K_t^{\alpha} L_t^{-\alpha} \tag{3.37}$$

$$R_t = \alpha A_t K_t^{\alpha-1} L_t^{1-\alpha} \tag{3.38}$$

$$\ln A_t = (1-\rho_A)\ln\overline{A} + \rho_A \ln A_{t-1} + \varepsilon_t \tag{3.39}$$

The structure of this model is very similar to the standard DSGE model and only one additional parameter, ϕ, reflecting the intensity of habit persistence need to be calibrated. The set of parameters to be calibrated is the following:

$$\Omega = \{\alpha, \beta, \delta, \gamma, \phi, \rho_A, \sigma_A\}$$

In order to compare the results from this model with the standard DSGE model, the values of the calibrated parameters will be the same than the ones used in the previous chapter. The only addi-

Table 3.1: Calibrated parameters

Parameter	Definition	Value
α	Technological parameter	0.350
β	Discount factor	0.970
γ	Preferences parameter	0.400
ϕ	Habit persistence	0.800
δ	Depreciation rate	0.060
ρ_A	TFP autorregressive parameter	0.950
σ_A	TFP standard deviation	0.010

tional parameter to be calibrated is the parameter that defines the intensity of consumption habits, ϕ. If the value of this parameter is zero, this would be in the standard case with no habit persistence. The higher the value of this parameter, the greater the intensity of habit formation. The summary of the calibration is shown in Table 3.1.

In the literature we find different values for the parameter representing habit persistence. For instance, Christiano, Eichenbaum and Evans (2005) estimate a value of 0.65 for the United States. Ravn, Schmitt-Grohé and Uribe (2005) used a value of 0.85. Smets and Wouters (2003) estimate a value of 0.54 for the eurozone, whereas Burriel, Fernández-Villaverde and Rubio (2009) estimate a value of 0.847 for the Spanish economy. In the simulation of the model, we use a value of 0.8, close to those estimated in the literature.

Table 3.2 shows the steady state values for the endogenous variables of the model economy. We find different steady state values with respect to the standard model, although the ratios with respect to total output do not change. We find larger steady-state values for all endogenous variables compared to the non-habit formation case.

Total Factor Productivity shock

In this section we study the effects of an aggregate productivity shock in our model economy with habit persistence. We expect that with habit persistence the dynamics of the variables to be different relative to the basic model. Indeed, the main differences are found in the responses of output and consumption, which are smoothed in impact. Starting with consumption, we observe that the impact

Table 3.2: Steady State

Variable	Value	Ratio to $\overline{Y}$
$\overline{Y}$	0.7994	1.000
$\overline{C}$	0.6148	0.769
$\overline{I}$	0.1846	0.231
$\overline{K}$	3.0773	3.849
$\overline{L}$	0.3869	-
$\overline{R}$	0.0909	-
$\overline{W}$	1.3431	-
$\overline{A}$	1.0000	-

effect of the shock is reduced, since consumption now shows a greater resistance to change. Moreover, we obtain a well persistent hump-shaped response of consumption. This may explain the observed excess smoothness of consumption to unanticipated shocks in income. This smoothness reaction of consumption turns into a higher sensitivity of investment to the shock, as the adjustment to the shock is done via saving. This differential behavior also affects the dynamics of the remaining variables.

We find that consumption habit persistence has important consequences on the dynamics of investment and, hence, on the process driving capital accumulation, amplifying the effects of the productivity shock on these variables. The explanation of this result is simple. Given a particular shock to the economy, habit persistence prevents the adjustment to be done via consumption and must be done via saving.

The estimated response of output reflects the importance of considering consumption habits in the DSGE model. We find that the level of production increases on impact but continues to increase in subsequent periods up to a maximum. Thus, in this case a hump-shaped response of output is also found. Now consumption moves slowly, causing higher investment in the initial periods which also leads to a further increase in capital stock. Volatility of investment and output increases due to the presence of habit persistence.

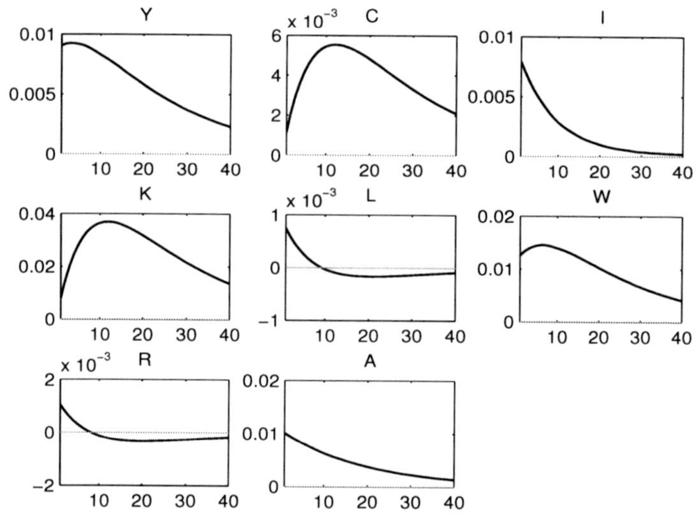

Figure 3.1: Impulse-response functions to a TFP shock with habit persistence

Conclusions

This chapter introduced habit formation into the basic DSGE model. This means that the utility function is not additively separable in time, as utility in a period does not only depend on consumption of that period but on a stock of habits formed by past consumption.

Consumption habit persistence could explain the observed excess smoothing of consumption to a (non-anticipated) change in income. Consumption habits implies the existence of an adjustment cost in consumption, measured in terms of utility. As a consequence, there are restrictions to the change in consumption when a particular shock hits the economy. Habit persistence causes the adjustment to be done via saving.

The literature has introduced habit persistence in DSGE models as a key feature to explain a number of empirically observed facts that standard models cannot account for. Indeed, habit persistence can be an important characteristic for explaining the business cycle.

Appendix A: Dynare code

The Dynare code corresponding to the model developed in this chapter, named *model3.mod*, is the following:

```
// Model 3:  Habits formation:
   // U[C(t)-phi*C(t-1),O(t)]
// Dynare code
// File:  model3.mod
// José L. Torres.  University of Málaga (Spain)
// Endogenous variables
var Y, C, I, K, L, W, R, A;
// Exogenous variables
varexo e;
// Parameters
parameters alpha, beta, delta, gamma, rho, phi;
// Calibration
alpha = 0.35;
beta  = 0.97;
delta = 0.06;
gamma = 0.40;
rho   = 0.95;
phi   = 0.80;
// Equations of the model
model;
(gamma/(C-phi*C(-1))-beta*gamma*phi/(C(+1)-phi*C))
  =(1-gamma)/((1-L)*(1-alpha)*Y/L);
(gamma/(C-phi*C(-1))-beta*gamma*phi/(C(+1)-phi*C))/
 (gamma/(C(+1)-phi*C)-beta*gamma*phi/(C(+2)-phi*C(+1)))
  =beta*(alpha*Y(+1)/K+(1-delta));
Y = A*(K(-1)^alpha)*(L^(1-alpha));
K = I+(1-delta)*K(-1);
I = Y-C;
W = (1-alpha)*A*(K(-1)^alpha)*(L^(-alpha));
R = alpha*A*(K(-1)^(alpha-1))*(L^(1-alpha));
log(A) = rho*log(A(-1))+ e;
end;
// Initial values
initval;
Y = 1;
C = 0.8;
```

```
L = 0.3;
K = 3.5;
I = 0.2;
W = (1-alpha)*Y/L;
R = alpha*Y/K;
A = 1;
e = 0;
end;
// Steady State
steady;
// Blanchard-Kahn conditions
check;
// Perturbation analysis
shocks;
var e; stderr 0.01;
end;
// Stochastic simulation
stoch_simul;
```

Bibliography

Abel, A. (1990): Asset prices under habit formation and catching-up with the Joneses. *American Economic Review*, 80(2), 38-42.

Boldrin, M., Christiano, L. and Fisher, J. (2001): Habit persistence, asset returns, and the business cycle. *American Economic Review*, 91(1), 149-166.

Burriel, P., Fernández-Villaverde, J. and Rubio-Ramírez, J. (2010): MEDEA: a DSGE model for the Spanish economy. *SERIEs*, 1(1-2), 175-249.

Campbell, J. and Cochrane, J. (1999): By force of habit: A consumption-based explanation of aggregate stock market behavior. *Journal of Political Economy*, 107(2), 205-251.

Carroll, C., Overland, J. and Weil, D. (2000): Saving and growth with habit formation. *American Economic Review*, 90(3), 341-355.

Christiano, L., Eichenbaum, M., and Evans, C. (2005): Nominal rigidities and the dynamic effects of a shock to monetary policy. *Journal of Political Economy*, 113(1), 1-45.

Constantinides, G. (1990): Habit formation: A resolution of the equity premium puzzle. *Journal of Political Economy*, 98(3), 519-543.

Deaton, A. (1992): *Understanding Consumption*. New York: Oxford University Press.

Duesenberry, J.S. (1949): *Income, Saving, and the Theory of Consumer Behavior*. Harvard University Press, Cambridge, Mass.

Fuhner, J. (2000): Optimal monetary policy in a model with habit formation. *American Economic Review,* 90(3), 367-390.

Heaton, J. (1993): The interaction between time-nonseparable preferences and time aggregation. *Econometrica,* 61(2), 353-385.

Pollak, R. (1970): Habit formation and dynamic demand functions. *Journal of Political Economy,* 78(4), 745-763.

Ravn, M., Schmitt-Grohé, S. and Uribe, M. (2006): Deep habits. *Review of Economic Studies,* 73(1), 1-24.

Schmitt-Grohé, S. and Uribe, M. (2008): What's News in Business Cycles. *NBER Working Papers,* 14215.

Smets, F. and Wouters, R. (2003): An estimated Dynamic Stochastic General Equilibrium model of the Euro Area. *Journal of the European Economic Association,* 1(5), 1123-1175.

Chapter 4

Non-Ricardian Agents

Introduction

One of the key assumptions made in DSGE models is that economic agents are rational forward-looking optimizers and that they can choose the optimal path of consumption over time to maximize their utility throughout their life cycle, breaking off period-by-period the level consumption from that of income. This is the core of the so-called permanent income-life cycle hypothesis. In this context, households use saving as a state variable to separate the temporal path of their consumption from the temporal path of their income, in order to maximize their utility. It is assumed that the consumption in a given point of time does not depend on the level of total income of that period, but on the level of income throughout the life cycle of the agent or, alternatively, on the so-called permanent income.

An implicit assumption is that agents have free access to the financial markets, for both to take income from the present to the future and to bring income from the future to the present. While the former is always true (just by not consuming a portion of the income), the latter may not be. In the real world we can find agents who would like to have a higher level of consumption in the present by borrowing, but they cannot carry out such an option by not having access to credit. When this happens, it is said that financial markets are not perfect and that a liquidity constraint exists.

Empirical evidence shows the existence of deviations from the permanent income-life cycle hypothesis. As pointed out in the previous chapter, two types of deviations are found in some empirical studies: Excess sensitivity of consumption to current income and excess smoothness of consumption to unanticipated changes in income. The first deviation implies the existence of some relationship between consumption in a period and income of that period. While there may be various elements that cause this kind of deviation from the theory of permanent income-life cycle, one possible explanation could be imperfect capital markets and liquidity constraints. This means that some households do not have access to credit so they cannot be optimizers, as they are unable to move future income to the present to finance current consumption.

One possibility to consider the existence of liquidity constraints is to assume that a portion of households cannot borrow. Here we develop a model economy in which there are two types of agents. The first type of agent is the standard so-called Ricardian agent, which is the one considered in the basic DSGE model. The second type of agent faces liquidity constraints and they may be called non-Ricardian or rule-of-thumb consumers. These latter agents can not borrow, so the level of consumption in each period is constrained by the income of that period. In this context, deviations from the permanent income-life cycle hypothesis will depend on the proportion of non-Ricardian agents that exist in the economy. The higher the proportion of non-Ricardian agents in the economy, the greater the relationship between current consumption and current income. This proportion will have important consequences when studying how the economy reacts to certain disturbances, particularly fiscal policy changes. In the model to be developed in this chapter there is no government, and hence, implications from the existence of rule-of-thumb households on fiscal policy are absent.

The structure of the rest of the chapter is as follows. Section 2 presents the characteristics of the two types of households who inhabited the economy: Ricardian and non-Ricardian agents. Section 3 presents a DSGE model in which the behavior of each agent is first analyzed separately and later they are aggregated. While the first group of agents are similar to those considered in the basic model, for the second type of agents it is assumed that the level of consumption in each period is equal to the income of that period, so they have no ability to save and to accumulate capital. Section 4 presents the equations defining the model and its calibration. Section 5 shows the results of a productivity shock. Finally, Section 6 outlines the main conclusions of the analysis.

Ricardian and Non-Ricardian Agents

The stand-in household described in the standard DSGE model is what is called in the literature a Ricardian agent. This is because the assumed behavior of these agents leads to the Ricardian equivalence theorem to hold.[1]

The assumptions made in the standard DSGE model imply that the representative household is a forward-looking optimizer agent and that he uses saving to maximize his utility throughout his life cycle. Thus, saving is considered as a variable that the agent uses to separate the temporal profile of their consumption from the temporal profile of income, in order to maximize utility. This causes the consumption of a given point of time does not depend on the income of that period, but depend on the level of income throughout the life cycle of the agent or permanent income.

The main assumption on which the above behavior is based, besides the fact that saving is only an instrumental variable to choose the optimal consumption at each point in time, is that agents can move income across time. Therefore, it is assumed that agents have free access to the financial markets, both to move income from the present to the future (saving) and to bring income from the future to the present (borrowing). While the former is always true, the latter may not be for some agents. Thus, we can find individuals who would like to have a higher level of consumption in the present, above their current income, but they can not carry out such an option by not having access to credit. When this happens it is said that financial markets are not perfect and that there are liquidity constraints.

In practice, many agents are subject to liquidity constraints on real economies, i.e., they are willing to borrow to increase their level of consumption in the present, but do not have access to credit. This implies that these agents may not maximize their intertemporal utility and their consumption is restricted by their current income. These agents are usually denoted as non-Ricardian agents or rule-of-thumb agents. Several empirical studies, both at macro and micro levels, show that a significant proportion of the population is subject to liquidity restrictions (see, for instance, Campbell and Mankiw, 1989; Deaton, 1992; Wolff, 1998; Souleles, 1999; and Johnson, Parker and Souleles, 2006).

The inclusion of the fact that a portion of the population is subject to liquidity constraints may have important implications for the ex-

[1]This designation refers to the principles of David Ricardo, according to which agents are intertemporal optimizers. Specifically, David Ricardo wondered what was the best way to finance a war, whether through taxes or through public debt, reaching the conclusion that the choice is irrelevant as both options are equivalent. The Lucas critique is a corollary of the Ricardian equivalence.

planatory power of the DSGE model. This is critical when assessing the effects of fiscal policy, as shown by Mankiw (2000). In the standard DSGE model with government, a positive shock in public spending causes a negative wealth effect, which forces the agents to reduce their consumption and increase their labor supply. This result is, in principle, in contradiction with the empirical literature, which predicts that a public spending shock has a positive, or at least not significant, effect on consumption. In the standard DSGE model, the negative wealth effect of a public spending shock is amplified by the fact that agents are "forward looking" and therefore their level of consumption depends on permanent income (Ricardian equivalence principle holds). The inclusion of non-Ricardian agents causes the level of aggregate consumption to increase in response to a public spending shock.

Galí *et al.* (2007) develop a DSGE model with Ricardian agents, which can separate their consumption path from their income path, and non-Ricardian agents, who are forced to consume their current income in each period. In this theoretical context, the effect of a public spending shock on private consumption depends on whether real wage increases or decreases on impact. However, to get a positive effect on private consumption, the percentage of non-Ricardian agents in the economy has to be above 60% in the case of a competitive labor market, while this percentage drops to 25% in the case of a non-competitive labor market. Therefore, even when non-Ricardian agents are considered, the ratio should be unrealistically high to the effects on consumption to be positive, especially if a competitive labor market is assumed.

Coenen and Straub (2005) introduce Ricardian and non-Ricardian agents to study the effects of fiscal policy, arriving at similar conclusions as in Galí *et al.* (2007). They suggest that although estimates of the share of non-Ricardian agents in the euro area is relatively low, the effects of fiscal policy would not be very different from those that would result from the standard model. Iwata (2009) makes a similar analysis applied to the Japanese economy, but including distortionary taxes instead of lump-sum taxes as in the previous works, showing that although the estimated percentage of non-Ricardian agents is relatively low, a rise in public spending causes an increase in private consumption, a result consistent with the empirical evidence.

Here we develop a simple model with the inclusion in the basic standard DSGE model of Ricardian and non-Ricardian agents. This simple exercise is interesting as in this framework both groups of agents behave differently but they cancel each other out, so at an aggregate level the model economy is similar to the standard Ricardian agent model.

The model

The model has a similar structure to the standard DSGE model except for the fact that the population is divided between two types of agents: Ricardian agents, which are the ones considered in the standard model and non-Ricardian agents which are assumed that do not have access to the financial market and are limited to consume in each period their income, as they cannot move income from the future to the present. Having described the behavior of each agent, the model proceed to the aggregation of the resulting behavior of each group to get the total economy behavior.

We assume that there is a continuum of consumers, indexed by $h \in [0,1]$. A proportion of the population, ω, are Ricardian agents who have access to financial markets and therefore do not face liquidity constraints. Therefore, this group of agents make decisions on savings and therefore can accumulate capital to be rent to the firms. These agents are noticed with the subscript $i \in [0,\omega]$. The other part of the population, $1-\omega$, is composed of non-Ricardian agents which face liquidity constraints and cannot make saving decisions since it is assumed that for each period consumption is equal to income. These agents are denoted with the subscript $j \in [\omega,1]$.

Ricardian Households

It is assumed that each Ricardian agent maximizes their intertemporal utility function is terms of consumption, $\{C_{i,t}\}_{t=0}^{\infty}$, and leisure, $\{1-L_{i,t}\}_{t=0}^{\infty}$. Ricardian agents' preferences are defined by the following utility function:

$$\sum_{t=0}^{\infty} \beta^t \left[\gamma \log C_{i,t} + (1-\gamma)\log(1-L_{i,t})\right] \tag{4.1}$$

where β is the discount factor and where $\gamma \in (0,1)$ is the proportion of consumption on total income.

Consumer's budged constraint states that consumption plus saving, $S_{i,t}$, cannot exceed the sum of labor and capital rental income:

$$C_{i,t} + S_{i,t} = W_t L_{i,t} + R_t K_{i,t} \tag{4.2}$$

where W_t is the wage and R_t is the rental price of capital. Capital stock holdings evolve according to:

$$K_{i,t+1} = (1-\delta) K_{i,t} + I_{i,t} \tag{4.3}$$

where δ is the depreciation rate of physical capital. Therefore, the budget constraint faced by Ricardian agents, assuming that $S_{i,t} = I_{i,t}$, can be written as:

$$C_{i,t} + K_{i,t+1} = W_t L_{i,t} + (R_t + 1 - \delta) K_{i,t} \tag{4.4}$$

The Lagrangian problem to be solved by households is to choose $C_{i,t}$, $L_{i,t}$, and $I_{i,t}$ so as to maximize:

$$\max_{(C_{i,t}, I_{i,t}, L_{i,t})} \mathcal{L} = \sum_{t=0}^{\infty} \beta^t \left\{ \begin{array}{c} \gamma \log C_{i,t} + (1-\gamma)\log(1-L_{i,t}) \\ -\lambda_t \left[\begin{array}{c} C_{i,t} + K_{i,t+1} - W_t L_{i,t} \\ -(R_t + 1 - \delta) K_{i,t} \end{array} \right] \end{array} \right\} \tag{4.5}$$

The first order conditions for the household are:

$$\frac{\partial \mathcal{L}}{\partial C_{i,t}} : \gamma C_{i,t}^{-1} - \lambda_t = 0 \tag{4.6}$$

$$\frac{\partial \mathcal{L}}{\partial L_{i,t}} : -\frac{(1-\gamma)}{1-L_{i,t}} + \lambda_t W_t = 0 \tag{4.7}$$

$$\frac{\partial \mathcal{L}}{\partial K_{i,t}} : \beta^t \lambda_t [R_t + 1 - \delta] - \beta^{t-1} \lambda_{t-1} \tag{4.8}$$

Combining expressions (4.6) and (4.7) we obtain the condition that equates the marginal rate of substitution between consumption and leisure to the opportunity cost of one additional unit of leisure:

$$\frac{1-\gamma}{\gamma} \frac{C_{i,t}}{1-L_{i,t}} = W_t \tag{4.9}$$

On the other hand, combining expressions (4.6) and (4.8) we arrive to the equilibrium condition that equates the marginal rate of consumption to the rate of return of investment:

$$\frac{1}{\beta}\frac{C_{i,t}}{C_{i,t-1}} = [R_t + 1 - \delta] \tag{4.10}$$

Non-Ricardian Households

Non-Ricardian agents have a simpler behavior. This is because they are subject to liquidity constraints, which do not allow them to move income from the future to the present. Given this restriction, we will assume that the consumption of these agents in each period is equal to the income of the period. In fact, they can move income from the present to the future, i.e., they can save, but they cannot borrow, i.e., they cannot bring future income to the present. As a consequence, non-Ricardian households are not optimizing agents and it is assumed that they consume their income on a period-by-period basis. This implies that this group of agents do not save and, hence, they do not accumulate capital.

The problem faced by this group of agents is the same than that of Ricardian agents, given by:

$$\sum_{t=0}^{\infty} \beta^t \left[\gamma \log C_{j,t} + (1-\gamma)\log(1 - L_{j,t})\right] \tag{4.11}$$

Given that non-Ricardian agents do not save, the budget constraint is given by:

$$C_{j,t} = W_t L_{j,t} \tag{4.12}$$

First order conditions for the non-Ricardian consumer problem are the following:

$$\frac{\partial \mathcal{L}}{\partial C_{j,t}} : \gamma C_{j,t}^{-1} - \lambda_t = 0 \tag{4.13}$$

$$\frac{\partial \mathcal{L}}{\partial L_{j,t}} : -\frac{(1-\gamma)}{1 - L_{j,t}} + \lambda_t W_t = 0 \tag{4.14}$$

Combining expressions (4.13) and (4.14) we obtain the condition that equates the marginal rate of substitution between consumption and leisure to the opportunity cost of one additional unit of leisure:

$$\frac{1-\gamma}{\gamma}\frac{C_{j,t}}{1-L_{j,t}} = W_t \tag{4.15}$$

which has the same form as the equivalent condition for the Ricardian agents.

Aggregation

Aggregate value (in per capita terms) for each variable related to households, $X_{h,t}$, is given by:

$$X_t = \int_0^1 X_{h,t}dh = \omega X_{i,t} + (1-\omega)X_{j,t} \tag{4.16}$$

given that it is assumed that all agents, independently the group they belong to, are identical. Therefore, aggregate consumption, C_t, is given by:

$$C_t = \omega C_{i,t} + (1-\omega)C_{j,t} \tag{4.17}$$

Similarly, total working time is given by:

$$L_t = \omega L_{i,t} + (1-\omega)L_{j,t} \tag{4.18}$$

On the other hand, as only Ricardian agents save and invest in physical capital, aggregate capital stock and aggregate investment are given by:

$$K_t = \omega K_{i,t} \tag{4.19}$$

$$I_t = \omega I_{i,t} \tag{4.20}$$

The firms

The problem of firms is to find optimal values for the utilization of labor and capital. The production of final output Y requires the services of labor L and K. The firms rent capital and employ labor in order to maximize profits at period t, taking factor prices as given. The technology is given by a constant returns to scale Cobb-Douglas production function,

$$Y_t = A_t K_t^{\alpha} L_t^{1-\alpha} \tag{4.21}$$

where A_t is a measure of total-factor, or sector-neutral, productivity and where $0 \leq \alpha \leq 1$.

The static maximization problem for the firms is:

$$\max_{(K_t, L_t)} \Pi_t = A_t K_t^{\alpha} L_t^{1-\alpha} - R_t K_t - W_t L_t \tag{4.22}$$

The first order conditions for the firms profit maximization are given by

$$\frac{\partial \Pi_t}{\partial K_t} : R_t - \alpha A_t K_t^{\alpha-1} L_t^{1-\alpha} = 0 \tag{4.23}$$

$$\frac{\partial \Pi_t}{\partial L_t} : W_t - (1-\alpha) A_t K_t^{\alpha} L_t^{-\alpha} = 0 \tag{4.24}$$

From the above first order conditions for profit maximization, the price for the production inputs is given by:

$$R_t = \alpha A_t K_t^{\alpha-1} L_t^{1-\alpha} \tag{4.25}$$

$$W_t = (1-\alpha) A_t K_t^{\alpha} L_t^{-\alpha} \tag{4.26}$$

Equilibrium of the model

The equilibrium of this economy is obtained by combining the first order conditions of the Ricardian agents with the first order condition of the non-Ricardian agents, given the price of the productive factors. From the Ricardian agents behavior we obtain that:

$$\frac{1-\gamma}{\gamma} \frac{C_{i,t}}{1-L_{i,t}} = (1-\alpha) A_t K_t^{\alpha} L_t^{-\alpha} \tag{4.27}$$

$$\frac{1}{\beta} \frac{C_{i,t}}{C_{i,t-1}} = \left[\alpha A_t K_t^{\alpha-1} L_t^{1-\alpha} + 1 - \delta\right] \tag{4.28}$$

whereas from the non-Ricardian agents the equilibrium condition is given by:

$$\frac{1-\gamma}{\gamma} \frac{C_{j,t}}{1-L_{j,t}} = (1-\alpha) A_t K_t^{\alpha} L_t^{-\alpha} \tag{4.29}$$

To close the model, the feasibility condition of the economy must hold:

$$Y_t = \omega C_{i,t} + (1-\omega) C_{j,t} + \omega I_{i,t} = C_t + I_t \tag{4.30}$$

First order conditions for the consumer problem, first order conditions from the profit maximization problem of the firm (4.25) and (4.26), together with the feasibility condition of the economy (4.30), characterize the competitive equilibrium of the economy.

Equations of the model and calibration

The competitive equilibrium of the model economy is obtained from a set of fourteen equations, for the macroeconomic endogenous variables, Y_t, C_t, $C_{i,t}$, $C_{j,t}$, I_t, $I_{i,t}$, K_t, $K_{i,t}$, L_t, $L_{i,t}$, $L_{j,t}$, W_t, R_t and for the variable A_t representing total factor productivity, which it is assumed to follow an autoregressive process of order 1. This set of equations is as follows:

$$\frac{1-\gamma}{\gamma}\frac{C_{i,t}}{1-L_{i,t}} = W_t \tag{4.31}$$

$$\frac{1-\gamma}{\gamma}\frac{C_{j,t}}{1-L_{j,t}} = W_t \tag{4.32}$$

$$\frac{C_{i,t}}{C_{i,t-1}} = \beta[R_t + 1 - \delta] \tag{4.33}$$

$$C_{j,t} = W_t L_{j,t} \tag{4.34}$$

$$C_t = \omega C_{i,t} + (1-\omega)C_{j,t} \tag{4.35}$$

$$L_t = \omega L_{i,t} + (1-\omega)L_{j,t} \tag{4.36}$$

$$Y_t = C_t + I_t \tag{4.37}$$

$$K_t = \omega K_{i,t} \tag{4.38}$$

$$I_t = \omega I_{i,t} \tag{4.39}$$

$$Y_t = A_t K_t^{\alpha} L_t^{1-\alpha} \tag{4.40}$$

$$W_t = (1-\alpha)Y_t / L_t \tag{4.41}$$

$$R_t = \alpha Y_t / K_t \tag{4.42}$$

$$K_{i,t+1} = (1-\delta)K_{i,t} + I_{i,t} \tag{4.43}$$

$$\ln A_t = (1-\rho_A)\ln \overline{A} + \rho_A \ln A_{t-1} + \varepsilon_t \tag{4.44}$$

Table 4.1: Calibrated parameters

Parameter	Definition	Value
α	Capital technological parameter	0.350
β	Discount factor	0.970
γ	Preference parameter	0.400
δ	Capital depreciation rate	0.060
ω	Ricardian agents proportion	0.500
ρ_A	TFP autoregressive parameter	0.950
σ_A	TFP standard deviation	0.001

The set of parameter to be calibrated are:

$$\Omega = \{\alpha, \beta, \delta, \gamma, \omega, \rho_A, \sigma_A\}$$

The only new parameter that we need to calibrate is ω, i.e., the proportion of Ricardian agents that exist in the economy. If $\omega = 1$, all households would be Ricardian agents. This particular case is the one considered in the standard DSGE model in which capital markets are perfect and there are no liquidity constraints. The closer to zero this parameter is, the greater the deviation from the permanent income-life cycle hypothesis, as a fraction of households are subject to liquidity constraints that prevent these group of agents to choose the optimal consumption-saving path.

In the literature we find different estimated values for this parameter. For instance, Coenen and Straub (2005) estimate a relative low proportion of non-Ricardian agents for the euro area, around 24%. Iwata (2009), for the Japanese economy, uses values ranging from a 100% of Ricardian agents as in the standard model to a proportion of 70%, that is, a 30% of agents subject to liquidity constraints. Galí *et al.* (2007) use a 50% of each type of agent as a benchmark. This is the proportion to be used in our exercise. Calibrated values for the parameter of the model economy are collected in Table 4.1.

Table 4.2 shows the steady state values of the variables of the model economy. The consumption/production ratio is 76.9% for the aggregate economy, while the saving rate is 23% of total output, which are equal to the steady state values of the standard DSGE models where all agents are Ricardian. We also observed that in the steady state the consumption of Ricardian agents is higher than that of non-Ricardian agents. This is simply because the non-Ricardian

Table 4.2: Steady State values

Variable	Value	Ratio to $\overline{Y}$
$\overline{Y}$	0.7446	1.000
$\overline{C}_i$	0.6081	0.817
$\overline{C}_j$	0.5372	0.721
$\overline{C}$	0.5727	0.769
$\overline{I}$	0.1719	0.231
$\overline{I}_i$	0.3439	0.462
$\overline{K}$	2.8664	3.849
$\overline{K}_i$	5.7329	7.699
$\overline{L}$	0.3603	-
$\overline{L}_i$	0.3207	-
$\overline{L}_j$	0.4000	-
$\overline{W}$	1.3431	-
$\overline{R}$	0.0909	-
$\overline{A}$	1.0000	-

agents have as the only source of income the labor rent, given that their savings are zero. Conversely, Ricardian agents have two sources of income: the income generated by labor and the income from renting accumulated capital.

The results in terms of consumption are also related to those in terms of hours worked. It can be observed that the proportion of time devoted to work is higher in the case of non Ricardian agents than for Ricardian agents. Hours devoted to work of non-Ricardian agents is 40% of the total available time, a value that will be kept fixed, regardless of the shocks afflicting the economy. This value is determined by the preferences parameter ($\gamma = 0.4$), and it is easy to show that in an economy without physical capital the parameter of preferences is equal to the fraction of discretionary time used in working activities, given the logarithmic specification for utility. In the case of Ricardian agents, the proportion of available time devoted to work is 32%. Combining both values, results in an aggregate hours worked rate of 36%. Comparing steady state values from this model for the aggregate variables with the ones from the standard DSGE model, we observe that they are equal, although each group of agents behaves differently: Non-Ricardian agents work more and Ricardian agents work less than the average.

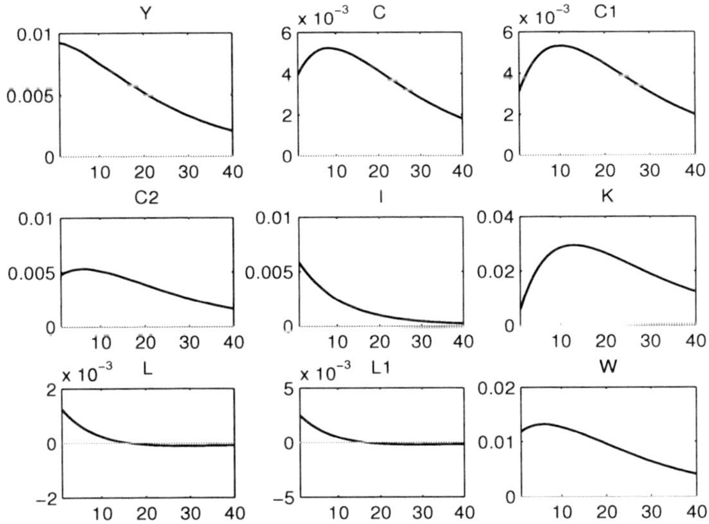

Figure 4.1: TFP shock with Ricardian and non-Ricardian agents

Total Factor Productivity shock

This section studies the effects of a positive productivity shock in the context of this DSGE model. Although the most interesting features of this model are related to the study of fiscal policy, it is also interesting to analyze what are the effects of an aggregate productivity shock over each group of agents. Figure 4.1 shows the results of a positive productivity shock on the relevant variables of the model, where the variables noted with a "1" refer to the Ricardian agents and with a "2" to the non-Ricardian agents. The aggregate productivity shock increases the level of production at impact and the supply of production factors given the rise in their returns. However, we must now take into account that only a fraction of total population saves and therefore makes investment in physical capital. Also, labor supply by non-Ricardian agents remains fixed (this is the reason why the evolution of "L2" is not shown, as its deviation from its steady state value is always zero).

The behavior of non-Ricardian in this model economy is very simple. Time devoted to work by non-Ricardian agents does not respond to this shock as it is a constant. Given the increases in the return to labor, they just consume more. Notice that the impulse response for "C2" is just a proportion of the impulse response for the wage. As we discussed earlier, without savings, the proportion of available time that non-Ricardian agents spend working is a constant derived from the fact that the utility of consumption is always equal to the disutility of labor. Regarding the Ricardian agents, the effects of this shock are similar to those obtained in the standard model. Both consumption and investment rise, leading to a process of accumulation of capital, while increasing hours worked given the increased utility in terms of consumption.

At the aggregate level, the behavior of the economy is identical to the standard model. In this sense, although only a fraction of the economy makes decisions on savings and therefore accumulates capital, its saving rate is higher, such that the total capital stock of the economy is similar to that obtained in an economy where all agents were Ricardian. In fact we can see how the steady state aggregate variables exactly match the steady state values that would be obtained in the standard model, being completely independent of the proportion of agents subject to liquidity constraints.

Conclusions

In this chapter we have developed a DSGE model in which there are two types of agents: Ricardian and non-Ricardian agents. While the first group of agents consists in forward-looking optimizing agents, the second group of agents is subject to liquidity constraints, so that they can borrow. The first type of agents is the one considered in the standard DSGE model, whereas the second group of agents implies a deviation from the permanent income-life cycle hypothesis.

The purpose of introducing these two groups of agents is to consider the effects of imperfect capital markets, or restrictions on the access to credit for a given proportion of the population. These liquidity constraints could have important implications in terms of the explanatory power of the model.

A major empirical results derived from the literature is the existence of excess sensitivity of consumption relative to current income. These deviations could be explained through the introduction of liquidity constraints. The existence of liquidity constraints is a key element to be taken into account when assessing the effects of fiscal policy. In the exercise done here, we studied the effects of a productivity shock, showing that, at the aggregate level, the results obtained are equivalent to those derived from the standard model.

Appendix A: Dynare code

The Dynare code corresponding to the model developed in this chapter, named *model4.mod*, is the following:

```
// Model 4:  Ricardian and non-Ricardian agents
// Dynare code
// File:  model4.mod
// José L. Torres.  University of Málaga (Spain)
// Endogenous variables
var Y, C, C1, C2, I, I1, K, K1, L, L1, L2, W, R, A;
// Exogenous variables
varexo e;
// Parameters
parameters alpha, beta, delta, gamma, omega, rho;
// Calibration of the parameters
alpha = 0.35;
beta  = 0.97;
delta = 0.06;
gamma = 0.40;
omega = 0.50;
rho   = 0.95;
// Equations of the model economy
model;
C1=(gamma/(1-gamma))*(1-L1)*W;
C2=(gamma/(1-gamma))*(1-L2)*W;
C2=W*L2;
C =omega*C1+(1-omega)*C2;
1 = beta*((C1/C1(+1))
 *(R(+1)+(1-delta)));
K = omega*K1;
L = omega*L1+(1-omega)*L2;
Y = A*(K(-1)^alpha)*(L^(1-alpha));
K1= I1+(1-delta)*K1(-1);
I1= W*L1+R*K1-C1;
I = omega*I1;
```

```
W = (1-alpha)*A*(K(-1)^alpha)*(L^(-alpha));
R = alpha*A*(K(-1)^(alpha-1))*(L^(1-alpha));
log(A) = rho*log(A(-1))+ e;
end;
// Initial values
initval;
Y = 1;
C = 0.8;
C1= 0.6;
C2= 0.2;
L = 0.3;
L1= 0.3;
L2= 0.3;
K = 3.5;
K1= 4;
I = 0.2;
I1= 0.3;
W = (1-alpha)*Y/L;
R = alpha*Y/K;
A = 1;
e = 0;
end;
 // Steady state
steady;
// Blanchard-Kahn conditions
check;
// Perturbation analysis
shocks;
var e; stderr 0.01;
end;
// Stochastic simulation
stoch_simul;
```

Bibliography

Campbell, J. and Mankiw, N. (1989): Consumption, income, and interest rates: Reinterpreting the time series evidence. *NBER Macroeconomics Annual*, MIT Press. Cambridge.

Coenen, G. and Straub, R. (2005): Non-Ricardian households and fiscal policy in an estimated DSGE model for the Euro area. *Computing in Economics and Finance*, 102.

Deaton, A. (1992): *Understanding consumption*. Clarendon Lectures in Economics, Clarendon Press: Oxford.

Galí, J., López-Salido, J., and Vallés, J. (2007): Understanding the effects of government spending on consumption. *Journal of the European Economic Association*, 5(1), 227-270.

Iwata, Y. (2009): Fiscal policy in an estimated DSGE model of the Japanese economy: Do non-Ricardian households explain all? *ESRI Discussion Paper Series* n. 216.

Johnson, D., Parker, J. and Souleles, N. (2006): Household expenditure and the income tax rebates of 2001. *American Economic Review*, 96(5), 1589-1610.

Mankiw, N. (2000): The savers-spenders theory of fiscal policy. *American Economic Review*, 90(2), 120-125.

Souleles, N. (1999): The response of household consumption to income tax refunds. *American Economic Review*, 89(4), 947-958.

Wolff, M. (2003): Recent trends in the size distribution of household wealth. *Journal of Economic Perspectives*, 12, 131-150.

Part III

Investment and Capital Accumulation

Chapter 5

Investment adjustment costs

Introduction

In the standard DSGE model it is assumed that capital stock can be changed from one period to another without any restriction, through the investment process. Thus, given a particular shock affecting optimal capital stock, agents can change their investment decisions such that the resulting capital stock would be again the optimal without any transformation cost. However, in the real world, physical capital is a special variable, because of its particular characteristics. We are speaking about factories, machines, ships, etc., that cannot be built up instantaneously or need to be installed to produce. One important aspect to be considered here is that the investment process is subject to implicit costs which are missing in the basic theoretical setup. This will cause additional rigidities in the capital accumulation process. This means that in the case that the capital stock is not at the optimal level, agents do not take an investment decision to completely cover the difference in a single period of time, but they change capital stock in a gradual process over time as investment is smoothed.

In the literature, the above issue has been studied using two alternative approaches: Considering the existence of adjustment costs in investment or, alternatively, by considering the existence of adjustment costs relative to the capital stock. In the first case, we face a cost associated with the variation in the level of investment compared to its steady state value. In the second case, we are talking about a cost in terms of the change in the capital stock. Both concepts are broadly equivalent, although they involve different specifications of the adjustment cost process. In this chapter, we will focus on the existence of adjustment costs associated with the investment process which are the more common adjustment cost considered in the literature. Investment decisions are costly in terms of loss of consumption given that a fraction of the output that goes to investment disappears, i.e., fails to be transformed into capital.

The structure of the rest of the chapter is as follows. Section 2 briefly reviews the concept of adjustment costs in investment and the different approaches used in the literature. Section 3 develops a DSGE model with adjustment costs in investment which are added to the capital accumulation equation. Section 4 presents the equations of the model and the calibration exercise. Section 5 studies the dynamic effects of a productivity shock. The chapter ends with some conclusions.

Investment adjustment costs

In the standard DSGE model the treatment given to the productive sector of the economy is very simple. Firms maximize profits period by period, by solving a static problem. In practice, firms take decisions on an intertemporal context, so the right thing would be to specify the problem in terms of maximizing the sum of all discounted profits. However, if we solve this dynamic problem, the result we get is exactly the same as in the static case, indicating that firms decisions today will not affect future profits, which does not seem to make much sense. This result occurs because the assumptions regarding the behavior of the firms are overly restrictive.

One of the shortcomings of the neoclassical analysis of the firm comes from the assumption that there is no restriction to the instantaneous variation in the capital stock and investment simply transforms into installed capital. However, in reality, firms face adjustment costs by altering their capital stock. The literature distinguishes between two types of adjustment costs: external and internal. External adjustment costs arise when firms face a perfectly elastic supply of capital. This will cause the price of capital to depend on the velocity of installation and/or on the quantity of new capital. By contrast, the internal adjustment costs are measured in terms of production losses. When new capital should be installed, a portion of the investment must be expended in the installation process which is costly or, alternatively, a fraction of the inputs already used in the production, basically labor, must be devoted to the installation of the new capital. These inputs will be not available to produce during the installation process, which implies forgone output.

Investment and capital accumulation analysis can take place either from the point of view of the firm or from the point of view of households, depending on the assumption about who is the owner of the capital stock. Strictly, the most realistic option appears to be the first, as it is firms that decide the level of investment in each period. This approach has been widely used to study the investment function, leading to the so-called Tobin's Q theory (Tobin, 1969; Hayashi, 1982), which allows to study the investment process based on the dynamics of the Q ratio that represents the ratio between the market value of the firm and the replacement cost of its installed capital. The alternative option, which is commonly used in DSGE models, involves studying the investment adjustment costs from the point of view of households. This is simply because we assume that the households are the owners of the capital stock.

In general, we can distinguish between capital adjustment costs and investment adjustment costs. Jorgenson (1963) introduced the existence of adjustment costs of investment as a lag structure associated with the investment process. Tobin (1969) developed a theory in which the investment decisions are taken depending on the value of a ratio named Q, defined as the market value of the firm relative to the replacement cost of installed capital. Hayashi (1982) shows that under certain conditions this ratio is equal to its marginal, the so-called q-ratio.

The existence of capital adjustment costs has been considered extensively in the literature on investment by Hayashi (1982), Abel and Blanchard (1993), Shapiro (1986), among others. Generally, we can define the following function for capital adjustment costs:

$$\Psi(\cdot) = \Psi(I_t/K_t) \tag{5.1}$$

where the adjustment cost function, $\Psi(\cdot)$, depends on the quantity of investment, I_t, relative to the installed capital stock, K_t, that is, on the ratio between the new capital to be installed and the capital stock already installed. This cost function has a number of features, such that:

$$\Psi(\delta) = 0$$
$$\Psi'(I_t/K_t) > 0$$
$$\Psi''(I_t/K_t) > 0$$

i.e., adjustment costs depend positively on investment relative to capital stock. If net investment is zero, gross investment is just equal to capital loss due to depreciation. Furthermore, its second derivative is positive, indicating that adjustment costs is convex. The existence of adjustment costs means a capital loss or an additional cost in the investment process. So for each dollar invested, it will transform into capital an amount less than one dollar, as a consequence of the adjustment costs. In this setting, the marginal productivity of capital is also a function of net investment adjustment costs.

Alternatively, the adjustment costs associated with investment refer to the existence of costs in terms of investment changes between periods. The usual way to define the adjustment cost of investment function is as follows (see, for instance, Christiano, Eichenbaum and Evans, 2005):

$$\Psi(\cdot) = \Psi\left(\frac{I_t}{I_{t-1}}\right) \tag{5.2}$$

where

$$\Psi(1) = 0$$
$$\Psi'(1) = 0$$
$$\Psi''(1) > 0$$

implying that there is a cost associated with changing the level of investment, that this cost is zero at steady state, and that this cost is increasing in the change in investment. Using this specification, the capital accumulation equation is defined as:

$$K_{t+1} = (1-\delta)K_t + \left[1 - \Psi\left(\frac{I_t}{I_{t-1}}\right)\right] I_t \tag{5.3}$$

In the literature we find a large number of DSGE models including the existence of adjustment costs either in capital or investment. Adjustment costs in capital have been considered, by Jermann (1998), Edge (2000), F-de-Córdoba and Kehoe (2000) and Boldrin, Christiano and Fisher (2001), among many others. For example, Edge (2000) shows that adjustment costs in capital together with habit persistence in consumption in a sticky-price monetary model is capable of generating a liquidity effect (a decline in short-term nominal interest rate in response to a positive monetary shock).

Adjustment costs in investment have been also considered extensively in the literature. For instance, Christiano *et al.* (2005) show that adjustment costs on investment can generate a hump-shaped response in investment, consumption and employment, consistent with the estimated response to a monetary policy shock. Finally, Burnside, Eichenbaum and Fisher (2004) show that an RBC model with adjustment costs in investment may explain the effects of a fiscal shock on hours worked and wages.

The model

The DSGE model presented here introduces the existence of adjustment costs in the investment process. This means that we will now alter the capital accumulation equation, including a cost function of investment adjustment. In this setting, consumers now must make a further decision as investment adjustment costs are incorporated in the budget constraint. This is because optimal capital stock decision and investment decision are now separated due to the existence of adjustment costs in the investment process.

Households

It is assumed that households maximize their intertemporal utility function in terms of consumption, $\{C_t\}_{t=0}^{\infty}$, and leisure, $\{1-L_t\}_{t=0}^{\infty}$, where L_t denotes labor. Consumers' preferences are defined by the following utility function:

$$\sum_{t=0}^{\infty} \beta^t \left[\gamma \log C_t + (1-\gamma)\log(1-L_t)\right] \tag{5.4}$$

where β is the discount factor and where $\gamma \in (0,1)$ is the proportion of consumption on total income.

Consumer's budget constraint states that consumption plus saving, S_t, cannot exceed the sum of labor and capital rental income:

$$C_t + S_t = W_t L_t + R_t K_t$$

where W_t is the wage, R_t is the rental price of capital and K_t is the physical capital stock. Investment adjustment costs are introduced by assuming the following equation for capital accumulation:

$$K_{t+1} = (1-\delta) K_t + \left[1 - \Psi\left(\frac{I_t}{I_{t-1}}\right)\right] I_t \tag{5.5}$$

where δ is the physical capital depreciation rate, I_t is gross investment and $\Psi(\cdot)$ is a cost function associated to investment. Smets and Wouters (2002) introduce an additional disturbance to the investment adjustment cost such as:

$$K_{t+1} = (1-\delta)K_t + \left[1 - \Psi\left(V_t \frac{I_t}{I_{t-1}}\right)\right] I_t \tag{5.6}$$

where V_t is assumed to follow an autorregressive process of order 1, $\log V_t = \rho_V \log V_{t-1} + \varepsilon_t^V$.

It is assumed that $S_t = I_t$. The Lagrangian function associated to the household maximization problem can be defined as:

$$Max \sum_{t=0}^{\infty} \beta^t \left\{ \begin{array}{c} [\gamma \log(C_t) + (1-\gamma)\log(1-L_t)] \\ -\lambda_t (C_t + I_t - W_t L_t - R_t K_{t-1}) \\ -Q_t \left(K_t - (1-\delta)K_{t-1} - \left[1 - \Psi\left(\frac{I_t}{I_{t-1}}\right)\right] I_t\right) \end{array} \right\} \tag{5.7}$$

where Q_t is the Lagrange's multiplier associated to the dynamics of capital stock. This multiplier, representing the shadow price of capital, is also known as the Tobin Q ratio and can be defined as the market value of the total installed capital over the replacement cost of that capital.

First order conditions for maximization are given by:

$$\frac{\partial \mathcal{L}}{\partial C} : \gamma \frac{1}{C_t} - \lambda_t = 0 \tag{5.8}$$

$$\frac{\partial \mathcal{L}}{\partial L_t} : -(1-\gamma) \frac{1}{1-L_t} + \lambda_t W_t = 0 \tag{5.9}$$

$$\frac{\partial \mathcal{L}}{\partial K} : \beta^t [\lambda_t R_t + (1-\delta) Q_t] - \beta^{t-1} Q_{t-1} = 0 \tag{5.10}$$

$$\frac{\partial \mathcal{L}}{\partial I_t} : \beta^t \left[Q_t - Q_t \Psi\left(\frac{I_t}{I_{t-1}}\right) - Q_t \Psi'\left(\frac{I_t}{I_{t-1}}\right) \frac{I_t}{I_{t-1}} - \lambda_t\right] + \beta^{t+1} Q_{t+1} \Psi'\left(\frac{I_{t+1}}{I_t}\right)\left(\frac{I_{t+1}}{I_t}\right)^2 = 0 \tag{5.11}$$

We can define the Tobin's Q marginal ratio, named q_t, as:

$$q_t = \frac{Q_t}{\lambda_t} \tag{5.12}$$

that is, the ratio of the two Lagrange's multipliers. Therefore, we get that $Q_t = q_t \lambda_t$. Using the FOC for the capital stock, we obtain:

$$\frac{\lambda_{t-1}}{\lambda_{t-1}} Q_{t-1} = \beta \left[\lambda_t R_t + (1-\delta) Q_t \frac{\lambda_t}{\lambda_t} \right]$$

or alternatively,

$$q_{t-1} = \beta \frac{\lambda_t}{\lambda_{t-1}} \left[q_t (1-\delta) + R_t \right]$$

The above expression indicates that the value of current installed capital depends on its future expected value, taking into account the depreciation rate and the expected rate of return.

Moreover, operating in the first order condition for investment, we obtain:

$$\beta^t \frac{\lambda_t}{\lambda_t} \left[Q_t - Q_t \Psi\left(\frac{I_t}{I_{t-1}}\right) - Q_t \Psi'\left(\frac{I_t}{I_{t-1}}\right) \frac{I_t}{I_{t-1}} - \lambda_t \right]$$
$$= -E_t \beta^{t+1} \frac{\lambda_{t+1}}{\lambda_{t+1}} Q_{t+1} \Psi'\left(\frac{I_{t+1}}{I_t}\right) \left(\frac{I_{t+1}}{I_t}\right)^2$$

and substituting,

$$\beta^t \left[q_t - q_t \Psi\left(\frac{I_t}{I_{t-1}}\right) - q_t \Psi'\left(\frac{I_t}{I_{t-1}}\right) \frac{I_t}{I_{t-1}} - 1 \right]$$
$$= -E_t \beta^{t+1} \frac{\lambda_{t+1}}{\lambda_t} q_{t+1} \Psi'\left(\frac{I_{t+1}}{I_t}\right) \left(\frac{I_{t+1}}{I_t}\right)^2$$

or

$$q_t - q_t \Psi\left(\frac{I_t}{I_{t-1}}\right) - q_t \Psi'\left(\frac{I_t}{I_{t-1}}\right) \frac{I_t}{I_{t-1}}$$
$$+ E_t \beta \frac{\lambda_{t+1}}{\lambda_t} q_{t+1} \Psi'\left(\frac{I_{t+1}}{I_t}\right) \left(\frac{I_{t+1}}{I_t}\right)^2 = 1$$

Notice that if $\Psi(\cdot) = 0$, that is, there are no adjustment costs in investment, and then $q_t = 1$, that is the Tobin's marginal Q should be equal to the replacement cost of installed capital in units of the final good.

By combining expressions (5.8) and (5.9) we obtain the condition that equates the marginal disutility of additional hours of work with the marginal return on additional hours:

$$\frac{1-\gamma}{\gamma}\frac{C_t}{1-L_t} = W_t$$

Combining (5.8) and (5.10) we obtain the following equilibrium condition for the consumption path that equates the marginal rate of consumption with the rate of return of investment:

$$q_{t-1} = \beta\frac{C_{t-1}}{C_t}\left[q_t(1-\delta)+R_t\right]$$

The firms

The problem of firms is to find optimal values for the utilization of labor and capital. The production of final output Y requires the services of labor L and K. The firms rent capital and employ labor in order to maximize profits at period t, taking factor prices as given. The technology is given by a constant return to scale Cobb-Douglas production function,

$$Y_t = A_t K_t^{\alpha} L_t^{1-\alpha} \tag{5.13}$$

where A_t is a measure of total-factor, or sector-neutral, productivity and where $0 \leq \alpha \leq 1$.

The static maximization problem for the firms is:

$$\max_{(K_t,L_t)} \Pi_t = A_t K_t^{\alpha} L_t^{1-\alpha} - R_t K_t - W_t L_t \tag{5.14}$$

The first order conditions for the firms profit maximization are given by

$$\frac{\partial \Pi_t}{\partial K_t} : R_t - \alpha A_t K_t^{\alpha-1} L_t^{1-\alpha} = 0 \tag{5.15}$$

$$\frac{\partial \Pi_t}{\partial L_t} : W_t - (1-\alpha) A_t K_t^{\alpha} L_t^{-\alpha} = 0 \tag{5.16}$$

From the above first order conditions, equilibrium wage and rental rate of capital are given by:

$$R_t = \alpha A_t K_t^{\alpha-1} L_t^{1-\alpha} \tag{5.17}$$

$$W_t = (1-\alpha) A_t K_t^{\alpha} L_t^{-\alpha} \tag{5.18}$$

Equilibrium of the model

For the equilibrium of the model, we first specify a particular functional form for the investment adjustment cost function. The literature offers a variety of different specifications. For instance, Christiano, Eichenbaum and Evans (2001) specify an adjustment cost function that satisfies the following properties $\Psi(1) = \Psi'(1) = 0$, $\Psi''(1) > 0$, $\Psi_{I_t}(\cdot) = 1$ and $\Psi_{I_{t-1}}(\cdot) = 0$. Christoffel, Coenen and Warne (2007) use the following functional form:

$$\Psi\left(\frac{I_t}{I_{t-1}}\right) = \frac{\psi}{2}\left(\frac{I_t}{I_{t-1}} - g_z\right)^2 \tag{5.19}$$

where $\psi > 0$ and g_z is the productivity growth rate in the long-run. Alternatively, Canzoneri, Cumby and Diba (2005) consider adjustment costs in capital, defining the following capital accumulation equation:

$$K_t - (1-\delta)K_{t-1} + I_t \quad \frac{\psi}{2}\frac{(I_t - \delta K_{t-1})^2}{K_{t-1}} \tag{5.20}$$

In our case, the investment adjustment cost function to be used is the following:

$$\Psi\left(\frac{I_t}{I_{t-1}}\right) = \frac{\psi}{2}\left(\frac{I_t}{I_{t-1}} - 1\right)^2 \tag{5.21}$$

Thus, the equilibrium condition for investment can be written as:

$$\begin{aligned} q_t - q_t\frac{\psi}{2}\left(\frac{I_t}{I_{t-1}} - 1\right)^2 - q_t\psi\left(\frac{I_t}{I_{t-1}} - 1\right)\frac{I_t}{I_{t-1}} \\ + \beta\frac{C_t}{C_{t+1}}q_{t+1}\psi\left(\frac{I_t}{I_{t-1}} - 1\right)\left(\frac{I_{t+1}}{I_t}\right)^2 = 1 \end{aligned}$$

Equations of the model and calibration

The competitive equilibrium of the model economy is given by a set of nine equations, driving the dynamics of the eight macroeconomic endogenous variables, Y_t, C_t, I_t, K_t, L_t, R_t, W_t, q_t plus the Total Factor Productivity, A_t, which it is assumed to follows an autorregressive process of order 1. This set of equations is the following:

$$(1-\gamma)\frac{1}{1-L_t} = \gamma\frac{1}{C_t}W_t \tag{5.22}$$

$$q_{t-1} = \beta \frac{C_{t-1}}{C_t} \left[q_t (1-\delta) + R_t \right] \tag{5.23}$$

$$Y_t = C_t + I_t \tag{5.24}$$

$$Y_t = A_t K_t^{\alpha} L_t^{1-\alpha} \tag{5.25}$$

$$K_{t+1} = (1-\delta) K_t + \left[1 - \frac{\psi}{2} \left(\frac{I_t}{I_{t-1}} \right)^2 \right] I_t \tag{5.26}$$

$$W_t = (1-\alpha) A_t K_t^{\alpha} L_t^{-\alpha} \tag{5.27}$$

$$R_t = \alpha A_t K_t^{\alpha-1} L_t^{1-\alpha} \tag{5.28}$$

$$q_t - q_t \frac{\psi}{2} \left(\frac{I_t}{I_{t-1}} - 1 \right)^2 - q_t \psi \left(\frac{I_t}{I_{t-1}} - 1 \right) \frac{I_t}{I_{t-1}} + \beta \frac{C_t}{C_{t+1}} q_{t+1} \psi \left(\frac{I_t}{I_{t-1}} - 1 \right) \left(\frac{I_{t+1}}{I_t} \right)^2 = 1 \tag{5.29}$$

$$\ln A_t = (1-\rho_A) \ln \overline{A} + \rho_A \ln A_{t-1} + \varepsilon_t \tag{5.30}$$

To calibrate the model economy, we need to assign values to the following parameters:

$$\Omega = \{\alpha, \beta, \gamma, \delta, \psi, \rho_A, \sigma_A\}$$

The only new additional parameter relative to the basic model is ψ, which represents the intensity of adjustment costs in investment. Table 5.1 shows the calibrated values of the parameters. Since the literature uses different specifications for investment adjustment cost function, this leads to different calibrated values for the parameters representing the intensity of the adjustment costs. Smets and Wouters (2003) estimate a parameter of 5.9 for an adjustment cost function similar to the one used here. Christoffel *et al.* (2008) estimate a value of 5.8. Here, we will use a value of 6 as in the above works.

Total Factor Productivity Shock

This section studies how the presence of investment adjustment costs influences the effects of a positive shock in total factor productivity. Impulse-response functions for the variables of the model economy are plotted in Figure 5.1. The dynamic responses of the

Table 5.1: Calibrated parameters

Parameter	Definition	Value
α	Capital technological parameter	0.350
β	Discount factor	0.970
γ	Preference parameter	0.400
δ	Capital depreciation rate	0.060
ψ	Investment adjustment cost	6.000
ρ_A	TFP autoregressive parameter	0.950
σ_A	TFP standard deviation	0.010

variables exhibit some notable differences compared to the ones obtained from the DSGE model without adjustment costs in investment. First, as expected, we observe a different response of investment to the shock. Impulse-response of investment is now hump-shaped, implying a different transmission mechanism of the shock to capital stock and output. This response is explained by the existence of adjustment costs associated with investment, which reduces the change in the amount invested from one period to another. This response of investment increases the persistence in the capital stock accumulation process.

Another interesting result is the q-ratio response to the productivity shock. The positive productivity shock causes this ratio to rise above its steady state value, which by definition is 1. This means that it is profitable to invest, since in this case the rise in the market value of the firms is larger than the cost of the new capital. As the capital stock increases, the q-ratio decreases (given the decreasing marginal productivity of capital).

Conclusions

This chapter develops a DSGE model with adjustment costs in the investment process. Without investment adjustment costs, firms can adjust their capital stock to the optimal level instantaneously. Adjustment costs introduce an additional cost in the investment process as installation of new capital is not free, and hence, any difference between the optimal capital stock and the already installed capital stock could not be compensated in each period. This implies a different response of investment to shocks (investment is

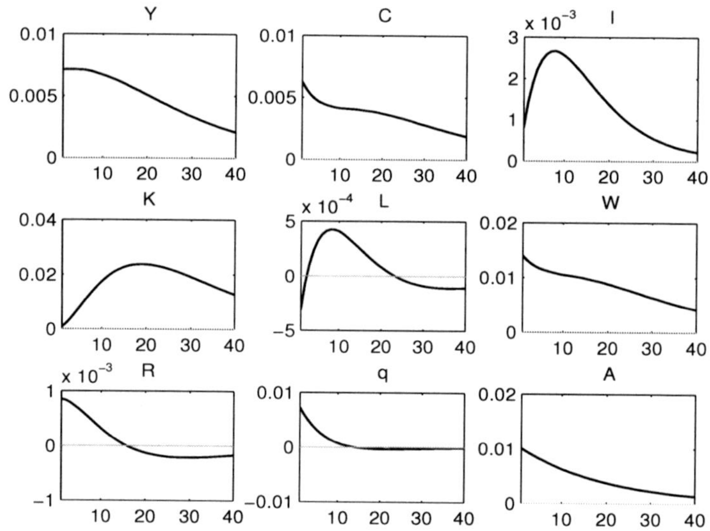

Figure 5.1: TFP shock with investment adjustment costs

smoother) which translates into a higher persistence in the capital stock accumulation process. Investment adjustment costs have been introduced in the standard DSGE model as an important factor to describe investment dynamics and to explain some business cycle facts. Irreversibility of capital stock, learning costs associated to the installation of new capital and labor adjustment costs are also important features to explaining capital and investment processes.

Appendix A: Dynare code

The Dynare code corresponding to the model developed in this chapter, named *model5.mod*, is the following:

```
// Model 5:  Investment adjustment costs
// Dynare code
// File:  model5.mod
// José L. Torres.  University of Málaga (Spain)
// Endogenous variables
var Y, C, I, K, L, W, R, q, A;
```

```
// Exogenous variables
varexo e;
// Parameters
parameters alpha, beta, delta, gamma, psi, rho;
// Calibration of the parameters
alpha = 0.35;
beta  = 0.97;
delta = 0.06;
gamma = 0.40;
psi   = 2.00;
rho   = 0.95;
// Equations of the model economy
model;
C=(gamma/(1-gamma))*(1-L)*W;
q=beta*(C/C(+1))*(q(+1)*(1-delta)+R(+1));
q-q*psi/2*((I/I(-1))-1)^2-q*psi*((I/I(-1))-1)
 *I/I(-1)+beta*C/C(+1)*q(+1)*psi*((I(+1)/I)-1)
 *(I(+1)/I)^2=1;
Y = A*(K(-1)^alpha)*(L^(1-alpha));
K = (1-delta)*K(-1)+(1-(psi/2*(I/I(-1)-1)^2))*I;
I = Y-C;
W = (1-alpha)*A*(K(-1)^alpha)*(L^(-alpha));
R = alpha*A*(K(-1)^(alpha-1))*(L^(1-alpha));
log(A) = rho*log(A(-1))+ e;
end;
// Initial values
initval;
Y = 1;
C = 0.8;
L = 0.3;
K = 3.5;
I = 0.2;
q = 1;
W = (1-alpha)*Y/L;
R = alpha*Y/K;
A = 1;
e = 0;
end;
 // Steady state
steady;
// Blanchard-Kahn conditions
```

```
check;
// Perturbation analysis
shocks;
var e; stderr 0.01;
end;
// Stochastic simulation
stoch_simul;
```

Bibliography

Abel, A. and Blanchard, O. (1983): An intertemporal equilibrium model of savings and investment. *Econometrica*, 51, 675-692.

Beaudry, P. and Portier, F. (2006): Stock prices, news, and economic fluctuations. *American Economic Review*, 96(4), 1293-1307.

Boldrin, M., Christiano, L. and Fisher, J. (2001): Habit persistence, asset returns and the business cycle. *American Economic Review*, 91, 149-166.

Burnside, C., Eichenbaum, M. and Fisher, J. (2004): Fiscal shocks and their consequences. *Journal of Economic Theory*, 115, 89-117.

Canzoneri, M., Cumby, R. and Diba, B. (2005): Price and wage inflation targeting: Variations on a theme by Erceg, Henderson and Levin. In Orphanides, A and Reifscheneider, D. (eds.), *Models and monetary policy: Research in the Tradition of Dale Henderson, Richard Porter and Peter Tinsley*. Washington, Board of Governors of the Federal Reserve System.

Chari, V., Kehoe, P. and McGrattan, E. (2000): Sticky price models of the business cycle: Can the contract multiplier solve the persistence problem? *Econometrica*, 68(5), 1151-1179.

Christiano, L., Eichenbaum, M., and Evans, C. (2005): Nominal rigidities and the dynamic effects of a shock to monetary policy. *Journal of Political Economy*, 113, 1-45.

Christoffel, K., Coenen, G. and Warne, A. (2008). The new area-wide model of the euro area - a micro-founded open-economy model for forecasting and policy analysis. *European Central Bank Working Paper Series* n. 944.

Edge, R. (2007): Time-to-build, time-to-plan, habit-persistence, and the liquidity effect. *Journal of Monetary Economics*, 54, 1644-1669.

F-de-Córdoba, G. and Kehoe, T. (2000): Capital flows and real exchange rate following Spain's entry into the European Community. *Journal of International Economics*, 51, 49-78.

Greenwood, J. and Hercowitz, Z. (1991): The allocation of capital and time over the business cycle. *Journal of Political Economy*, 99(6), 1188-1214.

Hayashi, F. (1982): Tobin's marginal q and average q: A neoclassical interpretation. *Econometrica*, 50(1), 213-224.

Jermann, U. (1998): Asset pricing in production economy. *Journal of Monetary Economics*, 41, 257-275.

Jorgenson, D. (1963): Capital theory and investment behavior. *American Economic Review*, 53(2), 247-259.

McCallum, B. and Nelson, E. (1999): Nominal income targeting in an open-economy optimizing model. *Journal of Monetary Economics*, 43, 553-578.

Shapiro, M. (1986): The dynamic demand for capital and labor. *Quarterly Journal of Economics*, 101, 512-542.

Smets, F. and Wouters, R. (2003): An estimated Dynamic Stochastic General Equilibrium model of the Euro Area. *Journal of the European Economic Association*, 1(5), 1123-1175.

Tobin, J. (1969): A general equilibrium approach to monetary theory. *Journal of Money, Credit and Banking*, 1(1), 15-29.

Chapter 6

Investment-Specific Technological Change

Introduction

The basic DSGE model introduces a number of very specific assumptions about the capital accumulation process. For instance, it is assumed that savings transform directly into physical capital through the investment process at no cost. This assumption has been relaxed in previous chapter. Additionally, the capital accumulation equation assumes that physical capital remains homogeneous over time and just new capital assets are added to the existing capital stock through investment.

However, in practice, technological progress changes the characteristics of physical capital, as technology is embodied in capital assets. When a new capital asset is incorporated to the economy through the investment process, these assets have different characteristics to those already existing, i.e., they are not homogeneous over time as different vintages of capital exist. Let us consider, as an example, the case of a computer, an equipment subject to technological progress that changes its technical and performance characteristics over time. Its relative price, in terms of goods production (or consumption, as is defined in the model) can be kept constant over time (or even reduced), but it is clear that a computer produced in 2010 is very different from a computer produced in 1990. Thus the cost of incorporating an additional computer to the production process may be the same over time, but its productivity is much higher. i.e., would be equivalent to having more capital units because it incorporates technological progress. This is the so-called investment-specific technological change (ISTC).

The neoclassical growth model predicts that in the long run, productivity growth is driven only by technological progress. Traditionally, the concept used in economics technological progress is associated with an increase in total factor productivity, affecting all of the factors of production. Because of that, it is called neutral technological change or Total Factor Productivity. However, there is also a specific technological progress associated to capital inputs, which depends on the investment process and occurs when new vintages of capital assets are incorporated to the capital stock.

This chapter introduces ISTC in the DSGE model, as a source of technological progress additional to neutral technological progress. While the second implies a change in aggregate productivity of the economy, the second type of technological progress refers to the amount of technology that can be acquired with the investment of a production unit.

The structure of the remainder of the chapter is as follows. Section 2 reviews the concept of investment-specific technological change. Section 3 presents a DSGE model with investment-specific technological change. Section 4 presents the equations of the model and the calibration. Section 5 studies the effects of a ISTC shock. The chapter ends with some conclusions.

Investment-specific technological change

The usual way to consider technological change in DSGE models is to assume the existence of a shock that affects the aggregate production function of the economy. This is the so-called Total Factor Productivity (TFP) shock or neutral technological change. However, another source of technological change derives from the fact that technical and performance characteristics of capital assets do not remain constant over time. In general, capital assets have embodied better technical and performance characteristics over time. This is especially true in the case of equipment (transport, telecommunications, machinery, etc.). This implies the existence of different vintages of capital assets, with different productivity.

Technological improvements in equipment have been impressive in the last two decades. Whereas there were some doubts at the beginning of the 1990s, now there is a wide consensus about the positive and significant effect of these improvements on growth and productivity. Neoclassical models predict that long-run productivity growth can only be driven by technological progress. Technology in turn can be differentiated into neutral progress and investment-specific progress. While the first of them is associated with multifactor productivity, the second one is the amount of technology that can be acquired by using one unit of a particular asset. In reality, the amount of technology that can be transferred to productivity widely differs among the different capital assets.

Greenwood, Hercowitz and Huffman (1988) are the first to develop a DSGE model with specific technological progress in the capital accumulation function as an exogenous stochastic process associated with investment. One simple way to introduce ISTC in a DSGE model is to define the capital accumulation process as follows:

$$K_{t+1} = (1-\delta)\,K_t + Z_t I_t \tag{6.1}$$

where δ is the physical capital depreciation rate and Z_t represents technological progress specific to investment. Following Greenwood *et al.* (1997), Z_t determines the amount of capital that can be purchased with a production unit, representing the current state of the technology to produce capital. In the standard neoclassical model would have to $Z_t = 1$ for all t, i.e., the amount of capital that can be purchased with a final production unit is constant over time. However, in reality the relative price of capital falls broadly, evidence that over time we can buy a larger amount of capital with the same amount of final production. Thus, the higher Z_t greater the amount of capital that can be incorporated into the economy with an investment unit, reflecting the fact that the quality of capital has increased. An increase in Z_t can be associated to a positive technology shock which reduces the slope of transforming the investment good in a consumption good (i.e. a reduction in the average cost of producing investment goods with respect to the average cost of producing consumption goods). To obtain a measure of technological progress specific to investment, it is necessary to have prices of capital assets adjusted for quality. This is what is called hedonic price, i.e., the price of a particular capital asset whose quality remains constant over time (see Gordon, 1990; and Cummins and Violante, 2002). For instance, we cannot directly compare the price of a car produced today relative to a car produced 20 years ago, because its quality has changed over time. In order to make this comparison possible, prices must be quality-adjusted.

DSGE models incorporating ISTC have been used to study the contribution to long-run productivity growth of the different sources of technological progress. Examples are Greenwood, Hercowitz and Krusell (2000), Kiley (2001), Cummins and Violante (2002), Pakko (2002a, 2005), Carlaw and Kosempel (2004), Bakhshi and Larsen (2005), Martínez, Rodríguez and Torres (2008, 2010), Rodríguez and Torres (2012), among others.

In the literature, we find a number of works studying the business cycle properties of ISTC shocks. Greenwood, Hercowitz and Krusell (2000) used a calibrated model on annual data from 1954-1990, finding that 30% of output fluctuations in this sample are caused by ISTC shocks. These results were later extended and confirmed by Cummins and Violante (2002). Several recent econometric papers – Fisher (2006), Arias, Hansen and Ohanian (2007), Justiniano and Primiceri (2008), Justiniano, Primiceri and Tambalotti (2011) – tackled the issue of the determinants of macroeconomic volatility during the period 1984 to 2008. Using the model developed by Greenwood *et al.* (2000), Fisher (2006) proposed a set of identifying conditions to disentangle neutral versus ISTC shocks. In the long run, the relative price of investment is assumed to be affected solely by ISTC shocks. Permanent neutral technology shocks can be identified if they are the only source of long-run changes in labor productivity. He finds that ISTC plays a crucial role in accounting for output fluctuations, explaining 42% of output variance from 1955:I-1979:II and 67% from 1982:III-2000:IV.

Arias *et al.* (2007) performed a calibration exercise that analyzes the moderation in volatilities around 1984 using a variety of shocks: TFP shocks, government spending shocks, a shock affecting the substitution between consumption and labor, and shocks to the intertemporal Euler equation. They estimated that the variances of these shocks were reduced after the first quarter of 1984 and showed that TFP shocks account for around 50% decline in cyclical volatility of output and labor since 1983. Justiniano and Primiceri (2008) estimated a DSGE model to analyze the different sources of U.S. fluctuations, which include technology shocks (both neutral and ISTC), preference shocks, fiscal shocks, and monetary policy shocks. They found that ISTC shocks can account for most output fluctuations and most of the decline in GDP volatility after 1984. They also found that the volatility of the series identified as ISTC technology stocks fell between 1/3 and 4/5 after 1984. Justiniano, Primiceri and Tambalotti (2011) extended previous analysis using the same estimated model but considering two different shocks to investment: an investment-specific shock, affecting the relative price between investment and consumption goods, and a shock to the marginal efficiency of investment, affecting the process by which investment goods are transformed into productive capital. They find that this last shock is the most important determinant of U.S. business cycle fluctuations during the post-war period, explaining between 60 and 85% of the variance of output, hours and investment. Nevertheless, Basu, Fernald and Kimball (2006) show that varying utilization of capital and labor can affect the validity of standard measures of TFP as proxies for technology change. Finally, Molinari, Rodríguez and Torres (2013) quantify the relative importance of different sources of technological progress as determinants of short-run fluctuations in the US economy. The particular focus is on the role of the technical innovations associated with information and communication technologies (ICT). The paper points to three main findings. First, neutral technical change is the main determinant of the US aggregate fluctuations, and its contribution remained constant throughout the postwar sample. Second, the importance of ICT increased significantly during the last decades of the considered sample, which nowadays is responsible for approximately 1/5 of GDP fluctuations. Third, the variance reduction of exogenous shocks typically associated with the last decades of the postwar sample, mainly comes from ICT and neutral shocks, whereas the volatility of innovations in traditional capital remained relatively stable.

The model

Here we present a very simple version of a DSGE model with specific technological change investment. The model includes two shocks: aggregate productivity, which measures the neutral technological change, and specific productivity, which measures technological change associated with new capital assets. Two changes are introduced in the basic model: First, the capital accumulation equation accounts now for changes in the quality of new vintages of capital through the investment process. Second, a new stochastic process must be defined for investment-specific shocks.

Households

The economy is inhabited by an infinitely lived, representative household who has time-separable preferences in terms of consumption of final goods, $\{C_t\}_{t=0}^{\infty}$, and leisure, $\{1-L_t\}_{t=0}^{\infty}$. Preferences are represented by the following utility function:

$$\sum_{t=0}^{\infty} \beta^t \left[\gamma \log C_t + (1-\gamma)\log(1-L_t)\right] \tag{6.2}$$

where β is the discount factor and where $\gamma \in (0,1)$ is the elasticity of substitution between consumption and leisure.

The budget constraint faced by the consumer says that consumption and saving, S_t, cannot exceed the sum of labor and capital rental income:

$$C_t + S_t = W_t L_t + R_t K_t \tag{6.3}$$

where W_t is the wage and R_t is the rental price of capital. To keep thing simple, we assume that saving transforms in investment at no cost, $I_t = S_t$.

The key point of the model is that capital holdings evolve according to:

$$K_{t+1} = (1-\delta) K_t + Z_t I_t \tag{6.4}$$

where δ is the depreciation rate of physical capital and where Z_t determines the amount of capital that can be purchased by one unit of output, representing the current state of technology for producing capital. Therefore, investment can be defined as:

$$I_t = \frac{K_{t+1} - (1-\delta) K_t}{Z_t} \tag{6.5}$$

and the budget constraint can be written as:

$$C_t + \frac{K_{t+1}}{Z_t} = W_t L_t + R_t K_t + \frac{(1-\delta) K_t}{Z_t} \tag{6.6}$$

The Lagrangian problem to be solved by households is to choose C_t, L_t, and I_t so as to maximize:

$$\max_{(C_t, I_t, L_t)} \mathcal{L} = \sum_{t=0}^{\infty} \beta^t \left\{ \begin{array}{c} \gamma \log C_t + (1-\gamma) \log(1-L_t) \\ -\lambda_t \left[C_t + \frac{K_{t+1}}{Z_t} - W_t L_t - R_t K_t - \frac{(1-\delta) K_t}{Z_t} \right] \end{array} \right\} \tag{6.7}$$

The first order conditions for the household are:

$$\frac{\partial \mathcal{L}}{\partial C_t} : \gamma C_t^{-1} - \lambda_t = 0 \tag{6.8}$$

$$\frac{\partial \mathcal{L}}{\partial L_t} : -\frac{(1-\gamma)}{1-L_t} + \lambda_t W_t = 0 \tag{6.9}$$

$$\frac{\partial \mathcal{L}}{\partial K_t} : \beta^t \lambda_t \frac{Z_{t-1}}{Z_t} [Z_t R_t + 1 - \delta] - \beta^{t-1} \lambda_{t-1} = 0 \tag{6.10}$$

Combining (6.8) and (6.9) we obtain the condition that equates the marginal rate of substitution between consumption and leisure to the opportunity cost of one additional unit of leisure,

$$\frac{1-\gamma}{\gamma}\frac{C_t}{1-L_t} = W_t \tag{6.11}$$

On the other hand, combining (6.8) with (6.10) yields:

$$\frac{1}{\beta}\frac{C_t}{C_{t-1}} = \frac{Z_{t-1}}{Z_t}\left[Z_t R_t + 1 - \delta\right] \tag{6.12}$$

that is, the equilibrium conditions that equates the marginal rate of consumption to the rate of return of investment, which now depends on the investment-specific technological change.

The firms

The problem of firms is to find optimal values for the utilization of labor and capital. The production of final output Y requires the services of labor L and K. The firms rent capital and employ labor in order to maximize profits at period t, taking factor prices as given. The technology is given by a constant return to scale Cobb-Douglas production function,

$$Y_t = A_t K_t^{\alpha} L_t^{1-\alpha} \tag{6.13}$$

where A_t is a measure of total-factor, or sector-neutral, productivity and where $0 \leq \alpha \leq 1$.

The static maximization problem for the firms is:

$$\max_{(K_t, L_t)} \Pi_t = A_t K_t^{\alpha} L_t^{1-\alpha} - R_t K_t - W_t L_t \tag{6.14}$$

The first order conditions for the firms profit maximization are given by

$$\frac{\partial \Pi_t}{\partial K_t} : R_t - \alpha A_t K_t^{\alpha-1} L_t^{1-\alpha} = 0 \tag{6.15}$$

$$\frac{\partial \Pi_t}{\partial L_t} : W_t - (1-\alpha) A_t K_t^{\alpha} L_t^{-\alpha} = 0 \tag{6.16}$$

From the above first order conditions for profit maximization, equilibrium prices for production inputs are given by:

$$R_t = \alpha A_t K_t^{\alpha-1} L_t^{1-\alpha} \tag{6.17}$$

$$W_t = (1-\alpha) A_t K_t^{\alpha} L_t^{-\alpha} \tag{6.18}$$

Equilibrium of the model

The equilibrium of the model economy is obtained by combining first order conditions for household with first order conditions for the firm, such as:

$$\frac{1-\phi}{\phi}\frac{C_t}{1-L_t} = (1-\alpha)\frac{Y_t}{L_t} \tag{6.19}$$

$$\frac{1}{\beta}\frac{C_t}{C_{t-1}} = \frac{Z_{t-1}}{Z_t}\left[Z_t \alpha \frac{Y_t}{K_t} + 1 - \delta\right] \tag{6.20}$$

To close the model, the feasibility constraint of the economy must be defined:

$$C_t + I_t = Y_t \tag{6.21}$$

A more formal definition of equilibrium is the following:

Definition 4 *A competitive equilibrium for this economy is a sequence of consumption, leisure and private investment for the consumers* $\{C_t, 1-L_t, I_t\}_{t=0}^{\infty}$, *a sequence of capital and labor utilization for the firm* $\{K_t, L_t\}_{t=0}^{\infty}$, *a sequence of the state of technology for producing each capital asset* $\{Z_t\}_{t=0}^{\infty}$, *such that given a sequence of prices* $\{W_t, R_t\}_{t=0}^{\infty}$.

i) The optimization problem of the consumer is satisfied.

ii) The first order conditions of the firm hold, and

iii) The feasibility constraint of the economy holds.

The balanced growth path

Although business cycle properties of ISTC shocks are of interest and will be studied later, long-run properties are also worth noting. In the literature we find a number of works studying the contribution to long-run growth of the different sources of technological progress using a DSGE growth model by computing the balance growth path.

Next, we define the balanced growth path, in which the steady state growth path of the model is an equilibrium satisfying the above set of equations of the model economy and where all variables grow at a constant rate. The balanced growth path requires that hours per worker must be constant. Given the assumption of no unemployment, this implies that total hours worked grow by the population growth rate, which is assumed to be zero.

According to the balanced growth path, output, consumption and investment must all grow at the same rate, which is denoted by g. However, the different types of capital would grow at a different rate depending on the evolution of their relative prices. From the production function, the balanced growth path implies that:

$$g = g_A g_K^{\alpha} \tag{6.22}$$

where g is the steady state productivity growth, g_A is the steady state exogenous growth of A_t and g_K is the steady state growth rate of capital. Then, from the law of motion (6.4), we have that the growth of capital input is given by:

$$g_K = \eta g \tag{6.23}$$

with η being the exogenous growth rate of Z_t. Therefore, the long run growth rate of output can be accounted for by neutral technological progress and by increases in the capital stock. In addition, expression (6.23) says that the capital stock growth also depends on technological progress in the process producing the capital goods. Therefore, it is possible to express output growth as a function of the exogenous growth rates of production technologies as:

$$g = g_A^{1/(1-\alpha)} \eta^{\alpha/(1-\alpha)} \tag{6.24}$$

Expression (6.24) implies that output growth can be decomposed as the weighted sum of the TFP (neutral technological progress) growth and embedded technological progress, as given by η. Along the balanced growth path, growth rate of each capital asset can be different, depending on the relative price of the new capital in terms of output. A particular capital asset with decreasing prices (specific technological progress) will display a growth rate higher than the output growth rate. On the contrary, capital assets whose relative prices increase, will grow over time at a lower rate than output.

On this basis, the following steady state ratios can be defined:

$$\rho \equiv \overline{Z}\frac{\overline{Y}}{\overline{K}} > 0 \tag{6.25}$$

$$s_i \equiv \frac{\overline{I}}{\overline{Y}} \in (0,1) \tag{6.26}$$

$$c \equiv \frac{\overline{C}}{\overline{Y}} \in (0,1) \tag{6.27}$$

$$l \equiv \overline{L} \in (0,1), \tag{6.28}$$

where the "upper bar" denotes its steady-state reference.

The balanced growth path is finally characterized by the following set of equations:

$$\eta g = \beta\left[\alpha\rho + 1 - \delta\right] \tag{6.29}$$

$$\eta g = \rho s + 1 - \delta \tag{6.30}$$

and

$$1 = c + s \tag{6.31}$$

$$c = (1-\alpha)\frac{\gamma}{1-\gamma}\left(\frac{1}{l} - 1\right). \tag{6.32}$$

Equations of the model and calibration

Competitive equilibrium of the model economy is given by a set of nine equations, driving the dynamics of the seven endogenous macroeconomic variables, Y_t, C_t, I_t, K_t, L_t, R_t, W_t, plus the two technologies A_t and Z_t which it is assumed to follow an AR(1) process. This set of equations is the following:

$$\frac{1-\gamma}{\gamma}\frac{C_t}{1-L_t} = W_t \tag{6.33}$$

$$\frac{1}{\beta}\frac{C_t}{C_{t-1}} = \frac{Z_{t-1}}{Z_t}\left[Z_t\alpha\frac{Y_t}{K_t} + 1 - \delta\right] \tag{6.34}$$

$$Y_t = C_t + I_t \tag{6.35}$$

$$Y_t = A_t K_t^{\alpha} L_t^{1-\alpha} \tag{6.36}$$

$$K_{t+1} = (1-\delta)K_t + Z_t I_t \tag{6.37}$$

$$W_t = (1-\alpha)A_t K_t^{\alpha} L_t^{-\alpha} \tag{6.38}$$

$$R_t = \alpha A_t K_t^{\alpha-1} L_t^{1-\alpha} \tag{6.39}$$

$$\ln A_t = (1-\rho_A)\ln \overline{A} + \rho_A \ln A_{t-1} + \varepsilon_t^A \tag{6.40}$$

$$\ln Z_t = (1-\rho_Z)\ln \overline{Z} + \rho_Z \ln Z_{t-1} + \varepsilon_t^Z \tag{6.41}$$

The model has two technology shocks, neutral or TFP technological change and investment-specific technological change. We assume that the two shocks are independent. However, since both perturbations represent technological change, alternatively it can be assumed that there may be some relationship between them. In particular, we can assume that the process followed by the two technologies is as follows:

$$\begin{matrix} \ln A_t \\ \ln Z_t \end{matrix} = \begin{bmatrix} \rho_A & \upsilon_{AZ} \\ \upsilon_{ZA} & \rho_Z \end{bmatrix} \begin{bmatrix} \ln A_{t-1} \\ \ln Z_{t-1} \end{bmatrix} + \begin{bmatrix} \varepsilon_t^A \\ \varepsilon_t^Z \end{bmatrix}$$

where $\left|\rho_i \pm \upsilon\right| < 1$, $i = A, Z$, in order to ensure stationarity, with $E(\varepsilon_t^i) = 0$ and $E(\varepsilon_t^i \varepsilon_t^i) = \sigma_i^2, \forall i$.

To calibrate the model, it is necessary to assign values to the following parameters:

$$\Omega = \{\alpha, \beta, \gamma, \delta, \rho_A, \sigma_A, \rho_Z, \sigma_Z\}$$

The only additional parameters appearing in this model are those corresponding to the stochastic process that follows the technology associated with the investment process in new capital. Table 6.1 shows the calibrated values of the parameters. It is assumed that the parameters defining the stochastic process for ISTC are exactly equal to the process for neutral shock. Greenwood *et al.* (2000) for the U.S. economy estimate an autoregressive parameter of 0.64 for ISTC. By contrast, Pakko (2005), also for the U.S., estimates values of 0.945 for the neutral technological change and 0.941 for the investment-specific technological change. Rodriguez and Torres (2010) estimate values of 0.95, 0.83 and 0.72 for the United States, Japan, and Germany, respectively.

Table 6.1: Calibrated parameters

Parameter	Definition	Value
α	Capital technological parameter	0.350
β	Discount factor	0.970
γ	Preference parameter	0.450
δ	Capital depreciation rate	0.060
ρ_A	TFP autoregressive parameter	0.950
σ_A	TFP standard deviation	0.010
ρ_Z	ISTC autoregressive parameter	0.950
σ_Z	ISTC standard deviation	0.010

Investment-Specific Technological shock

This section studies the dynamics effects of a ISTC shock. Figure 6.1 shows the impulse-response of different variables to a positive investment-specific technological shock. As it can be observed, this type of technological shock generates dynamic responses of the relevant variables different relative to an aggregate productivity shock. Main differences are found in the response of consumption and input prices.

Impact effect on consumption is negative. This is because the shock makes profitable to invest in new capital, as its productivity is higher than productivity of the installed capital stock. This causes a rise in investment which accumulated into capital stock. The ISTC shock causes the investment units to be cheaper in relation to consumer units. This provokes an intertemporal substitution effect between consumption and saving and an intratemporal substitution effect between consumption and leisure.

Input prices, reflecting the dynamics of the marginal productivity of production factors, show a different behaviour. Rental rate of capital rises in impact, but the response is negative afterward. This is because, capital stock increases, but the gain in productivity are only associated to the new capital invested, which represent a small fraction of total capital stock. On the other hand, the effect on labor is positive by the intratemporal substitution between consumption and leisure, which reduces wages in impact.

In summary, ISTC shocks generate an intertemporal substitution between investment and consumption and an intratemporal substitution between consumption and leisure that all together push

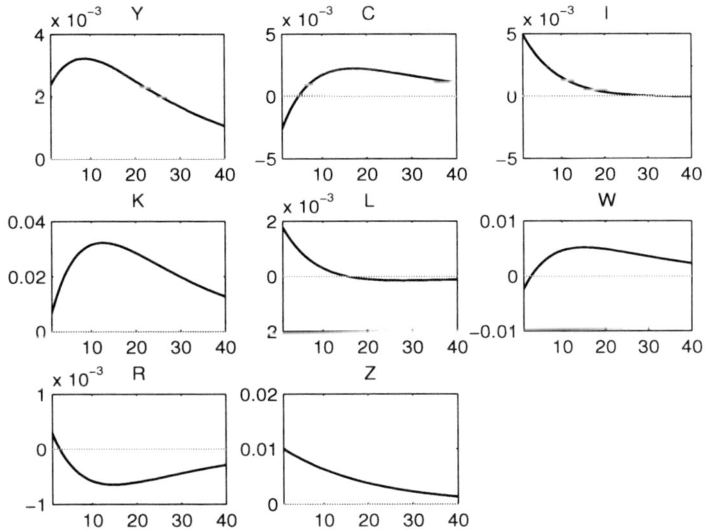

Figure 6.1: Investment-specific technological shock

upwards the response of output. Neutral and ISTC shocks cannot be identified by looking at the sign of the response of output, and should instead be identified by looking at the sign of the response of labor productivity, which increases after a neutral shock but decreases after an ISTC shock in the short run. Notice that the reduction in labor productivity after an ISTC shock is determined by the substitution effect between consumption and leisure, opposite to the one observed after a neutral shock, which implies that working hours reduce in the short run.

Conclusions

This chapter develops a DSGE model in which two technological shocks are considered: the standard neutral (TFP) technological change and embodied technological change to new capital assets or investment-specific technological change (ISTC). Compared to TFP changes that affect the aggregate productivity of the economy, ISTC does not affect productivity of capital assets already installed, but only new vintages of capital assets.

ISTC can be introducing in a DSGE model using alternative specifications. One possibility is to consider a two sector model: one sector producing consumption goods and the other sector producing investment goods, with specific productivity shock to each sector. Another possibility is the way shown in this chapter, introducing ISTC in the law of motion for capital stock.

A key result derived from this analysis is that the importance of TFP shock in explaining both short-run dynamics of the economy and long-run growth is reduced. This is because traditionally, embodied technological change in equipment has not been taken into account, and was thus, attributed to TFP changes. This could be an initial step toward a theory of TFP.

Appendix A: Dynare model file

The Dynare code corresponding to the model developed in this chapter, named *model6.mod*, is the following:

```
// Model 6:  Investment Specific Technological
// Change
// K(t+1)=(1-delta)*K(t)+Z(t)*I(t)
// Dynare code
// File:  model6.mod
// José L. Torres.  University of Málaga (Spain)
// Endogenous variables
var Y, C, I, K, L, W, R, A, Z;
// Exogenous variables
varexo e, u;
// Parameters
parameters alpha, beta, delta, gamma, rho1, rho2;
// Calibration of the parameters
alpha = 0.35;
beta = 0.97;
delta = 0.06;
gamma = 0.40;
rho1 = 0.95;
rho2 = 0.95;
// Equations of the model economy
model;
C = (gamma/(1-gamma))*(1-L)*(1-alpha)*Y/L;
```

```
1 = beta*(Z*C/(Z(+1)*C(+1)))
 *(Z*alpha*Y(+1)/K+(1-delta));
Y = A*(K(-1)^alpha)*(L^(1-alpha));
K = Z*I+(1-delta)*K(-1);
I = Y-C;
W = (1-alpha)*A*(K(-1)^alpha)*(L^(-alpha));
R = alpha*A*(K(-1)^(alpha-1))*(L^(1-alpha));
log(A) = rho1*log(A(-1))+e;
log(Z) = rho2*log(Z(-1))+u;
end;
// Initial values
initval;
Y = 1;
C = 0.8;
L = 0.3;
K = 3.5;
I = 0.2;
W = (1-alpha)*Y/L;
R = alpha*Y/K;
A = 1;
Z = 1;
e = 0;
u = 0;
end;
 // Steady state
steady;
// Blanchard-Kahn conditions
check;
// Perturbation analysis
shocks;
var e; stderr 0.01;
var u; stderr 0.01;
end;
// Stochastic simulation
stoch_simul;
```

Bibliography

Arias, A., Hansen, G. and Ohanian, L. (2007): Why have business cycle fluctuations become less volatile? *Economic Theory*, 32(1), 43-58.

Bakhshi, H. and Larsen, J. (2005): ICT-specific technological progress in the United Kingdom. *Journal of Macroeconomics* 27, 648-669.

Basu, S., Fernald, J. and Shapiro, M. (2001): Productivity growth in the 1990s: technology, utilization, or adjustment? *Carnegie-Rochester Conference Series on Public Policy*, 55, 117-165.

Carlaw, K. and Kosempel, S. (2004): The sources of total factor productivity growth: Evidence from Canadian data. *Economic Innovation and New Technology* 13, 299-309.

Cummins, J.G. and Violante, G. L. (2002): Investment-specific technical change in the U.S. (1947-2000): Measurement and macroeconomic consequences, *Review of Economic Dynamics*, 5(2), 243-284.

Fisher, J. (2006): "The dynamic effects of neutral and investment-specific technology shocks". *Journal of Political Economy*, 114(3), 413-451.

Gordon, R. (1990): The measurement of durable goods prices. University of Chicago Press.

Greenwood, J., Hercowitz, Z. and Huffman, G. (1988): Investment, capacity utilisation and the real business cycle. *American Economic Review*, 78(3), 402-417.

Greenwood, J., Hercowitz, Z. and Krusell, P. (1997): Long-run implication of investment-specific technological change, *American Economic Review,* 87(3), 342-362.

Greenwood, J., Hercowitz, Z. and Krusell, P. (2000): The role of investment-specific technological change in the business cycle, *European Economic Review,* 44(1), 91-115.

Justiniano, A. and G. Primiceri (2008): The time varying volatility of macroeconomic fluctuations, *American Economic Review,* 98(3), 604-641.

Justiniano, A.,Primiceri, G. and Tambalotti, A. (2011): Investment Shocks and the Relative Price of Investment. *Review of Economic Dynamics,* 14(1), 101-121.

Kiley, M. (2001): Computers and growth with frictions: aggregate and disaggregate evidence. *Carnegie-Rochester Conference Series on Public Policy,* 55, 171-215.

Martínez, D., J. Rodríguez and Torres, J.L. (2008): The productivity paradox and the new economy: The Spanish case". *Journal of Macroeconomics,* 30(4), 1169-1186.

Martínez, D., J. Rodríguez and Torres, J.L. (2010): ICT-specific technological change and productivity growth in the US: 1980–2004. *Information Economics and Policy,* 22(2), 121-129.

Molinari, B., J. Rodríguez and Torres, J.L. (2013): Information and Communication Technologies over the Business Cycle. *The B.E. Journal of Macroeconomics,* 13(1).

Pakko, M.R., (2005): Changing technology trends, transition dynamics, and growth accounting, *The B.E. Journal of Macroeconomics, Contributions,* 5(1), Article 12.

Rodríguez, J. and Torres, J.L. (2012): Technological sources of productivity growth in Germany, Japan, and the U.S. *Macroeconomic Dynamics,* 16(1), 133-156.

Part IV

The government

Chapter 7
Taxes

Introduction

In the DSGE models studied in previous chapters we considered the existence of two economic agents: Households and firms. Nevertheless, in all economies there exists another very important economic agent: The government. In this chapter and in the following two chapters, this third economic agent will be incorporated to our theoretical framework in order to study some effects of different government decisions on the economy. The government can be introduced in the basic DSGE model in a large variety of ways, since this economic agent is involved in virtually all areas of the economy, controlling a large number of variables. In this chapter we focus on the role of the government regarding fiscal revenues, that is, considering the existence of taxes.

In general, two types of taxes can be considered. First, lump-sum taxes which are non-distortionary taxes and do not change households and firms decisions. Second, distortionary taxes, such as income taxes or consumption taxes, as they affect the market price of goods and production inputs, and hence change private agents' economic decisions. Specifically, here we consider the existence of three types of taxes: a consumption tax, a labor income tax, and a tax on capital income, which are those that directly affect households.

In the DSGE model that is developed here, the key aspect is that these taxes introduce a distortion to the economy as they affect the relative price of production factors and the price of the final good. As a consequence, economic decisions of private agents will change in response to the tax code. In this framework we can study the effects of fiscal policies through public revenues. In the DSGE model that is developed here the government decides the tax policy and consumers and firms make their decisions accordingly, taking taxes set by the government as given. In order to simplify the theoretical framework, we assume that public revenues are returned to the economy in the form of an exogenous sequence of lump-sum transfers.

This model allows to us to study a variety of different interesting questions regarding taxation. First, we can use this model to compute Laffer curves for the economy, as the relationship between fiscal revenues and the tax rate in the steady-state. Second, we can study the dynamics effects of a change in the tax rates, changes that can be either permanent or temporary and anticipated or unanticipated. Finally, we will study the effects of an aggregate productivity shock in an economy with distortionary taxes.

The structure of the rest of the chapter is as follows. Section 2 defines the tax structure of the economy and how taxes can be introduced in the DSGE model. Section 3 presents the model with three taxes: consumption tax, labor income tax and capital income tax. Section 4 presents the equations of the model and the calibration exercise. In Section 5 steady state Laffer curves are estimated. Section 6 studies the effect of a change in taxes. In particular, we study the case of a change in consumption tax. Section 7 studies the dynamic effects of a TFP shock. Finally, Section 8 presents some conclusions.

Taxes

The introduction of taxes in the DSGE model requires the modification of the consumers budget constraint and/or the profit function for the firms, depending on the particular tax(es) to be considered. In reality, there exist a large variety of taxes: Lump-sum taxes, income taxes, consumption taxes including excises and corporate profit taxes. In pay-as-you go systems, contributions to Social Security are included in fiscal revenues and so they can be considered as an additional tax.

Lump-sum taxes can be introduced in the following way:

$$C_t + S_t = Y_t - T_t \tag{7.1}$$

where C_t is consumption, S_t is saving, Y_t is income and T_t is a fixed amount tax which it is not related to any macroeconomic variable. An alternative is to consider an income tax. In this case, the households budget constraint is defined as:

$$C_t + S_t = (1 - \tau^y) Y_t \tag{7.2}$$

where τ^y is the income tax rate. A consumption tax and a saving tax can also be considered as:

$$(1+\tau^c)C_t + (1+\tau^s)S_t = (1-\tau^y)Y_t \tag{7.3}$$

where τ^c is the consumption tax rate and τ^s is the saving tax rate.

Overall, we can distinguish between two types of taxes: direct taxes and indirect taxes. Direct taxes are income taxes. Examples are a labor income tax, a capital income tax or a corporate tax. Consumption taxes are indirect taxes, and cause the price of goods to be higher. Examples are the Value Added Tax (VAT), import taxes, and excises.

Computational macroeconomic models of fiscal policy crucially depend on realistic measures of tax rates. Agents' decisions depend on marginal tax and therefore effective marginal taxes should be used in the calibration. However, estimating marginal tax rates is a difficult task and, as pointed out by Mendoza, Razin and Tesar (1994), is often impractical at an international level given the limitations due to data availability and difficulties in dealing with the complexity of tax systems. Mendoza *et al.* (1994) proposed a method to estimate effective average taxes and show that these are within the range of marginal tax rates estimated in other works and display very similar trends. On the other hand, these authors argue that their definition of effective average tax rates can be interpreted as an estimation of specific tax rates that a representative agent, in a general equilibrium context, takes into account. Authors estimating marginal tax rates are Gouveia and Strauss (1994) and Calonge and Conesa (2003), although they obtain implausible results. Average effective tax rates involves the use of conservative values (smaller implied behavioral responses) relative to marginal taxes.

In the calibration of the model, we use effective average tax rates, borrowed from Boscá *et al.* (2009), who used the methodology proposed by Mendoza *et al.* (1994). Table 7.1 shows the estimated average tax rates reported by Boscá *et al.* (2009) for the year 2005 for some OECD countries, including consumption tax rates, labor tax rates and capital tax rates. It can be observed how the tax code can be very different to one country to another. Also the tax burden is different across countries. Overall, we can distinguish two groups of countries. First, there is a group of countries where the labor income tax is higher than the tax on capital income. These countries are Austria, Finland, France, Germany, Italy, Netherlands, Spain and Sweden, i.e., continental Europe. By contrast, another

Table 7.1: Effective average taxes (2005)

	τ_c	τ_l	τ_k
Australia	0.095	0.218	0.450
Austria	0.147	0.482	0.176
Canada	0.098	0.299	0.334
Denmark	0.199	0.397	0.448
Finland	0.176	0.451	0.256
France	0.129	0.430	0.298
Germany	0.120	0.374	0.177
Italy	0.107	0.431	0.283
Japan	0.062	0.257	0.356
Netherlands	0.146	0.359	0.192
Spain	0.116	0.348	0.252
Sweden	0.166	0.523	0.301
UK	0.124	0.255	0.325
USA	0.039	0.221	0.299

Source: Boscá *et al.* (2009)

group of countries where taxes on labor income are much lower than capital income taxes. These countries are Australia, Canada, Japan, the United Kingdom and the United States.

Introducing taxes in a DSGE model is rather simple, as the main structure of the model does not change, except for the consideration of a new economic agent: The government. The analysis of what the government does with fiscal revenues is more complex. In the model we will simple assume that fiscal revenues are returned to the economy just as a lump-sum transfer. Specifically, we consider the existence of three types of taxes over households: a consumption tax, a labor income tax and a capital income tax. In a competitive environment where households are the owner of the production inputs, there is no room for a corporate tax as firms profit are zero. The consumer budget constraint can be written as:

$$(1+\tau_t^c)C_t + S_t = (1-\tau_t^l)W_t L_t + (1-\tau_t^k)R_t K_t + G_t \tag{7.4}$$

where τ_t^c is the tax rate on consumption τ_t^l is the tax rate on labor income and τ_t^k is the tax rate on income the capital. The budget constraint indicates that final consumption including excises and value added taxes plus saving cannot exceed the sum of net labor income and net capital rental income plus transfers received from the government, G_t. Note that transfers enter as a constant (a fixed amount) in the consumer budget constraint, so it will not have any influence on decisions at the margin. This does not happen with tax rates, as they will affect consumption-saving and labor-leisure decisions.

Finally, to simplify our analysis we assume that government budget constraint is satisfied period-to-period. Therefore, transfers received by consumers, G_t, are exactly equal to tax revenue:[1]

$$G_t = \tau_t^c C_t + \tau_t^l W_t L_t + \tau_t^k (R_t - \delta) K_t \tag{7.5}$$

The model

Here we develop a DSGE model with taxes. Together to consumers and firms, we consider the government as an additional economic agent. Nevertheless, in this framework the government's role will be very simple, affecting only the consumer budget constraint. In particular, the government taxes private consumption goods, capital income and labor income to finance an exogenous sequence of lump-sum transfers, $\{T_t\}_{t=0}^{\infty}$.

Households

Consider a model economy where the decisions made by consumers are represented by a stand-in consumer, whose preferences are represented by the following instantaneous utility function:

$$U(C_t, N_t\overline{H} - L_t) = \gamma \log C_t + (1-\gamma)\log(1 - L_t) \tag{7.6}$$

Private consumption is denoted by C_t. Leisure is defined $1 - L_t$, that is the number of effective hours minus the number of hours worked, L_t, where total availability of time is normalized to 1. The parameter γ $(0 < \gamma < 1)$ is the proportion of private consumption to total private income. The budget constraint faced by the stand-in con-

[1] Notice that the corresponding part of the depreciation of physical is deducted from the tax on the income generated by the capital. We will define later how we arrive to that expression.

sumer, as defined above, is:

$$(1+\tau_t^c)C_t + S_t = (1-\tau_t^l)W_tL_t + (1-\tau_t^k)R_tK_t + G_t \tag{7.7}$$

where G_t is the transfer received by consumers from the government, K_t is the private capital stock, W_t is the compensation to employees, R_t is the rental rate, and $\tau_t^c, \tau_t^l, \tau_t^k$, are the private consumption tax, the labor income tax, and the capital income tax, respectively.[2] The budget constraints indicate that total consumption and saving cannot exceed the sum of labor and capital rental income net of taxes and lump sum transfers.

Capital stock evolves according to:

$$K_{t+1} = (1-\delta)\,K_t + I_t \tag{7.8}$$

where δ is the capital depreciation rate which is modelled as tax deductible and where I_t is gross investment.

The problem faced by the stand-in consumer is to maximize the value of her lifetime utility given by:

$$Max_{\{C_t,L_t\}_t^\infty} \sum_{t=0}^{\infty} \beta^t \left[\gamma \log C_t + (1-\gamma)\log(1-L_t)\right] \tag{7.9}$$

subject to the budget constraint, given the assumption that $S_t = I_t$:

$$(1+\tau_t^c)C_t + K_t - K_{t-1} = (1-\tau_t^l)W_tL_t + (1-\tau_t^k)(R_t - \delta_K)K_{t-1} + G_t \tag{7.10}$$

given $\tau_t^c, \tau_t^l, \tau_t^k$ and K_0 and where $\beta \subset (0,1)$, is the consumer's discount factor.

The Lagrangian problem to be solved by households is to choose C_t, L_t, and K_t so as to maximize:

$$\max_{(C_t,I_t,L_t)} \mathscr{L} = \sum_{t=0}^{\infty} \beta^t \left\{ \begin{array}{c} \gamma \log C_t + (1-\gamma)\log(1-L_t) \\ -\lambda_t \left[\begin{array}{c} (1+\tau_t^c)C_t + K_{t+1} - (1-\tau_t^l)W_tL_t \\ -(1-\tau_t^k)(R_t-\delta)K_t - K_t - G_t \end{array} \right] \end{array} \right\} \tag{7.11}$$

First order conditions for the household maximization problem

[2] Tax rates are constants and can be interpreted as average marginal tax rates. Jonsson and Klein (1996) use an isoelastic specification of the tax schedule rather than a linear one in order to capture the progressivity of income taxation.

are:

$$\frac{\partial \mathcal{L}}{\partial C_t} : \gamma \frac{1}{C_t} - \lambda_t \left(1 + \tau_t^c\right) = 0 \tag{7.12}$$

$$\frac{\partial \mathcal{L}}{\partial L_t} : -\left(1 - \gamma\right) \frac{1}{1 - L_t} + \lambda_t \left(1 - \tau_t^l\right) W_t = 0 \tag{7.13}$$

$$\frac{\partial \mathcal{L}}{\partial K_t} : \beta^t \lambda_t \left[\left(1 - \tau_t^k\right)(R_t - \delta) + 1\right] - \lambda_{t-1}\beta^{t-1} = 0 \tag{7.14}$$

where $\beta^t \lambda_t$ is the Lagrange multiplier assigned to the budget constraint at time t. Combining equations (7.12) and (7.13), we obtain the condition that equates the marginal rate of substitution between consumption and leisure to the opportunity cost of one additional unit of leisure:

$$\frac{1}{1 - L_t} = \frac{\gamma}{\left(1 - \gamma\right)} \frac{\left(1 - \tau_t^l\right)}{\left(1 + \tau_t^c\right)} \frac{W_t}{C_t} \tag{7.15}$$

Combining expression (7.12) with (7.14) we find the intertemporal equilibrium condition that equates the marginal rate of consumption with the rate of return of investment:

$$\frac{\left(1 + \tau_t^c\right) C_t}{\left(1 + \tau_{t-1}^c\right) C_{t-1}} = \beta\left[\left(1 - \tau_t^k\right)(R_t - \delta) + 1\right] \tag{7.16}$$

which represents the consumption optimal path. Notice that if we assume that the consumption tax is fixed over time, this particular tax will not affect the households consumption-saving decision.

The firms

The problem of firms is to find optimal values for the utilization of labor and capital. The production of final output Y requires the services of labor L and K. The firms rent capital and employ labor in order to maximize profits at period t, taking factor prices as given. The technology is given by a constant return to scale Cobb-Douglas production function,

$$Y_t = A_t K_t^{\alpha} L_t^{1-\alpha} \tag{7.17}$$

where A_t is a measure of total-factor, or sector-neutral, productivity and where $0 \leq \alpha \leq 1$.

The static maximization problem for the firms is:

$$\max_{(K_t,L_t)} \Pi_t = A_t K_t^{\alpha} L_t^{1-\alpha} - R_t K_t - W_t L_t \tag{7.18}$$

The first order conditions for the firms profit maximization are given by

$$\frac{\partial \Pi_t}{\partial K_t} : R_t - \alpha A_t K_t^{\alpha-1} L_t^{1-\alpha} = 0 \tag{7.19}$$

$$\frac{\partial \Pi_t}{\partial L_t} : W_t - (1-\alpha) A_t K_t^{\alpha} L_t^{-\alpha} = 0 \tag{7.20}$$

From these FOCs we obtain the price for the production inputs:

$$R_t = \alpha A_t K_t^{\alpha-1} L_t^{1-\alpha} \tag{7.21}$$

$$W_t = (1-\alpha) A_t K_t^{\alpha} L_t^{-\alpha} \tag{7.22}$$

The government

Finally, we consider the role of the government as a tax-levying entity. It is assumed that the government uses tax revenues to finance lump-sum transfers paid out to the consumers. We assume that the government balances its budget period-by-period by returning revenues from distortionary taxes to the agents via lump-sum transfers, T_t.

The government obtains resources from the economy by taxing consumption and income from labor and capital, whose effective average taxes are τ_t^c, τ_t^l, τ_t^k, respectively. The government budget in each period is given by,

$$\tau_t^c C_t + \tau_t^l W_t L_t + \tau_t^k (R_t - \delta_K) K_t = G_t \tag{7.23}$$

The government keeps a fiscal balance in each period. This assumption is made to highlight the distortionary effects of taxes, mainly on capital accumulation.[3]

[3] This assumption has been used by Barro (1990), Glomm and Ravikumar (1994), Cassou and Lansing (1998), among others. They argue that this setup may represent a closer approximation to actual constraints than one which allows the government to borrow or lend large amounts.

Equilibrium of the model

By combining equilibrium conditions for both households and firms, we find that:

$$\frac{\left(1+\tau_t^c\right) C_t}{\left(1+\tau_{t-1}^c\right) C_{t-1}} = \beta\left[\left(1-\tau^k\right)\left(\alpha A_t K_t^{\alpha-1} L_t^{1-\alpha} - \delta\right) + 1\right] \tag{7.24}$$

$$\frac{C_t}{1-L_t} = \frac{\gamma}{(1-\gamma)} \frac{\left(1-\tau_t^l\right)}{\left(1+\tau_t^c\right)} (1-\alpha) A_t K_t^{\alpha} L_t^{-\alpha} \tag{7.25}$$

Finally, the feasibility condition of the economy must hold:

$$C_t + I_t = Y_t \tag{7.26}$$

Definition 5 *A competitive equilibrium for this economy is a sequence of consumption, leisure, and private investment* $\{C_t, 1-L_t, I_t\}_{t=0}^{\infty}$ *for the consumers, a sequence of capital and labor utilization for the firm* $\{K_t, L_t\}_{t=0}^{\infty}$*, and a sequence of government transfers* $\{G_t\}_{t=0}^{\infty}$*, such that, given a sequence of prices,* $\{W_t, R_t\}_{t=0}^{\infty}$*, and a sequence of taxes,* $\{\tau_t^c, \tau_t^k, \tau_t^l\}_{t=0}^{\infty}$:

i) The optimization problem of the consumer is satisfied.

ii) Given prices for capital and labor, and given a sequence for public inputs, the first-order conditions of the firm are satisfied with respect to capital and labor.

iii) Given a sequence of taxes, the sequence of public transfers are such that the government constraint is satisfied.

iv) The feasibility constraint of the economy is satisfied.

Notice that according to the definition of equilibrium for our model economy, the government enters completely parameterized, and fiscal policy is made consistent to the model and the data. In other words, in our model the private sector reacts optimally to policy changes, and these policy changes are given exogenously.

Equations of the model and calibration

The equilibrium of our model economy is very similar to the standard models, as the total number of endogenous variables and thus, the number of equations does not change. The only difference is the existence of three new exogenous variables, which are treated as constant. The competitive equilibrium of the model economy is defined by a set of eight equations, representing the dynamics of the endogenous variables, Y_t, C_t, I_t, K_t, L_t, R_t, W_t, and the total factor productivity A_t and where three additional exogenous variables are included: τ_t^c, τ_t^l, τ_t^k. This set of equations is the following:

$$\frac{1}{1-L_t} = \frac{\gamma}{(1-\gamma)} \frac{\left(1-\tau_t^l\right)}{\left(1+\tau_t^c\right)} \frac{W_t}{C_t} \tag{7.27}$$

$$\frac{\left(1+\tau_t^c\right) C_t}{\left(1+\tau_{t-1}^c\right) C_{t-1}} = \beta\left[\left(1-\tau_t^k\right)(R_t-\delta)+1\right] \tag{7.28}$$

$$Y_t = C_t + I_t \tag{7.29}$$

$$Y_t = A_t K_t^{\alpha} L_t^{1-\alpha} \tag{7.30}$$

$$K_{t+1} = (1-\delta)K_t + I_t \tag{7.31}$$

$$W_t = (1-\alpha)A_t K_t^{\alpha} L_t^{-\alpha} \tag{7.32}$$

$$R_t = \alpha A_t K_t^{\alpha-1} L_t^{1-\alpha} \tag{7.33}$$

$$\ln A_t = (1-\rho_A)\ln \overline{A} + \rho_A \ln A_{t-1} + \varepsilon_t^A \tag{7.34}$$

To calibrate this model economy we only need additional information about tax rates, which are assumed to be constants. The model parameters to be calibrated are:

$$\Omega = \left\{\alpha, \beta, \gamma, \delta, \rho_A, \sigma_A, \tau^c, \tau^l, \tau^k\right\}$$

Table 7.2 shows the calibrated parameters we use to simulate the model economy. Tax rates are effective average rates for a particular economy (Spain) estimated by Boscá *et al.* (2009), following the methodology of Mendoza *et al.* (1994). These tax rates for the year 2005 are: $\tau^c = 0.116$, $\tau^c = 0.225$, and $\tau^c = 0.348$.

The Laffer curve

One very interesting instrument regarding taxes is the so-called Laffer curve (Laffer, 1981). The Laffer curve refers to the relationship between the level of taxes and the level of tax receipts (fiscal revenues) for an economy. If taxes are zero, it is no doubts that the level of fiscal revenues will also be zero. The same would occur in

Table 7.2: Calibrated parameters

Parameter	Definition	Value
α	Technological parameter	0.350
β	Discount factor	0.970
γ	Preferences parameter	0.450
δ	Capital depreciation rate	0.060
ρ_A	TFP autoregressive parameter	0.950
σ_A	TFP standard deviation	0.010
τ^c	Consumption tax rate	0.116
τ^l	Labor income tax rate	0.348
τ^k	Capital income tax rate	0.225

the extreme case in which the (income) tax rate is 100%, since in this case the activity level would be zero: Who is willing to work (freely) when the government takes all that is produced? Therefore, plotting the tax rate in the abscissa and the fiscal revenues in the ordinate axis, the Laffer curve has a growing section and a decreasing section. Although this argumentation is generally attributed to Laffer, hence its name, the fact is that this relationship is very old, perhaps because is so intuitive. The Laffer curve was originally developed by Ibn Khaldum, Minister of Economy and Finance of Tunisia, who lived between the years 1332 and 1406, who is also regarded as a forerunner of Marxism. In his book *Muqaddimah* (Προλεγόμενα *or Prolegómena* in Greek) he made a number of contributions to economic analysis, developing a labor theory of value and a variety of analysis about the role of the public sector. Among his proposals is that an increase in taxes by the government may not lead to higher fiscal revenues when such increases cause important adverse affects on the economic activity, while a decrease in taxes would increase the level of production and, hence, fiscal revenues, which corresponds to a situation reflected by the decreasing part of the Laffer curve.

The importance of the Laffer curve lies in the fact that it is an essential tool for studying the impact of tax changes on fiscal revenues. Knowing the position of the economy along the Laffer curve is a key aspect in designing the optimal tax policy to maximize fiscal revenues. If an economy is positioned in the decreasing part of the Laffer curve, then the optimal fiscal policy should be reducing tax rates, as this would expand economic activity and fiscal revenues.

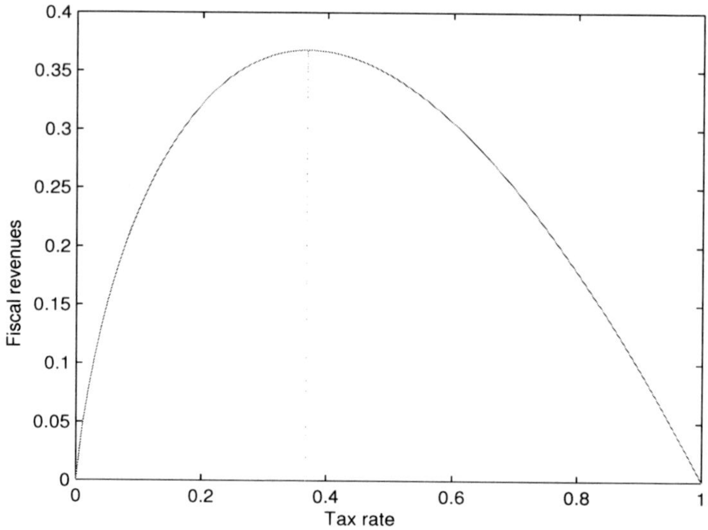

Figure 7.1: The Laffer cuve

However, if an economy is positioned in the increasing part of the Laffer curve, then a decrease in tax rates would lead to an expansion of economic activity, but at the expense of a decrease in tax revenues. Moreover, knowledge of the Laffer curve would allow the government to choose the optimal fiscal tax menu in order to obtain the higher fiscal revenues with the least possible negative distortions on the economic activity.

What the Laffer curve really represents is the elasticity of fiscal revenues to changes in tax rates and the optimal taxes rates to maximize fiscal revenues. For low tax rates levels, the elasticity of tax revenue is greater than unity. This elasticity decreases as the tax rate is increasing up to a value of zero, which corresponds to the point at which tax revenues are maximized. If the tax rate continues to rise, the elasticity becomes negative, decreasing tax revenues. Implicit in this reasoning is the fact that tax rates negatively affect economic activity. Thus, starting from a very low level of taxation, increasing taxes causes an increase in fiscal revenues due to the fact that the negative impact on economic activity is lower than the impact in generating revenues for the government. However, as we increase the tax rates the distortionary effects are larger, and the negative effects on economic activity are increase, so that fiscal revenues rise at a slower rate. This effect occurs until taxes reach a level where economic activity is severely affected, causing losses in the level of fiscal revenues.

Despite the fact that with a DSGE model at hand it is very easy to compute the Laffer curve for a particular economy, it is surprisingly difficult to find this thrilling exercise in the literature. The usual way of presenting the Laffer curve is through the realization of a graph that relates the level of tax revenues with the tax rate. Figure 7.1 plots a prototype Laffer curve. The asymmetry of the curve is intentional to notice that the maximum need not necessary be located in a tax rate of around 50%, and that the slope of both sections could be different.

Once we have calibrated a DSGE model for a particular economy, the numerical estimation of the Laffer curve is relatively simple, since it is possible to compute the steady-state values of all variables, including fiscal revenues, for each tax rate. This exercise can be done for a set of tax rates staring from zero. An application of this exercise is conducted by F-de-Córdoba and Torres (2012), who estimate Laffer curves for a number of European Union countries.

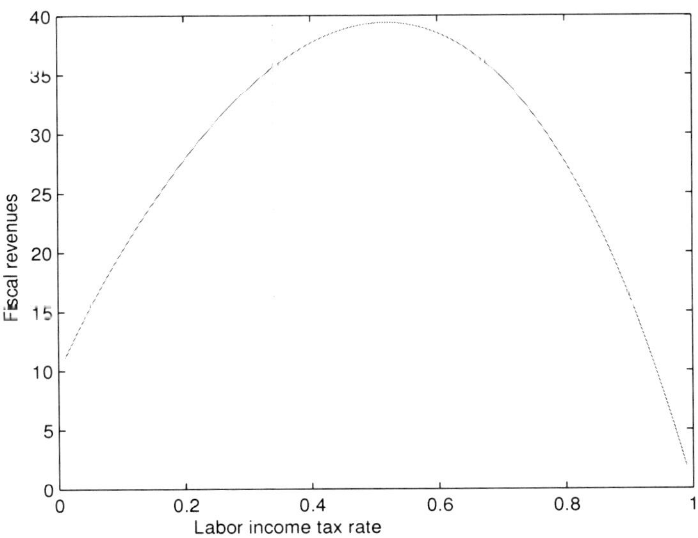

Figure 7.2: Labor income tax Laffer curve

Figures 7.2, 7.3 and 7.4, plot one-dimensional individual Laffer curves for the three tax rates considered: consumption, labor income and capital income taxes. These estimates represent the fiscal revenues at the steady state for each tax rate. The computation is very simple. Just to calculate the steady-state of our model economy for a value of the tax rate from 0 to 100%.

Figure 7.2 plots the Laffer for the labor income tax. As this is an income tax, possible values of the rate are between 0 and 1. As it can be observed, this Laffer curve has a standard shape, very similar to that used in theory. The vertical line indicates the calibrated level for the on labor income tax used in the simulation, a 34.4%, falling in the increasing part of the curve, indicating that there is some room to increase fiscal revenues by increasing this tax rate.

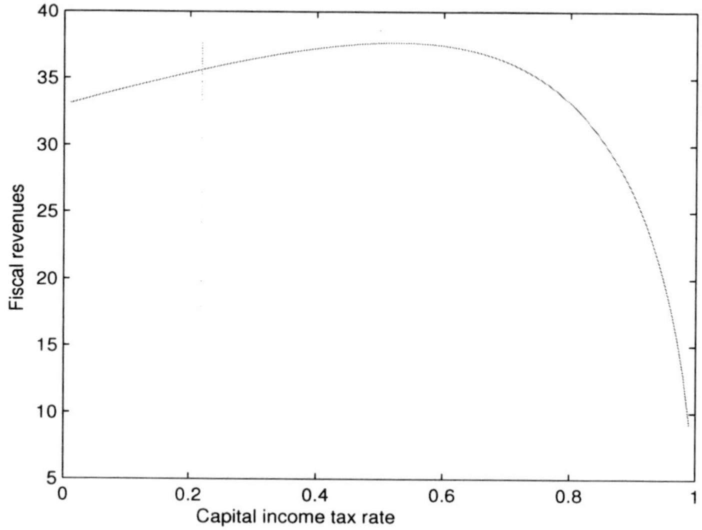

Figure 7.3: Capital income tax Laffer curve

Figure 7.3 plots the Laffer curve for a tax on capital income. In this case we observe a very flat curve at the increasing part but very steeper in the decreasing part. This type of relationship is caused by the distortionary effects caused by this tax on the process of capital accumulation, and hence, on the level of economic activity. Starting from a zero rate, as we increase the tax rate on capital income, fiscal revenues also increase, but do so by a very small amount. This is also because capital income is only a small proportion of total income of the economy. On the contrary, when it reaches the maximum of the curve, further increases in the tax rate makes fiscal revenues to decrease rapidly, as distortions on the process of capital accumulation become significant.

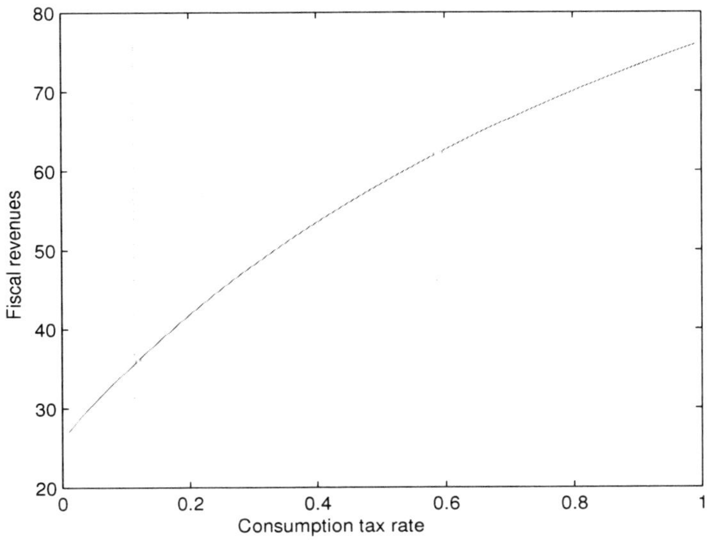

Figure 7.4: Consumption tax Laffer curve

Finally, Figure 7.4 plots the corresponding Laffer curve to the tax rate on consumption (VAT, excise duties, etc.). Steady-state computations have been done for a tax rate from 0 to 1, although this particular tax rate may exceed 1 given that this is an *ad-valorem* tax and not a percentage on income, which of course is limited to 100%. Nevertheless, a consumption tax of 100% is high enough for our purposes. It can be observed how the Laffer curve is always positive for this tax rate, that is, the elasticity of fiscal income with respect to the consumption tax rate is always greater than 1, and no maximum exists. The reason for this result is that this tax does not adversely affect economic activity through the supply of production factors. It is a tax on spending (or properties), introducing a premium on the price of goods and services. The explanation of this always positive relationship between fiscal revenues and consumption taxes can be found in the fact that, at the end, income will be spent in consump-

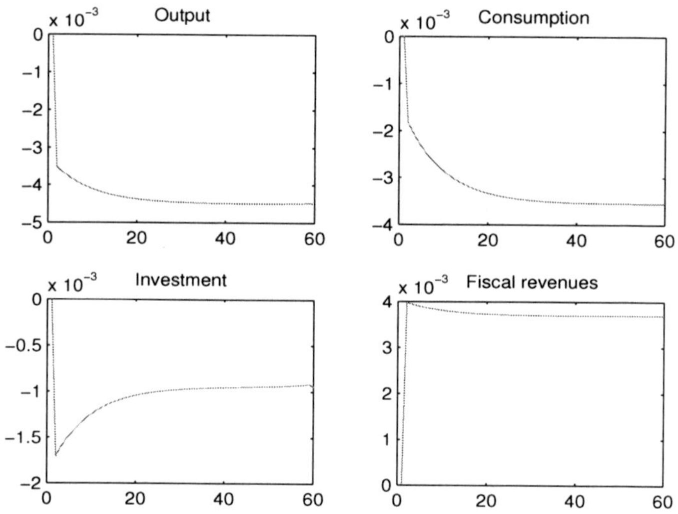

Figure 7.5: Unanticipated permanent increases in consumption tax(I)

tion. Increasing the consumption tax rate decreases consumption but in a lower proportion than the change in the tax rate.

Taxes changes

In this section we study the effects of a change in the tax rates. Specifically, we will study the effects of a change on the consumption tax. In particular, we study the effects of an unanticipated permanent increase in consumption tax. Other simulation exercises can be done, such as an anticipated permanent change in the consumption tax; an unanticipated transitory increase in consumption tax; and an anticipated transitory increase in consumption tax. Similar exercises can be done for the cases of labor income and capital income taxes.

Let us consider the case of a non-announced permanent increase in the consumption tax. Specifically, in the simulation it is assumed that the initial consumption tax is 11.6% and changes to 13 %, i.e., an increase of 1.4 percentage points. Figure 7.5 shows the effects of the rise in the tax on output, consumption, investment and tax revenues. Output reduces instantaneously, followed by a slow de-

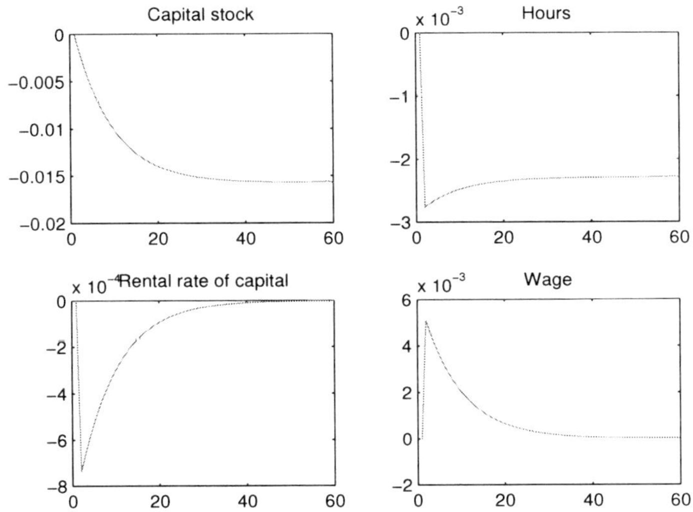

Figure 7.6: Unanticipated permanent increases in consumption tax(II)

cline to the new steady state, which is about 0.4% lower than the initial steady state. A similar behavior is observed for consumption. In the case of investment, we observe an overshooting effect, as investment is reduced in impact by an amount larger than that corresponding to its new steady state value. Finally, fiscal revenues increase almost instantaneously to its new steady state value.

The observed dynamics of the economy to this disturbance comes from the distortionary effects caused by this tax rate through intertemporal effects in which there is a substitution between consumption and leisure and a change in investment decisions. It can be observed that the adjustment of the economy to the new steady state is relatively fast for output and fiscal revenues, but slower for consumption and investment. Notice that this particular model does not consider income or wealth effects caused by a change in taxes as it is assumed that tax revenues collected by the government return to consumers as lump-sum transfers.

Figure 7.6 plots the dynamics for capital stock, labor, rental rate of capital and wages. Observed dynamics are determined by the existence of an intertemporal substitution effects between consumption and saving and by the existence of a substitution effect between leisure and labor. The rise in the tax reduces the purchasing power of wages, thereby reducing labor supply. The reduction in labor plus the reduction in capital stock causes the negative effect on output. Finally, steady state values for the relevant variables are reduced as a result of higher tax rates, except for the prices of production factors, which are independent of the taxes in the long-run.

Total Factor Productivity shock

Finally, this section studies the effects of an aggregate productivity shock when the economy is subjected to distortionary effects generated by the three types of taxes considered. This exercise shows how taxes generate distortions on the agent's decisions affecting how the economy responds to that shock. This can be done just comparing the impulse-response functions generated by our model economy with the ones obtained from the model without taxes.

The summary of results is presented in Figure 7.7. As can be observed, impact effect on output is much lower, in quantitative terms, than the one that would be obtained in an economy without a tax system, although the response is qualitatively similar. This is due to the distorting effects caused by taxes on the agents' decisions. In particular, the productivity shock has a positive effect on investment, but smaller under the presence of taxes. This makes capital stock's steady state value increase in small claims compared to the case without taxes.

The reason for the above results can be found in the change in inputs net of taxes income. Prices of production factors, reflecting their marginal productivity, behave exactly as in the model without taxes. That is, the rise in both the rental rate of capital and the wage are quantitatively the same as those obtained in the basic model without taxes, since they depend directly on the productivity shock. However, the net of taxes income generated by production factors is different, since a fraction of the income goes to the government (although later is returned to households as lump-sum transfers). This will change agents decisions about factors supply compared to an environment without taxes.

Finally, as expected, a positive productivity shock causes an expansion of economic activity and, given the calibrated values for taxes, its also increases fiscal revenues, indicating that the economy is positioned in the increasing part of the Laffer curve. Recall that

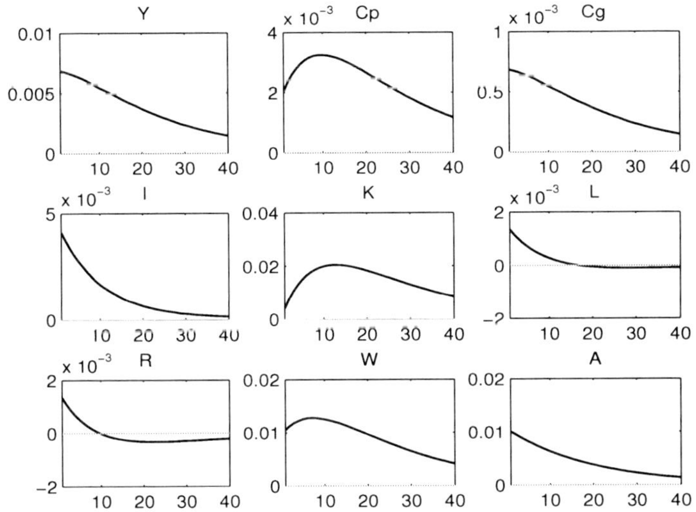

Figure 7.7: TFP shock with taxes

total increase in tax revenues can be broken down into three types of fiscal revenues, one for each tax.

Conclusions

In this chapter we have introduced taxes in the DSGE model, which in practice means the introduction of a third economic agent, the government, in addition to households and firms. In particular, we considered the existence of three different taxes: a consumption tax, a labor income tax and a capital income tax. In standard fiscal systems, there are other type of taxes, such as corporate profits taxes, lump-sum taxes, and in pay-as-you-go schemes, contributions to Social Security can also be considered as an additional tax.

In this simple framework, the only role assigned to the government is to achieve a certain level of fiscal revenues by taxing inputs income and consumption, and then return fiscal revenues to consumers as lump-sum transfers, with the additional assumption that the government budget constraint is fulfilled period to period. The key point in the analysis is that these taxes have distortionary effects on the decisions of individuals. Both the labor income tax and the consumption tax affect directly the labor supply. On the other hand, capital income tax (and changes in the consumption tax) affects directly investment decisions.

The chapter shows that using this DSGE model is very easy the computation of Laffer curves for each type of tax and for the whole fiscal system, for a particular calibrated economy. Second, we have studied the effects of changes in taxes. This exercise can be done considering both permanent and temporary changes, and both anticipated and non-anticipated changes. Finally, we analyzed the effects of an aggregate productivity shock on the economy when taxes are in place. The distortionary effects caused by taxes are represented by the result that a positive productivity shock on the economy have less expansionary effects compared to a situation without taxes.

Appendix A: Dynare code

Dynare codes for the model presented in this chapter, named *model7a.mod*, for a non-anticipated permanent change in the consumption tax is the following:

```
// Model 7a. Taxes. Non-announced permanent change
// in the consumption tax rate
// Dynare code
// File: model7a.mod
// José L. Torres. University of Málaga (Spain)
// Endogenous variables
var Y, C, I, F, K, L, R, W, A,
// Exogenous variables
varexo e, tauc, taul, tauk;
// Parameters
parameters alpha, beta, delta, gamma, rho;
// Calibrated parameters
alpha = 0.35;
beta = 0.97;
delta = 0.06;
gamma = 0.40;
rho = 0.95;
// Equations of the model
model;
(1+tauc)*C=(gamma/(1-gamma))*(1-L)*(1-taul)*
```

```
 (1-alpha)*Y/L;
1 = beta*((((1+tauc)*C)/((1+tauc(+1))*C(+1)))
 *((1-tauk)*(R(+1)-delta)+1)));
Y = A*(K(-1)^alpha)*(L^(1-alpha));
K = I+(1-delta)*K(-1);
I = Y-C;
W = (1-alpha)*A*(K(-1)^alpha)*(L^(-alpha));
R = alpha*A*(K(-1)^(alpha-1))*(L^(1-alpha));
F = tauc*C+taul*W*L+tauk*(R-delta)*K;
log(A) = rho*log(A(-1))+ e;
end;
// Initial values
initval;
Y = 1;
C = 0.8;
L = 0.3;
K = 3.5;
I = 0.2;
W = (1-alpha)*Y/L;
R = alpha*Y/K;
A = 1;
e = 0;
tauc = 0.116;
tauk = 0.225;
taul = 0.344;
end;
 // Steady state
steady;
SS0=oo_.steady_state;
// Blanchard-Kahn conditions
check;
// Final values
endval;
Y = 1;
C = 0.8;
L = 0.3;
K = 3.5;
I = 0.2;
W = (1-alpha)*Y/L;
R = alpha*Y/K;
A = 1;
```

```
e = 0;
tauc = 0.130;
tauk = 0.225;
taul = 0.344;
end;
 // Steady state
steady;
// Disturbance:  change in the consumption tax
shocks;
var tauc;
// Period of the change
periods 0;
// Change is the tax rate with respect to the
// final value
values 0;
end;
// Deterministic simulation
simul(periods=38);
// Figures
figure;
subplot(2,2,1);
plot(Y-SS0(1));
title('Output');
subplot(2,2,2);
plot(C-SS0(2));
title('Consumption');
subplot(2,2,3);
plot(I-SS0(3));
title('Investment');
subplot(2,2,4);
plot(F-SS0(4));
title('Fiscal revenues');
figure;
subplot(2,2,1);
plot(K-SS0(5));
title('Capital stock');
subplot(2,2,2);
plot(L-SS0(6));
title('Worked hours');
subplot(2,2,3);
plot(R-SS0(7));
```

```
title('Interest rate');
subplot(2,2,4);
plot(W-SS0(8));
title('Wage');
```

Bibliography

Aschauer, D. (1988): The equilibrium approach to fiscal policy. *Journal of Money, Credit, and Banking*, 20(1), 41-62.

Barro, R.J. (1989): The neoclassical approach to fiscal policy, en R. Barro (ed.), *Modern Business Cycle Theory*. Cambridge: Harvard University Press.

Barro, R.J. (1990): Government spending in a simple model of endogenous growth. *Journal of Political Economy*, 98(5), S103-126.

Baxter, M. and King, R. (1993): Fiscal policy in general equilibrium. *American Economic Review*, 83(3), 315-334.

Boscá, J., García, J. and Taguas, D. (2009): Taxation in the OECD: 1965-2004, Working Paper, Ministerio de Economía y Hacienda, Spain.

Braun, R. (1994): Tax disturbances and real economic activity in the Postwar United States. *Journal of Monetary Economics*, 33(3), 441-462.

Calonge, S. and Conesa, J.C. (2003): Progressivity and effective income taxation in Spain: 1990 and 1995. WP Centre de Recerca en Economia del Benestar.

Cassou, S. and Lansing, K. (1998), Optimal fiscal policy, public capital and the productivity slowdown. *Journal of Economic Dynamics and Control*, 22(6), 911-935.

F-de-Córdoba, G. and Torres, J.L. (2012): Fiscal harmonization in the European Union with public inputs. *Economic Modelling*, 29(5), 2024-2034.

Glomm, G. and Ravikumar, B. (1994), Public investment in infrastructure in a simple growth model. *Journal of Economic Dynamics and Control,* 18(6), 1173-1187.

Gouveia, M. and Strauss, R. (1994): Effective federal individual income tax functions: An exploratory empirical analysis. *National Tax Journal,* 47(2), 317-339.

Jonsson, G. and Klein, P. (1996): Stochastic fiscal policy and the Swedish business cycle. *Journal of Monetary Economics,* 38(2), 245-268.

Laffer, A. (1981): Government exactions and revenue deficiencies. *Cato Journal,* 1, 1-21.

Mendoza, E., Razin, A. and Tesar, L. (1994): Effective tax rates in macroeconomics. Cross-country estimated of tax rates on factor incomes and consumption, *Journal of Monetary Economics,* 34(2), 297-323.

McGrattan, E. (1994): The macroeconomic effects of distortionary taxation. *Journal of Monetary Economics,* 33(3), 573-601.

Chapter 8

Public Spending

Introduction

As pointed out in the previous chapter, the government can be introduced in DSGE models in a variety of alternative ways. This is because the public sector influences the economy through a large set of variables. In the previous chapter government was considered simply as a tax levying entity, focusing on the distortionary effects causes by income and consumption taxes. Fiscal revenues were returned to households as a lump-sum transfer. This chapter extends the analysis by considering some aspects regarding what the government does with revenues derived from taxes, i.e., government spending.

In the real world, fiscal revenues can be expended as transfers to households, in the consumption of goods and services demanded by the government, invested in public capital, expended in the provision to households of public or private goods and services, to pay debt services, etc. Here, we focus on government spending in goods and services. This means that now the state competes with private agents for goods and services that are produced in the economy and that some of the goods and services the households consume are provided by the public sector. So, now we have to distinguish between private consumption and public consumption or consumption of public provided goods, that can be public goods (defense, etc.) or private goods provided by the government (education, health, etc.).

A key element of this analysis is to determine how public spending or public consumption affects households' utility. For instance, we can assume that public consumption enters into the utility function of the individual, along with private consumption. This is because public spending on public consumption goods ends up being consumed by households. Some authors consider that government spending does not affect the utility of individuals since they are private goods that are consumed by the public sector. Other authors consider that public consumption positively affects the utility of individuals, but to a lesser extent than does private consumption. This would imply that an increases in government consumption crowd-out private consumption, which affects negatively consumers' utility.

Examples of DSGE models with government spending are developed by Hall (1980), Barro (1981), Aschauer (1985), Christiano and Eichembaum (1992), Baxter and King (1993), McGrattan (1994), among others. These authors introduce government spending using a variety of ways, with the general result that an increase in government spending reduces private consumption. This result is in contrast with empirical studies on the effects of public spending on private consumption, in which the effect of public spending on private consumption is positive or zero.

The structure of the rest of the chapter is the following. Section 2 reviews the various alternatives ways employed in the literature when modeling public consumption. Section 3 presents a DSGE model with public consumption. Section 4 shows the model equations and the calibration. Section 5 analyzes the effects of a disturbance in public consumption, assuming that this is a fixed variable. Finally, Section 6 ends with some conclusions.

Public spending

Public spending is a variable that is difficult to introduce correctly in DSGE models. As a matter of fact, relatively few DSGE models consider public spending as a factor to be taken into account when modeling the economy. Nevertheless, empirical evidence shows that public spending on goods and services is relatively important in the overall consumption basket of an economy, and that government decisions about expenditures may have important implications on the dynamics of other macroeconomic variables. In a simple theoretical environment, public consumption is transformed into goods and services that are subsequently consumed by households. These can be public goods, but also private goods the provision of which is decided by the government. The question here is how are these government provided goods (public goods or not) introduced in the household's utility function, and whether public consumption affects the marginal utility of private consumption.

In general we can distinguish two different ways of introducing public spending in a DSGE model. First, public spending can be considered as an element that diverts resources from the economy but does not affect the households' utility. This is the assumption used by, for instance, Christiano and Eichenbaum (1992) and Ljungqvist and Sargent (2004). Clearly, this is a very restrictive assumption.

Alternatively, the way that seems most appropriate is to consider that public spending on goods and services becomes consumption by households and thus, must be included into their utility function. We can assume that the utility function of the individuals now has two components:

$$U(C_{P,t}, O_t) + V(C_{G,t}) \tag{8.1}$$

where $U(\cdot)$ is the standard utility function as defined previously but now only includes private consumption, $C_{P,t}$, and leisure, O_t, and $V(\cdot)$ is an utility function depending on public consumption, $C_{G,t}$. This means that total utility not only depends on private consumption but also on public consumption. For instance, Baxter and King (1993) use the following utility function:

$$U\left[\log C_{P,t} + \gamma \log L_t + \Gamma(C_{G,t})\right] \tag{8.2}$$

where $\Gamma(\cdot)$ is an increasing function of public spending.

An alternative functional form consists in defining total consumption as:

$$C_t = C_{P,t} + \pi C_{G,t} \tag{8.3}$$

where π is a parameter which measures the contribution of public spending to total consumption. This functional form is used by Barro (1981), Aschauer (1985), Christiano and Eichenbaum (1992), and McGrattan (1994), among others. In this case we define the total consumption of the individual as a linear combination of private consumption and public consumption. The elasticity of substitution between the two types of goods is constant, and is determined by the parameter π. The above specification indicates that public spending can influence consumer utility whenever π is nonzero. If $\pi > 0$, the marginal utility of consumption decreases with an increase in public spending. The opposite occurs if $\pi < 0$. Thus, a public consumption unit would produce the same utility as π units of private consumption. Again public consumption would cause a shift in private consumption. The effect on consumer welfare will depend on the parameter π. If π is equal to unity, the total consumption of the individual and therefore welfare would not change.

This is because the parameter equal to unity implies that the utility of public goods is the same as that of private property. However, in the case where this parameter take a value less than unity, then public consumption would have negative effects on welfare.

Existing DSGE models with public spending indicate that an increase in public spending causes a negative income effect, leading the agents to increase their labor supply and reduce private consumption, as shown for example by Aiyagari, Christiano and Eichenbaum (1992), and Baxter and King (1993). However, a number of empirical studies that estimate VAR models find that private consumption increases in response to a positive shock in government consumption. Examples are Fatas and Mihov (2001), Blanchard and Perotti (2002) and Perotti (2007).

The model

Here, we introduce public consumption in a DSGE model. First, we develop a model in which the individual's total consumption is a CES of private consumption and public consumption. Second, we specify a utility function in which the total consumption is a linear function of private consumption and public consumption.

Households

Consumer's utility function can be defined as:

$$U(C_t) = U(C_{P,t}, C_{G,t}) \tag{8.4}$$

in which total utility depends on total consumption which it is a composite of private consumption, $C_{P,t}$, and public consumption, $C_{G,t}$. It is assumed that private consumption is not a perfect substitute of public consumption. Hence, total consumption can be defined as:

$$C_t = \left[\omega C_{P,t}^{\eta} + (1-\omega) C_{G,t}^{\eta}\right]^{\frac{1}{\eta}} \tag{8.5}$$

where η is a parameter representing the elasticity of substitution between private and public consumption. Notice that in this environment, households only decide over a portion of total consumption, the private consumption, whereas the other portion is given for households as it is decided by the government. In order to finance public expenditure, fiscal revenues are necessary. So, we consider the budget constraint of households used in the previous chapter:

$$(1+\tau_t^c)C_t + S_t = (1-\tau_t^l)W_t L_t + (1-\tau_t^k)R_t K_t + G_t \tag{8.6}$$

where τ_t^c is the tax rate on consumption τ_t^l is the tax rate on labor income and τ_t^k is the tax rate on capital income, and G_t, are lump-sum transfers which now are only a fraction of fiscal revenues.

The household problem can be defined as:

$$Max_{\{C_t,L_t\}_t^\infty} \sum_{t=0}^{\infty} \beta^t \left[\begin{array}{c} \gamma \log(\left[\omega C_{P,t}^\eta + (1-\omega) C_{G,t}^\eta\right]^{\frac{1}{\eta}}) \\ +(1-\gamma)\log(1-L_t) \end{array} \right] \tag{8.7}$$

subject to the budget constraint given by (8.6). Capital stock evolves according to:

$$K_{t+1} = (1-\delta) K_t + I_t \tag{8.8}$$

where δ is the physical capital depreciation rate and where I_t is gross investment. Assuming that $I_t = S_t$ and substituting expression (8.8) in (8.6), the budget constraint can be defined as:

$$(1+\tau_t^c)C_t + K_{t+1} - K_t = (1-\tau_t^l)W_t L_t + (1-\tau_t^k)(R_t-\delta)K_t + T_t \tag{8.9}$$

The Lagrangian problem to be solved by households is to choose $C_{P,t}$, L_t, and I_t so as to maximize:

$$\max_{(C_{p,t},I_t,L_t)} \mathscr{L} = \sum_{t=0}^{\infty} \beta^t \left\{ \begin{array}{c} \gamma \log(\left[\omega C_{P,t}^\eta + (1-\omega) C_{G,t}^\eta\right]^{\frac{1}{\eta}}) \\ +(1-\gamma)\log(1-L_t) \\ -\lambda_t \left[\begin{array}{c} (1+\tau_t^c)C_t + K_{t+1} - (1-\tau_t^l)W_t L_t \\ -(1-\tau_t^k)(R_t-\delta)K_t - K_t - T_t \end{array} \right] \end{array} \right\} \tag{8.10}$$

First order conditions for the above maximization problem are given by:

$$\frac{\partial \mathcal{L}}{\partial C_t}: \frac{\gamma\eta\omega C_{P,t}^{\eta-1}}{\left[\omega C_{P,t}^{\eta} + (1-\omega)C_{G,t}^{\eta}\right]} - \lambda_t\left(1+\tau_t^c\right) = 0 \tag{8.11}$$

$$\frac{\partial \mathcal{L}}{\partial L_t}: -(1-\gamma)\frac{1}{1-L_t} + \lambda_t(1-\tau_t^l)W_t = 0 \tag{8.12}$$

$$\frac{\partial \mathcal{L}}{\partial K_t}: \beta^t\lambda_t\left[(1-\tau_t^k)(R_t-\delta)+1\right] - \lambda_{t-1}\beta^{t-1} = 0 \tag{8.13}$$

where $\beta^t\lambda_t$ is the Lagrange multiplier corresponding to the budget constraint at time t, and thus, the shadow price of consumption is given by:

$$\lambda_t = \frac{\gamma\eta\omega C_{P,t}^{\eta-1}}{(1+\tau_t^c)\left[\omega C_{P,t}^{\eta} + (1-\omega)C_{G,t}^{\eta}\right]}$$

Notice that the above maximization problem is solved by choosing the optimal level of private consumption, taking public consumption as given, which is exogenously determined by the government. This could imply a loss in households welfare if, as is assumed, private consumption and public consumption are not perfect substitutes. The alternative is to solve the problem in a central planning environment, where the planner chooses both types of consumption in order to maximize social welfare.

Combining expressions (8.11) and (8.12) we obtain the condition that equates the marginal rate of substitution between consumption and leisure to the opportunity cost of one additional unit of leisure:

$$\frac{\gamma\eta\omega C_{P,t}^{\eta-1}(1-\tau_t^l)W_t}{(1+\tau_t^c)\left[\omega C_{P,t}^{\eta} + (1-\omega)C_{G,t}^{\eta}\right]} = \frac{(1-\gamma)}{1-L_t} \tag{8.14}$$

Combining FOC (8.11) with FOC (8.13) we obtain the following intertemporal equilibrium condition, representing optimal consumption path:

$$\frac{\frac{(1+\tau_t^c)C_{P,t}^{\eta-1}}{\left[\omega C_{P,t}^{\eta}+(1-\omega)C_{G,t}^{\eta}\right]}}{\frac{(1+\tau_{t-1}^c)C_{P,t-1}^{\eta-1}}{\left[\omega C_{P,t-1}^{\eta}+(1-\omega)C_{G,t-1}^{\eta}\right]}} = \beta\left[\left(1-\tau_t^k\right)R_t + 1 - \delta\right] \tag{8.15}$$

The firms

The problem of firms is to find optimal values for the utilization of labor and capital. The production of final output Y requires the services of labor L and K. The firms rent capital and employ labor in order to maximize profits at period t, taking factor prices as given. The technology is given by a constant return to scale Cobb-Douglas production function,

$$Y_t = A_t K_t^{\alpha} L_t^{1-\alpha} \tag{8.16}$$

where A_t is a measure of total-factor, or sector-neutral, productivity and where $0 \leq \alpha < 1$.

The static maximization problem for the firms is:

$$\max_{(K_t, L_t)} \Pi_t = A_t K_t^{\alpha} L_t^{1-\alpha} - R_t K_t - W_t L_t \tag{8.17}$$

The first order conditions for the firms profit maximization are given by:

$$\frac{\partial \Pi_t}{\partial K_t} : R_t - \alpha A_t K_t^{\alpha-1} L_t^{1-\alpha} = 0 \tag{8.18}$$

$$\frac{\partial \Pi_t}{\partial L_t} : W_t - (1-\alpha) A_t K_t^{\alpha} L_t^{-\alpha} = 0 \tag{8.19}$$

The government

Finally, we consider the role of the government as a tax-levying entity and as a supplier of goods and services. It is assumed that the government uses tax revenues to finance both lump-sum transfers paid out to the consumers and public spending on goods and services. We assume that the government balances its budget period-by-period. The government obtains resources from the economy by taxing consumption and income from labor and capital, whose effective average taxes are τ_t^c, τ_t^l, τ_t^k, respectively. The government budget in each period is given by,

$$\tau_t^c C_t + \tau_t^l W_t L_t + \tau_t^k (R_t - \delta) K_t = G_t + C_{G,t} \tag{8.20}$$

The government decides the amount of public consumption in goods and services. Hence, $C_{G,t}$ can be considered as an exogenous variable, which is taken as given by households. An alternative, following McGrattan *et al.* (1997), is to assume that public spending in goods and services follows is a stochastic process given by:

$$C_{G,t} = \xi_t Y_t \tag{8.21}$$

where ξ_t is a random variable indicating the proportion of total output.

Equilibrium of the model

Combining first order conditions for households and firms we obtain:

$$\frac{\frac{(1+\tau_t^c)C_{P,t}^{\eta-1}}{\left[\omega C_{P,t}^{\eta}+(1-\omega)C_{G,t}^{\eta}\right]}}{\frac{(1+\tau_{t-1}^c)C_{P,t-1}^{\eta-1}}{\left[\omega C_{P,t-1}^{\eta}+(1-\omega)C_{G,t-1}^{\eta}\right]}} = \beta\left[\left(1-\tau^k\right)\alpha A_t K_t^{\alpha-1} L_t^{1-\alpha} + 1 - \delta\right]$$

$$\frac{\omega C_{P,t}^{\eta} + (1-\omega)C_{G,t}^{\eta}}{\gamma\eta\omega C_{P,t}^{\eta-1}} = \frac{\gamma}{(1-\gamma)}\frac{(1-\tau_t^l)}{(1+\tau_t^c)}(1-L_t)(1-\alpha)A_t K_t^{\alpha} L_t^{-\alpha}$$

Finally, the feasibility condition of the economy must hold:

$$C_{P,t} + C_{G,t} + I_t = Y_t \tag{8.22}$$

$$C_t + I_t = Y_t \tag{8.23}$$

Definition 6 *A competitive equilibrium for this economy is a sequence of private consumption, leisure, and private investment $\{C_{P,t}, 1-L_t, I_t\}_{t=0}^{\infty}$ for the consumers, a sequence of capital and labor utilization for the firm $\{K_t, L_t\}_{t=0}^{\infty}$, and a sequence of government transfers and public spending in goods and services $\{G_t, C_{G,t}\}_{t=0}^{\infty}$, such that, given a sequence of prices, $\{W_t, R_t\}_{t=0}^{\infty}$, and a sequence of taxes, $\{\tau_t^c, \tau_t^k, \tau_t^l\}_{t=0}^{\infty}$:*

i) The optimization problem of the consumer is satisfied.

ii) Given prices for capital and labor, and given a sequence for public inputs, the first-order conditions of the firm are satisfied with respect to capital and labor.

iii) Given a sequence of taxes, the sequence of public transfers and the sequence of public spending in goods and services are such that the government constraint is satisfied.

iv) The feasibility constraint of the economy is satisfied.

Notice that according to the definition of equilibrium for our model economy, the government enters completely parameterized, and fiscal policy is made consistent to the model and the data. In other words, in our model the private sector reacts optimally to policy changes, and these policy changes are given exogenously.

An alternative functional form for aggregate consumption

An alternative way of introducing public spending in the household's utility function also widely used in the literature, consists in defining total consumption as:

$$C_t = C_{P,t} + \pi C_{G,t} \tag{8.24}$$

where π is a parameter that indicates the contribution of public spending to marginal utility of total consumption. Total consumption is a linear combination of private consumption and public consumption. The elasticity of substitution between the two types of goods is constant, and is determined by the parameter π.

In this case, the households' utility function is given by:

$$U(C_t, O_t) = \gamma \log(C_{P,t} + \pi C_{G,t}) + (1-\gamma)\log(1-L_t) \tag{8.25}$$

The auxiliary Lagrange function associated to the above problem is:

$$\max_{(C_{P,t}, I_t, L_t)} \mathcal{L} = \sum_{t=0}^{\infty} \beta^t \left\{ \begin{array}{c} \gamma \log(C_{P,t} + \pi C_{G,t}) + (1-\gamma)\log(1-L_t) \\ -\lambda_t \left[\begin{array}{c} (1+\tau_t^c)C_t + K_{t+1} - (1-\tau_t^l)W_t L_t \\ -(1-\tau_t^k)(R_t - \delta)K_t - K_t - T_t \end{array} \right] \end{array} \right\} \tag{8.26}$$

First order conditions are given by:

$$\frac{\partial \mathcal{L}}{\partial C_t} : \frac{\gamma}{\left[C_{P,t} + \pi C_{G,t}\right]} - \lambda_t \left(1 + \tau_t^c\right) = 0 \tag{8.27}$$

$$\frac{\partial \mathcal{L}}{\partial L_t} : -\left(1-\gamma\right)\frac{1}{1-L_t} + \lambda_t (1-\tau_t^l) W_t = 0 \tag{8.28}$$

$$\frac{\partial \mathcal{L}}{\partial K_t} : \beta^t \lambda_t \left[(1-\tau_t^k)(R_t - \delta) + 1\right] - \lambda_{t-1}\beta^{t-1} = 0 \tag{8.29}$$

Combining first order conditions we obtain the following two equilibrium conditions:

$$\frac{(1-\gamma)}{1-L_t} = \frac{\gamma}{[C_{P,t} + \pi C_{G,t}]} \frac{(1-\tau_t^l)}{(1+\tau_t^c)} W_t \tag{8.30}$$

$$\beta \frac{(1+\tau_{t-1}^c)[C_{P,t-1} + \pi C_{G,t-1}]}{(1+\tau_t^c)[C_{P,t} + \pi C_{G,t}]} \left[(1-\tau_t^k)(R_t - \delta) + 1\right] = 1 \tag{8.31}$$

Equations of the model and calibration

The competitive equilibrium of the model economy is defined by a set of nine equations, representing the sequences of the endogenous variables, Y_t, $C_{P,t}$, $C_{G,t}$, I_t, K_t, L_t, R_t, W_t, plus A_t, and the following four exogenous variables: ξ_t, τ_t^c, τ_t^l, τ_t^k. It is assumed that these four exogenous variables are constants.

Using the version in which total consumption is a linear combination of private consumption and public consumption with a constant elasticity of substitution, the model economy is defined by the following set of equations:

$$\frac{(1-\gamma)}{1-L_t} = \frac{\gamma}{[C_{P,t} + \pi C_{G,t}]} \frac{(1-\tau_t^l)}{(1+\tau_t^c)} W_t \tag{8.32}$$

$$\beta \frac{(1+\tau_{t-1}^c)[C_{P,t-1} + \pi C_{G,t-1}]}{(1+\tau_t^c)[C_{P,t} + \pi C_{G,t}]} \left[(1-\tau_t^k)(R_t - \delta) + 1\right] = 1 \tag{8.33}$$

$$Y_t = C_{P,t} + I_t + C_{G,t} \tag{8.34}$$

$$Y_t = A_t K_t^{\alpha} L_t^{1-\alpha} \tag{8.35}$$

$$K_{t+1} = (1-\delta)K_t + I_t \tag{8.36}$$

$$W_t = (1-\alpha) A_t K_t^{\alpha} L_t^{-\alpha} \tag{8.37}$$

$$R_t = \alpha A_t K_t^{\alpha-1} L_t^{1-\alpha} \tag{8.38}$$

$$C_{G,t} = \xi_t Y_t \tag{8.39}$$

$$\ln A_t = (1-\rho_A)\ln \overline{A} + \rho_A \ln A_{t-1} + \varepsilon_t^A \tag{8.40}$$

Table 8.1: Calibrated parameters

Parameter	Definition	Value
α	Technological parameter	0.350
β	Discount factor	0.970
γ	Preferences parameter	0.450
δ	Capital depreciation rate	0.060
π	Elasticity of substitution between differentiated goods	0.500
ξ	Public consumption/output ratio	0.100
ρ_A	TFP autoregressive parameter	0.950
σ_A	TFP standard deviation	0.001
τ^c	Consumption tax rate	0.116
τ^l	Labor income tax rate	0.348
τ^k	Capital income tax rate	0.225

The set of parameters to be calibrated are:

$$\Omega = \left\{\alpha, \beta, \gamma, \delta, \pi, \xi, \rho_A, \sigma_A, \tau^c, \tau^l, \tau^k\right\}$$

Two additional parameters need to be calibrated: the ratio of public consumption on total output, ξ, which is assumed to be a constant, and the elasticity of substitution between private consumption and public consumption, π. Table 8.1 shows the selected values.

Aschauer (1985) estimates a value of π between 0.3 and 0.4 for the U.S. Christiano and Eichembaum (1992) simply assume that $\pi = 0$, which implies that public consumption does not affect utility. McGrattan (1994) estimates a negative value for this parameter, -0.026, although not significantly different from zero. Here, we assume an arbitrary value of 0.5. Finally, the public consumption/output ratio is assumed to be 0.1. This value can also be defined in terms of the proportion of public consumption over total fiscal revenues.

Public consumption change

This section studies the effects of a (permanent) positive shock on public consumption. It is assumed that the share of government consumption on output is deterministic, i.e., it is a constant, and

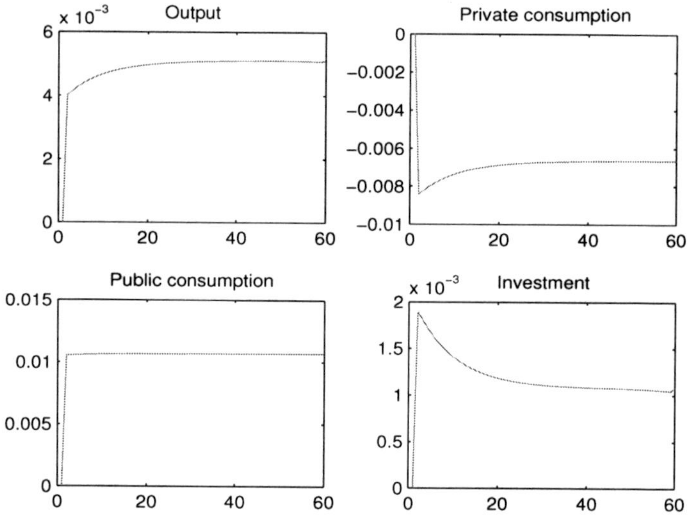

Figure 8.1: Permanent public consumption change (I)

changes from an initial value of 0.10 to a value of 0.12. This means that the model economy is deterministic, since the only shock we consider in this exercise is a public consumption change. The dynamic effects of this shock are shown in Figures 8.1 and 8.2.

First, the rise in public consumption has a positive effect on output, but of negligible amount. This result is consistent with the empirical evidence that a rise in public consumption causes a very limited rise in output. It also has a very slight positive effect on investment. These results are expected given the structure of the model, in which public consumption has limited effects on growth, although public consumption has indirect positive effects on both capital stock and worked hours, as can be observed in Figure 8.2.

The most significant effect is observed relative to private consumption. Public consumption causes a substitution of private consumption, virtually the same amount. That is, there is an almost complete crowding-out effect of private consumption by public consumption. The explanation for this result is simple. Final output remains almost unchanged, but the rise in public consumption can only be achieved by reducing private consumption by a similar amount. This is the so-called crowding-out effect on the private

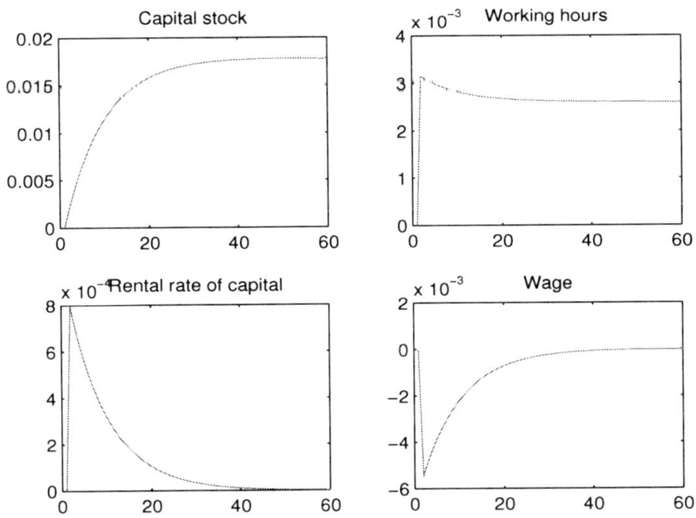

Figure 8.2: Permanent public consumption change (II)

sector by the public sector and one of the main neoclassical results regarding the effects of fiscal policy.

Results from this basic setting are in contradiction with some observed empirical evidence that public consumption has a positive effect on private consumption. Nevertheless, it is important to note that the model includes a large number of simplifying assumptions, such as that the government budget constraint holds period-by-period or a closed economy, which have important implications for the results from the simulation of the model economy.

Conclusions

This chapter introduces public expenditure in the DSGE model with taxes. In this framework, the government does not only decide the tax menu and the level of fiscal revenues but also what to do with those fiscal revenues. Here, it is assumed that a fraction of total fiscal revenues is returned to the economy in the form of lump-sum transfers whereas another proportion is expended in public consumption. The key element of this analysis is to define how government spending on goods and services enters in the household utility function. Several alternative hypotheses are used in the literature.

In the model developed in this chapter, we have assumed that government consumption is part of the utility function of the individual, being an additional element to private consumption. The model is used to study the effect of a permanent public consumption change, which is assumed to be an exogenous fixed amount. The model reproduces the well-known crowding-out effect of private consumption by public consumption. Additional exercises can be done, by assuming a transitory public consumption change or to study business cycle properties of stochastic public consumption shocks.

Appendix A: Dynare code

Dynare code for the model developed in this chapter, named *model8a.mod*, is the following:

```
// Model 8a:  Permanent change in public consumption
// Dynare code
// File:  model8a.mod
// José L. Torres.  University of Málaga (Spain)
// Endogenous variables
var Y, Cp, Cg, I, K, L, R, W, A;
// Exogenous variables
varexo e, tauc, taul, tauk, zita;
// Parameters
parameters alpha, beta, delta, gamma, pi, rho;
// Calibration of parameters
alpha = 0.35;
beta  = 0.97;
delta = 0.06;
gamma = 0.40;
pi    = 0.50;
rho   = 0.95;
// Equations of the model economy
model;
(1+tauc)*(Cp+pi*Cg)=(gamma/(1-gamma))
    *(1-L)*(1-taul)*W;
1 = beta*((1+tauc)*(Cp+pi*Cg)
    /((1+tauc)*(Cp(+1)+pi*Cg(+1)))
```

```
  *((1-tauk)*(R(+1)-delta)+1));
Y = A*(K(-1)^alpha)*(L^(1-alpha));
K = I+(1-delta)*K(-1);
I = Y-Cp-Cg;
W = (1-alpha)*A*(K(-1)^alpha)*(L^(-alpha));
R = alpha*A*(K(-1)^(alpha-1))*(L^(1-alpha));
Cg = zita*Y;
log(A) = rho*log(A(-1))+ e;
end;
// Initial values
initval;
Y = 1;
Cp = 0.8;
Cg = 0.1;
L = 0.3;
K = 3.5;
I = 0.2;
W = (1-alpha)*Y/L;
R = alpha*Y/K;
A = 1;
e = 0;
zita = 0.100;
tauc = 0.116;
tauk = 0.225;
taul = 0.344;
end;
 // Steady state
steady;
SS0=oo_.steady_state;
// Blanchard and Khan conditions
check;
// Final values
endval;
Y = 1;
Cp = 0.8;
Cg = 0.1;
L = 0.3;
K = 3.5;
I = 0.2;
W = (1-alpha)*Y/L;
R = alpha*Y/K;
```

```
A = 1;
e = 0;
zita = 0.120;
tauc = 0.116;
tauk = 0.225;
taul = 0.344;
end;
 // Steady state
steady;
// Shock analysis
shocks;
var zita;
// Disturbance periods
periods 0;
// Change to final value
values 0;
end;
// Deterministic simulation
simul(periods=58);
// Figures
figure;
subplot(2,2,1);
plot(Y-SS0(1));
title('Output');
subplot(2,2,2);
plot(Cp-SS0(2));
title('Private consumption');
subplot(2,2,3);
plot(Cg-SS0(3));
title('Public consumption');
subplot(2,2,4);
plot(I-SS0(4));
title('Investment');
figure;
subplot(2,2,1);
plot(K-SS0(5));
title('Capital stock');
subplot(2,2,2);
plot(L-SS0(6));
title('Working hours');
subplot(2,2,3);
```

```
plot(R-SS0(7));
title('Rental rate of capital');
subplot(2,2,4);
plot(W-SS0(8));
title('Wage');
```

Bibliography

Aschauer, D. (1985): Fiscal policy and aggregate demand. *American Economic Review*, 75(1), 117-127.

Aiyagari, S., Christiano, L. and Eichenbaum, M. (1992): The output, employment, and interest rate effects of government consumption. *Journal of Monetary Economics*, 30(1), 73-86.

Aschauer, D. (1989), Is public expenditure productive? *Journal of Monetary Economics*, 23, 177-200.

Barro, R. (1981): Output effects of government purchases. *Journal of Political Economy*, 89, 1086-1121.

Barro, R. (1989): The neoclassical approach to fiscal policy, in R. Barro (ed.), *Modern Business Cycle Theory*. Cambridge: Harvard University Press.

Barro, R. and King, R. (1984): Time-separable preferences and intertemporal substitution models of the business cycle. *Quarterly Journal of Economics*, 99, 817-839.

Baxter, M. and King, R. (1993): Fiscal policy in general equilibrium. *American Economic Review*, 83(3), 315-334.

Blanchard, O. and Perotti, R. (2002): An empirical characterization of the dynamic effects of change in government spending and taxes on output. *Quarterly Journal of Economics* 117(4), 1329-1368.

Braun, R. (1994): Tax disturbances and real economic activity in the Postwar United States. *Journal of Monetary Economics*, 33, 441-462.

Chari, V., Kehoe, P. and McGrattan, E. (2000): Sticky price models of the business cycle: Can the contract multiplier solver the persistence problem? *Econometrica*, 68(5), 1151-1179.

Christiano, L. and Eichenbaum, M. (1992): Current real business cycle theories and aggregate labor market fluctuations. *American Economic Review*, 82(3), 430-450.

Christiano, L., Eichenbaum, M., and Evans, C. (2005): Nominal rigidities and the dynamic effects of a shock to monetary policy. *Journal of Political Economy*, 113(1), 1-45.

Fatás, A. and Mihov, I. (2001): The effects of fiscal policy on consumption and employment: Theory and Evidence. *CEPR Discussion Paper* n. 2760.

Hall, R.E. (1980): Labor supply and aggregate fluctuations. *Carnegie-Rochester Conference Series on Public Policy*, 12, 7-33.

McGrattan, E. (1994): The macroeconomic effects of distortionary taxation. *Journal of Monetary Economics*, 33(3), 573-601.

McGrattan, E., Rogerson, R. and Wright, R. (1997): An equilibrium model of the business cycle with household production and fiscal policy. *International Economic Review*, 38(2), 267-290.

Perotti, R. (2007): In search of the transmission mechanism of fiscal policy. Mimeo.

Chapter 9

Public Capital

Introduction

This chapter introduces the government in a DSGE model from an alternative point of view: as a supplier of public inputs. In this context, the government uses tax revenues to finance spending in public investment which accumulates in public capital (i.e., infrastructure) and raises total productivity of private factors. Thus, similar to the previous chapter, we consider a dual role for the government: as a tax-levying entity and a supplier of public inputs. In the real world, final output of the economy does not only depend on the quantity of private productive factors, but also is affected by a large variety of public inputs, from courts to roads. In this setting, the production function of the economy includes three productive factors: labor, private capital and public capital. Although public capital stock can play an important role in the final output of an economy, in the literature only a few DSGE models consider the role of public inputs.

The relationship between public capital and economic growth remains an open question which is of great interest, both academically and politically. Although there exists an extensive literature on the subject, there is still no consensus on the quantitative importance of the stock of public capital on the level of output of an economy. However, it is generally accepted that public infrastructure have a positive effect on the level of output in an economy.

This chapter presents a DSGE model with public capital. We consider a production function that relates the level of aggregate output of the economy with three production factors: labor, private capital and public capital. The government sets a tax on consumption, capital income and labor income in order to finance an exogenous sequence of transfers and a sequence of public investment. The key question here is how are the returns to scale under the presence of public capital as an additional production input. We can maintain the assumption of constant returns to scale or, alternatively, we can assume constant returns to scale associated to private factors, and thus, increasing returns to scale in the aggregate.

The remainder of the chapter is structured as follows. Section 2 briefly reviews the literature on public capital. Section 3 presents a DSGE with public capital as an additional input into the aggregate production function. Section 4 shows the equations of the model and the calibration. Section 5 studies the effects of a public investment shock. Finally, Section 6 includes some relevant conclusions.

Public capital

Investment decisions on physical capital are not taken only by households (or firms) but also by the government. Public capital could be an important input in the aggregate production function. The branch of the literature has focused on the relationship between public investment in capital and economic growth. Public capital (infrastructure) was incorporated into the aggregate production function of the economy in the early 70s, with the works of Arrow and Kurz (1970), Weitzman (1970) and Pestieau (1974). However, it is the work of Barro (1990), where these first attempts were revived, causing a growing interest in introducing public capital as an additional input in growth models. Barro (1990) introduces public expenditure into the aggregate production function with constant returns to scale, showing that there is no transition to the steady state, but considering public spending as a flow rather than a stock variable. Examples of theoretical developments are Barro and Sala-i-Martin (1992), Finn (1993), Glomm and Ravikumar (1994), Cashin (1995) and Low (2000), among others. For instance, Glomm and Ravikumar (1994) introduced public capital in the production function, although with the assumption that public capital fully depreciates period to period, which in practice is equivalent to considering public capital as a flow variable as in Barro (1990). Cashin (1995) developed a model in which public capital is a stock variable, similar to private capital.

The first empirical analysis of the effects of public capital on output growth was made by Mera (1973) for the Japanese economy. Mera (1973) considers different Cobb-Douglas type production functions with public capital for the 9 regions of Japan, by industry and type of capital, obtaining an average value of the elasticity of output with respect to public capital of 0.2 (0.22 for the primary sector, 0.2 for the industrial sector, 0.5 for transport and communications and between 0.12 and 0.18 for the services sector). Subsequently, Ratner (1983) performed a similar analysis for the U.S. economy, for the period 1949 to 1973, obtaining an elasticity of output with respect to public capital of 0.058 (while the estimated elasticity with respect to private capital was 0.22). However, it was the work of Aschauer (1989) which put this topic in the agenda.

The work of Aschauer (1989) had a great impact because it advanced the idea that the productivity slowdown observed in the U.S. since the 70s was due to the decrease in the stock of public capital. Aschauer (1989) found that about 60% of the observed slowdown in productivity growth in the United States were due to the decline in public investment in infrastructure, estimating a value of the elasticity of output with respect to public capital between 0.25 and 0.56, with a mean value of 0.39, even higher than the estimated output elasticity with respect to private capital. Munnell (1990a), studied also the U.S. and found a very similar value for the output elasticity to public capital, of 0.34, while Munnell (1990b), using disaggregated data for the States obtained values between 0.06 and 0.15, which are lower than previous estimation at an aggregate level, a result that also appears in other works that use a higher level of disaggregation and attributed to the existence of spillover effects.

Based on previous works, there is a large empirical literature estimating production functions in which public capital is included, but with ambiguous results.[1] For example, Ford and Poret (1991) for 11 OECD countries obtained values between 0.29 and 0.66, similar to previous estimations. However, other authors such as Aaron (1990), Tatom (1991), Holtz-Eakin (1994) and Evans and Karras (1994) obtained opposed results, estimating values of the elasticity of output with respect to public capital which are not significantly different from zero. For instance, Holtz-Eakin (1994) replicated the above analyses using the same estimation procedure but controlling for unobserved variables, and found no relationship between public capital and output. Evans and Karras (1994) estimate several specifications of the production function for different definitions of public capital and for a set of countries, finding no evidence that public capital is productive, except education spending. García-Milá, McGuire and Porter (1996) performed a similar analysis using different specifications and different definitions of public capital, obtaining again the result that the elasticity is not significantly different from zero. These authors conclude that previous empirical studies reflect spurious correlations between the level of

[1] A critical review of the literature is, for instance, Romp and de Haan (2007).

production and public capital.

Business cycle properties of public investment in capital have been also studied empirically with the estimation of vector autoregressive (VAR) models to quantify output response to changes in public capital. Again, we find mixed results. On the one hand, authors such as Clarida (1993) and Batina (1998, 1999), among others, have found positive effects of public capital on output. By contrast, authors such as McMillin and Smith (1994), Otto and Voss (1996) and Voss (2002) find a negative relationship.

However, these analyzes do not take into account the behavior of economic agents and the implications of the provision of public capital in a general equilibrium context, which can lead to biased estimates of the elasticity of output with respect to public capital. In this sense, Finn (1993) and Cassou and Lansing (1998) are exceptions. Finn (1993) estimates a DSGE model with public transport infrastructure, in order to study whether the productivity growth stagnation in the United States during the 1970s was due to a lack of public investment, as suggested by Aschauer (1989). Using the Generalized Method of Moments (GMM), Finn estimated a value of the elasticity of production with respect to public capital of 0.16 (although very imprecise, with values between 0.32 and 0.001). Guo and Lansing (1997) in a model of optimal fiscal policy obtained a value of 0.0525. Cassou and Lansing (1998) use values between 0.1 and 0.123. These values are closer to the initial analysis of Mera (1973) and Ratner (1983) than to those of Aschauer (1989) and Munnell (1990a). Feehan and Matsumoto (2002) develop a model with public investment in infrastructure and human capital formation.

The key point when adding public capital to the aggregate production function is how the returns to scale are. We can consider that the aggregate production function of the economy is represented by a nested C.E.S. with a standard Cobb-Douglas production function augmented by public capital given by:

$$Y_t = A_t \left[\sigma Z_t^{\rho} + (1-\sigma)\left(K_t^{\alpha} L_t^{1-\alpha}\right)^{\rho} \right]^{1/\rho} \tag{9.1}$$

where the production of final output, Y, requires labor services, L, and two types of capital: private capital, K, and public capital (public infrastructures), Z. A_t is a measure of total-factor productivity, α is the private capital share of output, σ measures the weight on public capital relative to private factors and $1/(1-\rho)$ is a measure of the elasticity of substitution between public inputs and private inputs. In the particular case when the elasticity of substitution between public and private inputs is unity ($\rho = 0$), the technology is given by:

$$Y_t = A_t Z_t^{\sigma} K_t^{\alpha(1-\sigma)} L_t^{(1-\alpha)(1-\sigma)} \tag{9.2}$$

Note that this functional form for the technology implies that the economy is subject to constant return to scale as $\sigma + \alpha(1-\sigma) + (1-\alpha)(1-\sigma) = 1$. An alternative would be to consider the existence of constant return to scale to private factors. In this case, the aggregate production function can be defined as:

$$Y_t = A_t Z_t^{\sigma} K_t^{\alpha} L_t^{1-\alpha} \tag{9.3}$$

which implies the existence of increasing returns to scale for the economy.

The model

We consider a production function that relates output to three inputs: labor, private capital and public capital. Our choice of the production function assumes that a positive level of public capital is necessary for production, which implies that there must be a minimum level of fiscal revenues for the output to be positive.[2] The government taxes private consumption goods, capital income and labor income to finance an exogenous sequence of lump-sum transfers, $\{G_t\}_{t=0}^{\infty}$, and a sequence of public investment, $\{I_{g,t}\}_{t=0}^{\infty}$. The public capital that is generated is used in the production process by firms as an additional factor to private production factors. The fact that the public production factor is used free of charge by the firms causes these extraordinary profits to be obtained. In our case, we will assume that these extra profits as additional remuneration of private production factors, which means that the price paid by private inputs will exceed its marginal productivity.

[2] For an analysis of the fiscal policy implications from general equilibrium models with public capital see for instance, Baxter and King (1993) and Greiner and Hanusch (1998).

Households

The problem faced by the stand-in consumer is to maximize the value of her lifetime utility given by:

$$Max_{\{C_t,L_t\}_{t=0}^{\infty}} \sum_{t=0}^{\infty} \beta^t \left[\gamma \log C_t + (1-\gamma)\log(1-L_t)\right] \tag{9.4}$$

subject to the budged constraint:

$$(1+\tau_t^c)C_t + I_t = (1-\tau_t^l)W_t^e L_t + (1-\tau_t^k)R_t^e K_t + G_t \tag{9.5}$$

Capital stock accumulation process is given by:

$$K_{t+1} = (1-\delta_K)K_t + I_t \tag{9.6}$$

where δ_K is the depreciation rate of physical private capital and where I_t is gross investment. Substituting capital accumulation equation into the budget constraint, we obtain:

$$(1+\tau_t^c)C_t + K_{t+1} - K_t = (1-\tau_t^l)W_t^e L_t + (1-\tau_t^k)(R_t^e - \delta_K)K_t + G_t \tag{9.7}$$

given K_0, the initial private capital stock and where $\beta \in (0,1)$, is the discount factor, G_t is the transfer received by consumers from the government, K_t is the private capital stock, W_t^e is the compensation to employees, R_t^e is the rental rate, δ_K is the capital depreciation rate which is modelled as tax deductible, and $\tau_t^c, \tau_t^l, \tau_t^k$, are the private consumption tax, the labor income tax, and the capital income tax, respectively. The budget constraints indicate that consumption and investment cannot exceed the sum of labor and capital rental income net of taxes and lump sum transfers. As it will be shown below, the relative price of private inputs, W_t^e and R_t^e, will be higher than their marginal productivity, denoted by W_t and R_t.

The Lagrangian function associated to the household maximization problem is:

$$\max_{(C_t,I_t,L_t)} \mathcal{L} = \sum_{t=0}^{\infty} \beta^t \left\{ \begin{array}{c} \gamma \log C_t + (1-\gamma)\log(1-L_t) \\ -\lambda_t \left[\begin{array}{c} (1+\tau_t^c)C_t + K_{t+1} - (1-\tau_t^l)W_t^e L_t \\ -(1-\tau_t^k)(R_t^e - \delta_K)K_t - K_t - G_t \end{array} \right] \end{array} \right\} \tag{9.8}$$

First order conditions for the household maximization problem

are:

$$\frac{\partial \mathcal{L}}{\partial C_t} : \gamma \frac{1}{C_t} - \lambda_t \left(1 + \tau_t^c\right) = 0 \tag{9.9}$$

$$\frac{\partial \mathcal{L}}{\partial L_t} : -\left(1 - \gamma\right) \frac{1}{1 - L_t} + \lambda_t \left(1 - \tau_t^l\right) W_t^e = 0 \tag{9.10}$$

$$\frac{\partial \mathcal{L}}{\partial K_t} : \beta^t \lambda_t \left[\left(1 - \tau_t^k\right) (R_t^e - \delta_K) + 1\right] - \lambda_{t-1} \beta^{t-1} = 0 \tag{9.11}$$

where $\beta^t \lambda_t$ is the Lagrange multiplier assigned to the budget constraint at time t. Combining equations (9.9) and (9.10), we obtain the condition that equates the marginal rate of substitution between consumption and leisure to the opportunity cost of one additional unit of leisure:

$$\frac{1}{1 - L_t} = \frac{\gamma}{\left(1 - \gamma\right)} \frac{\left(1 - \tau_t^l\right) W_t^e}{\left(1 + \tau_t^c\right) C_t} \tag{9.12}$$

Combining expression (9.9) with (9.11) we find the intertemporal equilibrium condition that equates the marginal rate of consumption to the rate of return of investment:

$$\frac{\left(1 + \tau_t^c\right) C_t}{\left(1 + \tau_{t-1}^c\right) C_{t-1}} = \beta \left[\left(1 - \tau_t^k\right) (R_t^e - \delta_K) + 1\right] \tag{9.13}$$

which represents the optimal path of consumption.

Firms

The problem of the firm is to find optimal values for the utilization of labor and capital given the presence of public inputs. The stand-in firm is represented by a standard Cobb-Douglas production function augmented by public capital, as in Cassou and Lansing (1998). The production of final output, Y, requires labor services, L, and two types of capital: private capital, K, and public capital (public infrastructures), Z. Goods and factors markets are assumed to be perfectly competitive. The firm rents capital and hires labor to maximize period profits, taking public inputs and factor prices as given. The technology exhibits a constant return to private factors and thus the profits are zero in equilibrium. However, the firms earn an economic profit equal to the difference between the value of output and the payments made to the private inputs.

We assume that these profits are distributed between the private inputs in an amount proportional to the private input share of output.[3] The technology is given by:

$$Y_t = A_t K_t^{\alpha_1} Z_t^{\alpha_2} L_t^{\alpha_3} \tag{9.14}$$

where A_t is a measure of total-factor productivity, and where α_j, $j = \{1,2,3\}$ are the technological parameters for each input. The existence of constant returns to scale is assumed, that is, $\alpha_1+\alpha_2+\alpha_3 = 1$. Other authors, for instance, Baxter and King (1993) assume constant returns to scale in private factors ($\alpha_1 + \alpha_3 = 1$) and thus, increasing returns to scale for the aggregate economy, $\alpha_1+\alpha_2+\alpha_3 > 1$.

The government

Finally, we consider the dual role of the government: as a tax-levying entity and as supplier of public inputs. The government uses tax revenues to finance spending in public investment (infrastructures) which raises total factor productivity and lump-sum transfers paid out to the consumers. We assume that the government balances its budget period-by-period by returning revenues from distortionary taxes to the agents via lump-sum transfers, G_t.

The government obtains resources from the economy by taxing consumption and income from labor and capital, whose effective average taxes are τ_t^c, τ_t^l, τ_t^k, respectively. The government budget in each period is given by,

$$\tau_t^c C_t + \tau_t^l W_t^e L_t + \tau_t^k (R_t^e - \delta_K) K_{t-1} = G_t + I_{Z,t}, \tag{9.15}$$

where $I_{Z,t}$, is public investment. This expenditure plus the transfers to consumers are the counterpart of fiscal income. The government keeps a fiscal balance in each period. Public investments accrue into the public structures stock. We assume the following accumulation process for the public capital:

$$Z_t = (1-\delta_Z) Z_{t-1} + I_{Z,t}, \tag{9.16}$$

which is analogous to the private capital accumulation process and where δ_Z is the depreciation rate of public physical capital.

---

[3] Guo and Lansing (1997), using a similar technology, assume that each household owns a single firm and that all households receive equal amounts of total profits.

To close the model, it is necessary to define how the government decides public capital investment. We assume that the investment decision in public capital is a random proportion of final output, such as:

$$I_{Z,t} = \theta_t Y_t \tag{9.17}$$

where θ_t, can be a constant or a random variable. In the simulation of the model economy, we will assume that public investment is stochastic using the following expression:

$$I_{Z,t} = B_t \theta Y_t \tag{9.18}$$

where B_t follows an AR(1) process.

Equilibrium of the model

Our model has three productive factors. However, the third factor, public capital, has no market price. This implies that the rent generated by the public input must be assigned to the private factors. Based on the firm profit maximization problem, the first-order conditions are:

$$R_t = \alpha_1 A_t K_t^{\alpha_1 - 1} Z_t^{\alpha_2} L_t^{\alpha_3} \tag{9.19}$$

$$W_t = \alpha_3 A_t K_t^{\alpha_1} Z_t^{\alpha_2} L_t^{\alpha_3 - 1} \tag{9.20}$$

On the other hand, taking the derivative of the profit function with respect to public capital, we obtain:

$$\frac{\partial Y_t}{\partial Z_t} = \alpha_2 A_t K_t^{\alpha_1} Z_t^{\alpha_2 - 1} L_t^{\alpha_3} \tag{9.21}$$

Notice that equation (9.21) is not properly a condition of the model since there is no agent to claim the income generated by the public input.

From the above equations we can obtain the following relations that will be useful for our calibration:

$$R_t K_t = \alpha_1 Y_t$$

$$W_t L_t = \alpha_3 Y_t$$

$$\frac{\partial Y_t}{\partial Z_t} Z_t = \alpha_2 A_t K_t^{\alpha_1} Z_t^{\alpha_2} L_t^{\alpha_3} = \alpha_2 Y_t$$

The firm will produce extraordinary profits of the magnitude $\alpha_2 Y_t$, since this amount is not charged to the owner of the factor. The government usually does not charge a price that covers the full cost of the services provided with the contribution of public inputs. Therefore a rent is generated.

Extraordinary profits

A first possibility, following Guo and Lansing (1997) and Cassou and Lansing (1998), is to consider that firms earn positive profits equal to the difference between the value of output and the rental cost of private factors. Under the assumption that households are the owner of firms, they receive the positive profits. In this particular case, profits π_t, can be defined as:

$$\pi_t = (1 - \alpha_1 - \alpha_3) Y_t$$

to be included in the household's budget constraint as a given amount, in a similar way to public transfers.

Private factors redistribution

A second alternative, the one used in our analysis, consists in assuming, following Feehan and Batina (2007), that this rent is dissipated and absorbed by the other factors as:

$$R_t^e K_t = \alpha_1 A_t K_t^{\alpha_1} Z_t^{\alpha_2} L_t^{\alpha_3} + s\alpha_2 A_t K_t^{\alpha_1} Z_t^{\alpha_2} L_t^{\alpha_3}$$
$$W_t^e L_t = \alpha_3 A_t K_t^{\alpha_1} Z_t^{\alpha_2} L_t^{\alpha_3} + (1-s)\alpha_2 A_t K_t^{\alpha_1} Z_t^{\alpha_2} L_t^{\alpha_3}$$

The effective return to capital R_t^e, includes a share s of the payment to the public input, and the effective return to labor W_t^e, absorbs the balancing $(1 - s)$. If we assume that $s = \alpha_1/(\alpha_1 + \alpha_3)$, then,

$$R_t^e K_t = \alpha_1 (1 + \frac{\alpha_2}{\alpha_1 + \alpha_3}) Y_t = \alpha Y_t \tag{9.22}$$

$$W_t^e L_t = \alpha_3 (1 + \frac{\alpha_2}{\alpha_1 + \alpha_3}) Y_t = (1 - \alpha) Y_t \tag{9.23}$$

where α is the private capital share of output and $(1 - \alpha)$ the labor share of output.

Thus, the economy satisfies the following feasibility constraint:

$$C_t + I_t + I_{Z,t} = R_t^e K_{t-1} + W_t^e L_t \tag{9.24}$$

Definition 7 *A competitive equilibrium for this economy is a sequence of consumption, leisure, and private investment* $\{C_t, 1-L_t, I_t\}_{t=0}^{\infty}$ *for the consumers, a sequence of capital and labor utilization for the firm* $\{K_t, L_t\}_{t=0}^{\infty}$*, and a sequence of government transfers* $\{G_t\}_{t=0}^{\infty}$*, such that, given a sequence of prices,* $\{W_t^e, R_t^e\}_{t=0}^{\infty}$*, taxes,* $\{\tau_t^c, \tau_t^k, \tau_t^l\}_{t=0}^{\infty}$ *and a sequence of public investments* $\{I_{Z,t}\}_{t=0}^{\infty}$*:*
i) The optimization problem of the consumer is satisfied.
ii) Given prices for capital and labor, and given a sequence for public inputs, the first-order conditions of the firm are satisfied with respect to capital and labor.
iii) Given a sequence of taxes, and government investment, the sequence of transfers and current spending are such that the government constraint is satisfied.
iv) The feasibility constraint of the economy is satisfied.

Notice that according to the definition of equilibrium for our model economy, the government enters completely parameterized, and fiscal policy is made consistent to the model and the data. In other words, in our model the private sector reacts optimally to policy changes, and these policy changes are given exogenously.

Equations of the model and calibration

The competitive equilibrium of the model economy is defined by a set of thirteen equations for the sequences of the endogenous variables Y_t, C_t, I_t, K_t, L_t, R_t, W_t, $I_{Z,t}$, Z_t, R_t^e, W_t^e, and A_t, B_t and the exogenous variables θ, τ^c, τ^l, τ^k. This set of equations is the following:

$$\frac{1}{1-L_t} = \frac{\gamma}{(1-\gamma)} \frac{\left(1-\tau_t^l\right)}{\left(1+\tau_t^c\right)} \frac{W_t^e}{C_t} \tag{9.25}$$

$$\frac{\left(1+\tau_t^c\right) C_t}{\left(1+\tau_{t-1}^c\right) C_{t-1}} = \beta\left[\left(1-\tau_t^k\right)(R_{t+1}^e - \delta_K) + 1\right] \tag{9.26}$$

$$Y_t = C_t + I_{K,t} + I_{Z,t} \tag{9.27}$$

$$Y_t = A_t K_t^{\alpha_1} Z_t^{\alpha_2} L_t^{\alpha_3} \tag{9.28}$$

$$K_{t+1} = (1-\delta_K)K_t + I_t \tag{9.29}$$

$$Z_{t+1} = (1-\delta_Z)Z_t + I_{Z,t} \tag{9.30}$$

$$I_{Z,t} = B_t \theta Y_t \tag{9.31}$$

$$W_t = \alpha_3 A_t K_t^{\alpha_1} Z_t^{\alpha_2} L_t^{\alpha_3 - 1} \tag{9.32}$$

$$R_t = \alpha_1 K_t^{\alpha_1 - 1} Z_t^{\alpha_2} L_t^{\alpha_3} \tag{9.33}$$

$$R_t^e = R_t + s\alpha_2 A_t K_t^{\alpha_1 - 1} Z_t^{\alpha_2} L_t^{\alpha_3} \tag{9.34}$$

$$W_t^e = W_t + (1-s)\alpha_2 A_t K_t^{\alpha_1} Z_t^{\alpha_2} L_t^{\alpha_3 - 1} \tag{9.35}$$

$$\ln A_t = (1-\rho_A)\ln \overline{A} + \rho_A \ln A_{t-1} + \varepsilon_t^A \tag{9.36}$$

$$\ln B_t = (1-\rho_B)\ln \overline{B} + \rho_B \ln B_{t-1} + \varepsilon_t^B \tag{9.37}$$

The set of parameters to be calibrated are:

$$\left\{\alpha_1, \alpha_2, \alpha_3, \alpha, \delta_K, \delta_Z, \beta, \gamma, \theta, \tau^c, \tau^l, \tau^k, \rho_A, \sigma_A, \rho_B, \sigma_B\right\}$$

Total capital income share α, is assumed to be 0.35 as in previous models. However, notice that in this framework this value does not correspond to the technological parameter of private capital, neither the share of labor income, $1-\alpha$, corresponds to the technological parameter of labor. In fact, the ratio of income shares for capital and labor are defined by:

$$\alpha = \alpha_1 (1 + \frac{\alpha_2}{\alpha_1 + \alpha_3})$$

$$1 - \alpha = \alpha_3 (1 + \frac{\alpha_2}{\alpha_1 + \alpha_3})$$

The empirical literature shows a wide range of values for the output elasticity of public capital ranging from a null value, according to which the public capital would have no effect on the level of output of the economy, to valuesthat are implausibly high or even higher than those obtained for private capital. Aschauer (1989) obtains valuesranging from 0.39 to 0.59, while Munnell (1990a) obtains a value of 0.34. By contrast, authors such as Aaron (1990), Tatom (1991), Holtz-Eakin (1994), Evans and Karras (1994a and b), Garcia-Milá *et al.* (1996), among others, get zero or very small values. Cassou and Lansing (1998) through the calibration of a general equilibrium model similar to ours obtained values between 0.1

Table 9.1: Calibrated parameters

Parameter	Definition	Value
α_1	Private capital technological parameter	0.315
α_2	Public capital technological parameter	0.585
α_3	Labor technological parameter	0.100
α	Technological parameter	0.350
β	Discount factor	0.970
γ	Preferences parameter	0.450
δ_K	Private capital depreciation rate	0.060
δ_Z	Public capital depreciation rate	0.020
θ_Z	Public investment/output ratio	0.050
ρ_A	TFP autoregressive parameter	0.950
σ_A	TFP standard deviation	0.010
ρ_A	Public investment autoregressive parameter	0.950
σ_A	Public investment standard deviation	0.010
τ^c	Consumption tax rate	0.116
τ^l	Labor income tax rate	0.348
τ^k	Capital income tax rate	0.225

and 0.123 for the United States. Guo and Lansing (1997), however, a smaller gain of value 0.0525. Meanwhile, Finn (1993) estimating by GMM a DSGE model gets a value of 0.158. Baxter and King (1993) use as reference a value of 0.05, calibrating a model for a range of valuesbetween 0 and 0.4.

In our case, we assume that public capital technological parameter is 0.1. Using the above expression, we find that the associated private capital technology parameter is $\alpha_1 = 0.315$, while the technology parameter for labor is $\alpha_3 = 0.585$.

An additional parameter to be calibrated is the depreciation rate of public capital. Calibrated value for private capital depreciation rate is 6%. However, we would expect this value to be different for the public capital stock, given the different composition of private and public capital. Structures depreciate at a different speed than equipment. Aggregate depreciation rate depends on the proportion of each capital asset in total. Given the composition of public capital, we would expect the depreciation rate to be lower than that of private capital. We assume a public capital depreciation rate of 2% per year.

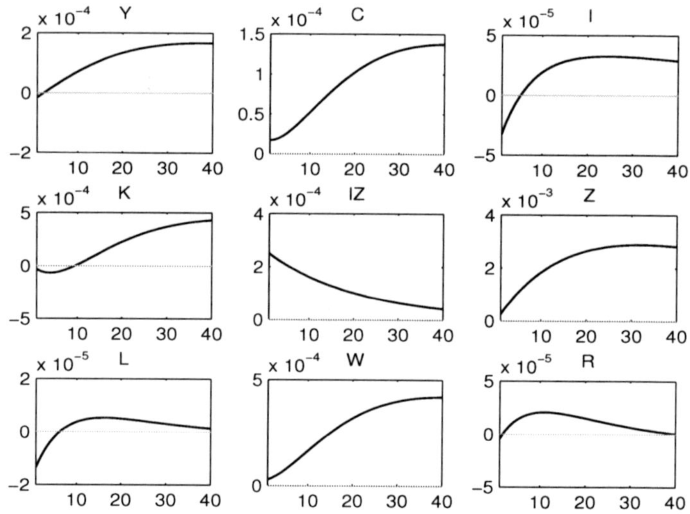

Figure 9.1: Public investment shock

Finally, we calibrate the parameter for public investment. As in the previous chapter for the case of public consumption, we have two possibilities: To assume a given percentage of fiscal revenues, or over total output, or to assume that public investment follows a particular stochastic process. In the previous chapter, public consumption was assumed to be deterministic. In this chapter we choose the second option and consider that public investment is stochastic. This is simply done by adding a disturbance to the pubic investment equation. In particular, we assume that 5% of final output is expended in public investment.

Public investment shock

This section studies the dynamic effects of a shock to public investment. In this exercise we assume that the stochastic process associated with public investment is similar to the process followed by total factor productivity. Impulse-response of the relevant variables are plotted in Figure 9.1.

First, we highlight the evolution of public investment, which increases initially to gradually decline until its steady state value, given the assumed stochastic process. This induces a process of public capital accumulation. The impact effect of the shock on private investment is negative, but it turns to positive in subsequent periods. The rise in both public and private capital stock causes a positive reaction of output, although labor is reduced in impact.

In summary, a positive public investment shock causes a rise in consumption and output. Given the assumed production function, the public investment shock is equivalent to a total factor productivity shock as it causes a rise in productivity of private inputs. As a consequence, also private investment and labor increase.

Conclusions

This chapter develops a DSGE model with public investment in physical capital. In this case the production function of the economy uses three factors of production: labor, private capital, and public capital. The existence of constant returns to scale is assumed. As firms do not pay for the public inputs, a positive profit is generated. It is assumed that this rent is dissipated and absorbed by the other two factors.

Public investment shocks can be deterministic or stochastic. Here, we assume the process for public investment to be stochastic. To study some of the implications of this model, we study the effects of a positive shock in public investment. Several noteworthy questions can be investigated. The optimal stock of public capital stock, the contribution to long-run growth, or changes in the fraction of government spending devoted to public investment, are all exercises that can be carried out within this theoretical framework.

Appendix A: Dynare code

Dynare code corresponding to the model developed in this chapter, named *model8.mod*, is the following:

```
// Model 9.  Public capital
// Dynare Code
// File:  model9.mod
// José L. Torres.  University of Málaga (Spain)
// Endogenous variables
var Y, C, I, K, IZ, Z, L, W, R, A, B;
// Exogenous variables
```

```
varexo e, u, tauc, taul, tauk;
// Parameters
parameters alpha, alpha1, alpha2, alpha3, beta,
 deltak, deltag, gamma, rho1, rho2;
// Calibrated parameters
alpha  = 0.35;
alpha1 = 0.315;
alpha2 = 0.100;
alpha3 = 0.585;
beta   = 0.97;
deltak = 0.06;
deltag = 0.02;
gamma  = 0.40;
rho1   = 0.95;
rho2   = 0.95;
// Equations of the model economy
model;
(1+tauc)*C=(gamma/(1-gamma))*(1-L)*
 (1-taul)*(1-alpha)*Y/L;
1 = beta*((((1+tauc)*C)/((1+tauc)*C(+1)))
 *((1-tauk)*alpha*Y(+1)/K+(1-deltak)));
Y = A*(K(-1)^alpha1)*(Z(-1)^alpha2)*(L^alpha3);
K = (Y-C)+(1-deltak)*K(-1);
Z = IZ+(1-deltag)*Z(-1);
I = Y-C-IZ;
IZ = B*0.05*Y;
W = (1-alpha)*A*(K(-1)^alpha1)*(Z(-1)^alpha2)*
 (L^(alpha3-1));
R = alpha*A*(K(-1)^(alpha1-1))*(Z(-1)^alpha2)*
 (L^(alpha3));
log(A) = rho1*log(A(-1))+e;
log(B) = rho2*log(B(-1))+u;
end;
// Initial values
initval;
Y = 1;
C = 0.75;
L = 0.3;
K = 3.5;
I = 0.25;
Z = 1;
```

```
IZ = 0.05*Y;
W = (1-alpha)*Y/L;
R = alpha*Y/K;
A = 1;
B = 1;
e = 0;
u = 0;
tauc = 0.116;
tauk = 0.225;
taul = 0.344;
end;
 // Steady state
steady;
// Blanchard-Kahn conditions
check;
// Disturbance analysis
shocks;
var u; stderr 0.01;
end;
 // Stochastic simulation
stoch_simul;
```

Bibliography

Aaron, H. (1990), Discussing of 'Why is infrastructure important?', in Munnell, A. (Ed.) *Is there a shortfall in public capital investment?*, Federal Reserve Bank of Boston.

Ai, C. and Cassou, S. (1995), A normative analysis of public capital. *Applied Economics*, 27, 1001-1209.

Arrow, K.J. and Kurz, M. (1970), *Public Investment, the Rate of Return and Optimal Fiscal Policy*, The Johns Hopkins Press: Baltimore.

Aschauer, D. (1989), Is public expenditure productive? *Journal of Monetary Economics*, 23, 177-200.

Barro, R. (1990), Government spending in a simple model of endogenous growth. *Journal of Political Economy*, 98, 103-125.

Barro, R. and Sala-i-Martin (1992), Public Finance in models of economic growth. *Review of Economic Studies*, 59, 645-661.

Batina, R. (1998), On the long run effects of public capital and disaggregated public capital on aggregate output. *International Tax and Public Finance*, 5(3), 263-281.

Batina, R. (1999), On the long run effects of public capital on aggregate output: estimation and sensitivity analysis. *Empirical Economics*, 24(4), 711-717.

Baxter, M. and King, R. (1993): Fiscal policy in general equilibrium. *American Economic Review*, 83(3), 315-334.

Cassou, S. and Lansing, K. (1998), Optimal fiscal policy, public capital and the productivity slowdown. *Journal of Economic Dynamics and Control*, 22(6), 911-935.

Cashin, P. (1995), Government spending, taxes, and economic growth. *International Monetary Fund Staff Papers*, 42(2), 237-269.

Clarida, R. (1993), International capital mobility, public investment and economic growth. *NBER Working Paper*, n. 4506.

Diewert, W. (1986), The measurement of the economic benefits of infrastructure services, in M. Beckmann and W. Krelle, (eds.), *Lecture Notes in Economics and Mathematical Systems*, n. 278, Berlin-Heidelberg.

Evans, P. and Karras, G. (1994), Is government capital productive? Evidence from a panel of seven countries. *Journal of Macroeconomics*, 16, 271-279.

Feehan, J.P. and Matsumoto, M. (2002): Distortionary taxation and optimal public spending on productive activities. *Economic Inquiry*, 40(1), 60-68.

Feehan, J.P. and Batina, R. (2007): Labor and capital taxation with public inputs as common property. *Public Finance Review*, 35, 626-642.

Finn, M. (1993), Is all government capital productive? *Federal Reserve Bank of Richmond Economic Quarterly*, 79(4), 53-80.

Ford, R. and Poret, P. (1991), Infrastructure and private sector productivity. *OECD Economic Studies*, 17, 63-89.

García-Milá, T., McGuire, T. and Porter, R. (1996), The effect of public capital in state-level production functions reconsidered. *Review of Economics and Statistic*, 78(1), 177-180.

Glomm, G. and Ravikumar, B. (1994), Public investment in infrastructure in a simple growth model. *Journal of Economic Dynamics and Control*, 18(6), 1173-1187.

Guo, J. and Lansing, K. (1997), Tax structure and welfare in a model of optimal fiscal policy. *Economic Review Federal Reserve Bank of Cleveland*, 1, 11-23.

Holtz-Eakin, D. (1994), Public-sector capital and the productivity puzzle. *Review of Economics and Statistics*, 76(1), 12-21.

Hulten, C.R. and Schwab, R.M. (1993), Infrastructure spending: where do we go from here? *National Tax Journal*, 46(3), 261-273.

McMillin, W. and Smith, D. (1994), A multivariate time series analysis of the United States aggregate production function. *Empirical Economics*, 19(4), 659-674.

Munnell, A. (1990a), Why has productivity growth declined?: Productivity and public investment. *New England Economic Review*, January/February, 3–22.

Munnell, A. (1990b), How does public infrastructure affect regional economic performance?, in A.H. Munnell (ed.). *Is There a Shortfall in Public Capital Investment?*, Federal Reserve Bank of Boston, Conference Series, 34, 60-103.

Mera, K. (1973), Regional production functions and social overhead capital: An analysis of the Japanese case. *Regional and Urban Economics*, 3(2), 157-186.

Otto, G. and Voss, G. (1996), Public capital and private sector productivity. *The Economic Record*, 70, 121-132.

Pestieau, P. (1974), Optimal taxation and discount rate for public investment in a growth setting. *Journal of Public Economics*, 3, 217-235.

Ratner, J. (1983), Government capital and the production function for U.S. private output. *Economics Letters*, 13(2-3), 213-217.

Romp, W, and de Haan, J. (2007), Public capital and economic growth: A critical survey. *Perspektien der Wirtschaftspolitik*, 8 (Special Issue), 6-52.

Sturm, J.E., Kuper, G.H. and de Haan, J. (1997), Modelling government investment and economic growth on a macro level: a review, in Brakman, S. and van Ees, H., (Eds.) *Market Behaviour and Macroeconomic Modelling*, MacMillan, London.

Tatom, J. (1991), Public capital and private sector performance. *Federal Reserve Bank of St. Louis Review*, 73(3), 3-15.

Voss, G. (2002), Public and private investment in the United States and Canada. *Economic Modelling*, 19(4), 641-664.

Weitzman, M. (1970), Optimal growth with scale economies in the creation of overhead capital. *Review of Economic Studies*, 37(4), 556-570.

Part V

Time Decisions

Chapter 10

Human Capital

Introduction

DSGE models usually introduce leisure as an argument of the households' utility function additionally to consumption. In this setting, the agent must decide how to divide its time endowment between work and leisure, so consumption-leisure decisions can be studied. In this chapter, we introduce human capital in the standard DSGE model. Human capital can be defined as the state-of-the-art about how to produce goods and services. From an economic point of view, this is a concept associated to the labor input and can be interpreted as the technology embodied in workers.

We assume that skill can be accumulated using time devoted to skill acquisition activities. Households devote time to skill acquisition through participation in both formal (schooling, training programs, etc.) and informal (education and training outside the job) activities. Skill acquisition activities have a cost in terms of foregone current income. On the other hand, education makes a worker more productive when the skills have been acquired. This implies a higher wage and a higher consumption in the future. In this setting, the model will include an additional intertemporal equilibrium condition regarding labor-education decisions. From a long-run approach, human capital accumulation is one of the main sources of output and productivity growth.

The remainder of the chapter is organized as follows. Section 2 briefly reviews how the literature introduces human capital in DSGE modelling. Section 3 presents the model with human capital. Section 4 presents the equations of the model and the calibration. Section 5 studies the effect of a TFP shock. Finally, Section 6 summarizes and concludes.

Human Capital

Human capital stock refers to the accumulated stock of knowledge or skills about how to produce. We can consider human capital as a type of technology embodied in labor. Human capital can be accumulated through an investment process in education and training. Experience (learning-by-doing) is another way of accumulating human capital. Whereas other types of technological progress are assumed to be exogenous, human capital accumulation is an endogenous process derived from agents' decisions about how much time (or foregone production) is devoted to skill acquisition activities.

Modern interest on human capital starts with the seminal works of Mincer (1958), Schultz (1961, 1963) and Becker (1962, 1964). Nevertheless, the interest on the economic consequences of investment in education is not new. The first work estimating the stock of human capital in an economy was conducted by William Petty in 1676 (see Kiker, 1966). In the literature we find a large number of works focusing on the role of human capital in a DSGE framework. Initial contributions are Uzawa (1965) and Lucas (1988).

This topic has been explored by, among others, DeJong and Ingram (2001) who find that a positive technology shock increases wage, rising the opportunity cost of leisure and education and therefore negatively impacts on the skill acquisition activities. They obtained a negative correlation of -0.31 over the period 1970-1996 between the growth rate of output and college enrollments in the US. They conclude that skill acquisition activities have clear macroeconomic implications and they are influenced by the business cycle. Other examples are He and Liu (2001), Dellas and Sakellaris (2003), or Malley and Woitek (2009), among others.

The key point of the model is how time devoted to education and skill acquisition transforms into human capital. In the literature, we find several alterative functional forms for the human capital investment process. We can use two general alternative specifications for the production of human capital. First, assuming that investing time in education is the only input needed, as in Heckman (1976) and Haley (1976). Indeed, this is exactly how Mincer (1958) specifies his return-to-schooling equation. One example of this type of human capital investment process could be the following

$$I_{H,t} = B_t E_t^{\theta} \tag{10.1}$$

where $\theta > 0$, that is, marginal returns of educations can be decreasing $(0 < \theta < 1)$, or even increasing $(\theta > 1)$, $I_{H,t}$ is the investment in human capital, E_t is the time devoted to skill acquisition activities and B_t is a productivity parameters. Second, both time in education and goods (human capital and/or physical capital) are needed as in

Ben-Porath (1967) and Trostel (1993). In this case, we can define investment in education as:

$$I_{H,t} = B_t (E_t H_t)^{\theta} \tag{10.2}$$

or:

$$I_{H,t} = B_t E_t^{\theta} H_t^{1-\theta} \tag{10.3}$$

where H_t is the stock of human capital. In this case, new investments in human capital are producing by combining the existing stock of human capital with the available time spent investing in education. The efficiency of new human capital production is governed by B_t and θ. As far as θ is positive but smaller than one, expressions (10.1) and (10.2) preserve the law of diminishing returns to education.

The Model

In the model, the representative agent allocates non-leisure time between production and learning. In this context, the balanced growth path equilibrium of the economy depends on the allocation of time to acquiring education. Two goods are produced in the economy: a final good and a human capital good. The final good can be used for three purposes: consumption, physical capital investment and education (or human capital investment).

Following Guvenen and Kuruscu (2006), we assume that the agent supplies two types of labor inputs to the market: raw labor and human capital. Raw labor is the constant labor input that the agent was born with, while human capital is the skills that are acquired by the agent either through formal schooling or through on the job training. This formulation of labor inputs allows us to discuss skills and human capital formation without having to introduce different types of agents, *e.g.*, high-skilled and low-skilled labor, as is done in some studies (see for instance, Krusell *et al.*, 2000).

Households

The economy is inhabited by an infinitely lived, representative household, who has preferences represented by the following utility function:

$$U(C_t, O_t) \tag{10.4}$$

where C_t is consumption and O_t is leisure.

Non-leisure time is split between time on the job (producing output), L_t, and time in education (producing human capital), E_t. The household time restriction is defined as

$$O_t + L_t + E_t = 1 \tag{10.5}$$

where total number of effective hours have been normalized to one.

The agent's utility function is given by

$$U(C_t, O_t) = \gamma \ln C_t + (1-\gamma)\ln(1 - L_t - E_t) \tag{10.6}$$

Each household saves in the form of investment in physical capital, $S_t = I_{K,t}$, and receives capital interest income $R_t K_t$ where R_t is the return to capital and K_t is the physical capital stock. Total labor earnings are given by $W_t H_t L_t$ where H_t is the households stock of human capital and W_t is the wage. Note that human capital only receives income if associated with working time. The household budget constraint is defined as:

$$C_t + S_t = R_t K_t + W_t H_t L_t \tag{10.7}$$

The law of motion for physical capital stock is given by:

$$K_{t+1} = (1-\delta_K) K_t + I_{K,t} \tag{10.8}$$

where δ_K is the depreciation rate of physical private capital.

The stock of human capital evolves according to:

$$H_{t+1} = (1-\delta_H) H_t + I_{H,t} \tag{10.9}$$

Human capital depreciation, $0 < \delta_H < 1$, reflects the aging and replacement of the population: new cohorts must be continually trained in order to maintain the stock of human capital. One can also see this model as one with vintage human capital. New skills are needed to design, introduce and/or use the new, more efficient capital equipment, while some skills become obsolete as older vintages of capital become obsolete. Investment in human capital is assumed to be:

$$I_{H,t} = B_t E_t^{\theta} \tag{10.10}$$

New investments in human capital are produced by devoting time to education and skill acquisition activities. The efficiency of new human capital production is governed by B_t and θ. B_t is a stochastic process defining technological efficiency of education. Human capital depreciation, $0 < \delta_H < 1$, reflects the aging and replacement of the population. That is, we have to continually train new cohorts in order to maintain the stock of human capital. One can also see this model as one with vintage human capital. New skills are needed to design, introduce and/or use the new, more efficient capital equipment, while some skills become obsolete as older vintages of capital become obsolete.

The Lagrangian auxiliary function to be solved by households is:

$$\max \mathcal{L} = \sum_{t=0}^{\infty} \beta^t \left\{ \begin{array}{c} \gamma \ln C_t + (1-\gamma)\ln(1-L_t-E_t) \\ -\lambda_t \left[C_t + K_{t+1} - (1-\delta_K)K_t - R_t K_t - W_t L_t H_t\right] \\ -\xi_t \left[H_{t+1} - (1-\delta_H)H_t - B_t E_t^{\theta}\right] \end{array} \right\} \tag{10.11}$$

The first order conditions for the households are:

$$\frac{\partial \mathcal{L}}{\partial C_t} = \gamma \frac{1}{C_t} - \lambda_t = 0 \tag{10.12}$$

$$\frac{\partial \mathcal{L}}{\partial L_t} = -\frac{1-\gamma}{1-L_t-E_t} + \lambda_t W_t H = 0 \tag{10.13}$$

$$\frac{\partial \mathcal{L}}{\partial E_t} = -\frac{1-\gamma}{1-L_t-E_t} + \xi_t \theta B_t E_t^{\theta-1} = 0 \tag{10.14}$$

$$\frac{\partial \mathcal{L}}{\partial K_t} = \beta^t \lambda_t (R_t + 1 - \delta_K) - \beta^{t-1}\lambda_{t-1} = 0 \tag{10.15}$$

$$\frac{\partial \mathcal{L}}{\partial H_t} = \beta^t \left[\lambda_t W_t L_t + \xi_t (1-\delta_H)\right] - \beta^{t-1}\xi_{t-1} = 0 \tag{10.16}$$

Lagrange multipliers are:

$$\frac{\gamma}{C_t} = \lambda_t \tag{10.17}$$

$$\xi_t = \frac{1-\gamma}{(1-L_t-E_t)\theta B_t E_t^{\theta-1}} \tag{10.18}$$

Combining FOCs (10.12) with (10.13) we obtain the condition that equates the marginal rate of substitution between consumption and leisure, as the opportunity cost of one additional unit of leisure:

$$\frac{1-\gamma}{\gamma}C_t = W_t H_t (1 - L_t - E_t) \tag{10.19}$$

Combining FOCs (10.14) with (10.16) we obtain the equation that equates the marginal rate of substitution between consumption and time devoted to education:

$$\begin{aligned} &\frac{1-\gamma}{(1-L_{t-1}-E_{t-1})\theta B_{t-1} E_{t-1}^{\theta-1}} \\ &= \frac{\beta\gamma W_t L_t}{C_t} + \beta \frac{(1-\gamma)(1-\delta_H)}{(1-L_t-E_t)\theta B_t E_t^{\theta-1}} \end{aligned} \tag{10.20}$$

Finally, combining FOCs (10.12) with (10.15) we find the condition that equates the marginal rate of consumption to the rate of return of investment in physical capital:

$$1 = \beta \frac{C_{t-1}}{C_t}(R_t + 1 - \delta_K) \tag{10.21}$$

Firms

The problem of the firms is to find optimal values for the utilization of capital and labor inputs. The firms rent capital and employ labor in order to maximize profits at period t, taking factor prices as given. The technology is given by a constant returns to scale Cobb-Douglas production function:

$$Y_t = A_t K_t^{\alpha} (L_t H_t)^{1-\alpha} \tag{10.22}$$

The problem of the firms is to maximize:

$$\Pi_t = A_t K_t^{\alpha} (L_t H_t)^{1-\alpha} - R_t K_t - W_t L_t H_t \tag{10.23}$$

From the first order conditions for the firms profit maximization, the rental price of inputs are given by:

$$R_t = \alpha A_t K_t^{\alpha-1} (L_t H_t)^{1-\alpha} \tag{10.24}$$

$$W_t = (1-\alpha) A_t K_t^{\alpha} (L_t H_t)^{-\alpha} \tag{10.25}$$

that is, the firms hire capital and labor inputs such that the marginal productivity of these factors must equate their competitive rental prices.

Equations of the model and calibration

The competitive equilibrium for this economy is defined by a set of twelve equations, representing the sequences of the endogenous variables, Y_t, C_t, $I_{K,t}$, K_t, H_t, $I_{H,t}$, E_t, L_t, R_t, W_t and two technologies, A_t and B_t, which are assumed to be endogenous and to follow an autoregressive process of order 1. This set of equations is the following:

$$(1-\gamma)\frac{1}{1-L_t-E_t} = \gamma\frac{1}{C_t}H_tW_t \tag{10.26}$$

$$\frac{C_t}{C_{t-1}} = \beta[R_{t+1}+1-\delta] \tag{10.27}$$

$$\frac{1-\gamma}{(1-L_{t-1}-E_{t-1})\theta B_{t-1}E_{t-1}^{\theta-1}} \tag{10.28}$$
$$= \frac{\beta\gamma W_tL_t}{C_t} + \beta\frac{(1-\gamma)(1-\delta_H)}{(1-L_t-E_t)\theta B_tE_t^{\theta-1}}$$

$$Y_t = C_t + I_t \tag{10.29}$$

$$Y_t = A_tK_t^{\alpha}(H_tL_t)^{1-\alpha} \tag{10.30}$$

$$K_{t+1} = (1-\delta_K)K_t + I_{K,t} \tag{10.31}$$

$$H_{t+1} = (1-\delta_H)H_t + I_{H,t} \tag{10.32}$$

$$I_{H,t} = E_t^{\theta} \tag{10.33}$$

$$W_t = (1-\alpha)A_tK_t^{\alpha}(H_tL_t)^{-\alpha} \tag{10.34}$$

$$R_t = \alpha A_tK_t^{\alpha-1}(H_tL_t)^{1-\alpha} \tag{10.35}$$

$$\ln A_t = (1-\rho_A)\ln\overline{A} + \rho_A\ln A_{t-1} + \varepsilon_t^A \tag{10.36}$$

$$\ln B_t = (1-\rho_B)\ln\overline{B} + \rho_B\ln B_{t-1} + \varepsilon_t^B \tag{10.37}$$

The set of parameters to be calibrated is the following:

$$\Omega = \left\{\alpha,\beta,\delta_K,\delta_H,\gamma,\theta,\rho_A,\sigma_A,\rho_B,\sigma_B\right\}$$

Table 10.1: Calibrated parameters

Parameter	Definition	Value
α	Technological parameter	0.350
β	Discount factor	0.970
γ	Preferences parameter	0.400
θ	Education productivity	0.800
δ_K	Physical capital depreciation rate	0.060
δ_H	Human capital depreciation rate	0.010
ρ_A	TFP autorregressive parameter	0.950
σ_A	TFP standard deviation	0.010
ρ_B	Human capital autorregressive parameter	0.950
σ_B	Human capital standard deviation	0.010

To numerically simulate the model, six additional parameters need to be calibrated. DeJong and Ingram (2001), using Bayesian techniques, estimate a DSGE model similar to the one developed here and find posterior mean values of $\theta = 1.04$, $\delta_H = 0.006$, $\rho_B = 0.86$, and $\sigma_B = 0.006$. We use values of $\theta = 0.8$ and $\delta_H = 0.01$. Finally, the parameters of the stochastic process for the shocks affecting skill investment are assumed to be similar to the TFP process.

Total Factor Productivity shock

This section studies the effects of a TFP shock. In particular, we are interested in studying how the decision about how much time is devoted to skill acquisition activities is affected by a productivity shock. The model can also be used to study the effects of a particular shock to the education sector.

Figure 10.1 plots the impulse-response functions to a positive TFP shock for the relevant variables of the model. The positive productivity shock rises the price of production factors, as expected. This provokes a rise in labor (working time) and investment. The key finding is that time devoted to education is reduced on impact. We observe an intertemporal substitution effect between working time and education time. Indeed, the productivity shock increases the profitability of devoting time to work and increases the cost (as foregone income) of allocating time to educational activities. Agents do not only substitute education by labor, but there is also a substitu-

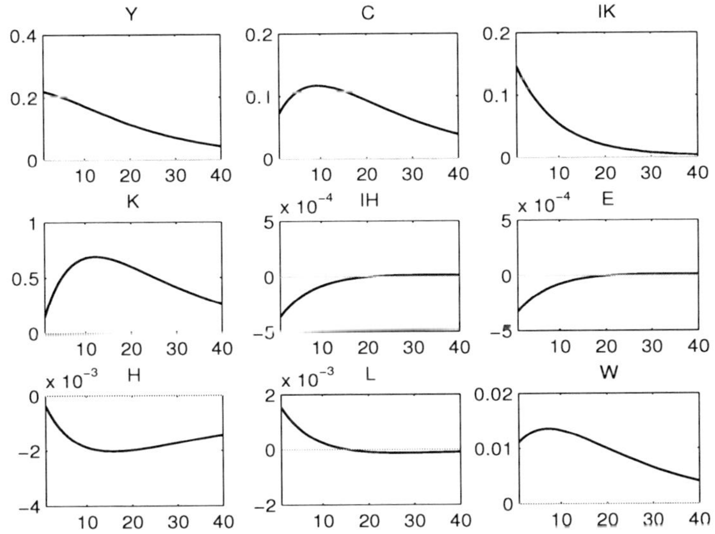

Figure 10.1: TFP shock with human capital

tion effect between leisure and labor.

The reduction in time devoted to skill acquisition activities causes a reduction in the stock of human capital. Therefore, we found that time devoted to skill acquisition activities is countercyclical. In good times, agents prefer working to spending time in skill acquisition. In bad times, agents return to school.

Finally, the effects of the productivity shock on output and consumption are positive and the reduction in human capital is compensated by higher labor and physical capital.

Conclusions

This chapter introduces human capital in the standard DSGE model. Labor input is now composed of raw labor (working time) and labor skills stock, i.e., human capital. The human capital accumulation process depends on skill investment. Skill investment is assumed to be a function of time devoted to education, which is an additional time allocation decision to be taken by households.

We studied the business cycle properties of skill acquisition activities. We found that a positive TFP shock causes a reduction in the time devoted to skill acquisition activities, and thus, to a reduction in the stock of human capital. This is due to the fact the productivity shock changes the cost, as income foregone, of educational activities.

In the model developed in this chapter, the skill investment process is assumed to be a function of the time devoted to education activities. An alternative would be to assume that the function that transforms skill investment into human capital also depends on the human capital stock. Finally, it would be of interest to study how shocks to the skill acquisition process affect the economy. Another interesting exercise would be to study how technological change embodied in new capital assets could cause a sudden depreciation in human capital stock as previous knowledge becomes obsolete.

Appendix A: Dynare code

Dynare code corresponding to the model developed in this chapter, named *model10.mod*, is the following:

```
// Model 10. Human capital
// Dynare code
// File: model10.mod
// José L. Torres. University of Málaga (Spain)
// Endogenous variables
var Y, C, IK, K, IH, H, L, E, W, R, A, B;
// Exogenous variables
varexo e, v;
// Parameters
parameters alpha, beta, deltak, deltah, gamma
 theta, rhoA, rhoB;
// Calibration
alpha  = 0.35;
beta   = 0.97;
deltak = 0.06;
deltah = 0.01;
gamma  = 0.40;
theta  = 0.80;
rhoA   = 0.95;
rhoB   = 0.95;
```

```
// Equations of the model
model;
C = (gamma/(1-gamma))*(1-L-E)*H*W;
1 = beta*((C/C(+1))*(R(+1)+(1-deltak)));
Y = A*(K(-1)^alpha)*((L*H)^(1-alpha));
K = (Y-C)+(1-deltak)*K(-1);
IK = Y-C;
H=IH+(1-deltah)*H(-1);
IH = B*(E)^theta;
(1-gamma)/((1-L-E)*theta*B*(E)^(theta-1))=
 beta*((gamma*W(+1)*L(+1))/C(+1)
 ((1-gamma)*(1-deltah)/(1-L(+1)-E(+1)*
 theta*B*(E+1)^(theta-1))));
W = (1-alpha)*A*(K(-1)^alpha)*((L*H)^(-alpha));
R = alpha*A*(K(-1)^(alpha-1))*((L*H)^(1-alpha));
log(A) = rhoA*log(A(-1))+ e;
log(B) = rhoB*log(B(-1))+ v;
end;
// Initial values
initval;
Y  = 1;
C  = 0.8;
L  = 0.3;
K  - 3.5;
IK = 0.2;
K  = 3.5;
E  = 0.15;
IK = 0.15^0.8;
H  = IK/deltah;
W  = (1-alpha)*Y/L;
R  = alpha*Y/K;
A  = 1;
B  = 1;
e  = 0;
v  = 0;
end;
// Steady State computation
steady;
// Blanchard-Kahn conditions
check;
// Shock analysis:  TFP shock
```

```
shocks;
var e; stderr 0.01;
end;
// Stochastic simulation
stoch_simul;
```

Bibliography

Becker, G. (1962): Investment in human capital: A theoretical analysis. *Journal of Political Economy,* 70(1), 9-49.

Becker, G. (1964): *Human capital.* Columbia University Press: New York.

Ben-Porath, Y. (1967): The Production of Human Capital and the Life Cycle of Earnings. *Journal of Political Economy,* 75(4), 352-365.

DeJong, D. and Ingram, B. (2001): The cyclical behavior of skill acquisition. *Review of Economic Dynamics,* 4(3), 536-561.

Dellas, H. and Sakellaris, P. (2003): On the cyclicality of the demand for education: Theory and evidence. *Oxford Economic Papers,* 55(1), 148-172.

Greenwood, J., Hercowitz, Z. and Krusell, P. (1997): Long-run implication of investment-specific technological change. *American Economic Review,* 87(3), 342-362.

Guvenen, F. and Kuruscu, B. (2006): Understanding wage inequality: Ben-Porath meets skill biased technological change. Mimeo.

Haley, W. (1976): Estimation of the Earnings Profile from Optimal Human Capital Accumulation. *Econometrica,* 44(6), 1223-1238.

Heckman, J. J. (1976): A Life-cycle Model of Earnings, Learning, and Consumption. *Journal of Political Economy,* 84(4), 11-44.

He, H. and Liu, Z. (2007): Investment-specific technological change, skill accumulation, and wage inequality. *Review of Economic Dynamics,* 11(2), 314-334.

Kiker, B. (1966): The historical roots of the concept of human capital. *Journal of Political Economy*, 74(5), 481-499.

Krusell, P., Ohanian, L., Ríos-Rull, J. and Violante, G. (2000): Capital-skill complementarity and inequality: A macroeconomic analysis. *Econometrica*, 68(5), 1029-1053.

Malley, J. and Woitek, U. (2009): Productivity shocks and aggregate cycles in an estimated endogenous growth model. *CESifo Working Paper Series* 2672.

Mincer, J. (1958): Investment in Human Capital and Personal Income Distribution. *Journal of Political Economy*, 66(4), 281–302.

Lucas, R. (1988): On the mechanics of economic development. *Journal of Monetary Economics*, 22, 3-42.

Schultz, T. (1961): Investment in human capital. *American Economic Review*, 51(1), 1-17.

Schultz, T. (1963): *The economic value of education*. Columbia University Press: New York.

Trostel, P. (1993): The Effect of Taxation on Human Capital. *Journal of Political Economy*, 101(2), 327-350.

Uzawa, H. (1965): Optimum technical change in an aggregate model of economic growth. *International Economic Review*, 6, 18-31.

Chapter 11

Home Production

Introduction

Standard DSGE models divide households' discretionary available time in two parts: work and leisure. The previous chapter introduced education as an additional activity which required time. This chapter focuses on time devoted to activities at home. Certain activities within the home cannot be considered as leisure. Time devoted to cooking, child rearing, house cleaning, etc., cannot be considered as leisure and they represent home production of goods and services produced and consumed by households. Therefore, available discretional time, which is usually defined as total time (24 hours per day) minus sleeping time and personal care time (which is assumed to be 8 hours per day), is now divided into three parts: working time, time spent doing homeworks and leisure.

In this context, households must take an additional decision: how much time to devote to home production, which is also a component of their utility function. We assume that house production is not perfect substitute for market goods and services. Therefore, this setting considers an economy with two productive sectors: the market sector and the homework sector.

In order to study the implications of homework, this chapter introduces these activities in a DSGE model. Examples of DSGE models with home production are Benhabid, Rogerson and Wright (1991) and McGrattan, Rogerson and Wright (1997). The introduction of the household sector increases the explanatory power of the standard DSGE model. One of the main implications is that, households can increase the number of hours devoted to work by decreasing homework time, while keeping leisure constant.

The structure of the rest of this chapter is as follows. Section 2 discusses the concept of home production and its economic implications. Section 3 presents a DSGE model with home production. Section 4 presents the equations of the model and the calibration. Section 5 studies the effects of a productivity shock. Finally, Section 6 ends with some conclusions.

Home Production

Becker's (1965) seminal paper on the theory of the allocation of time demonstrated that there was margin for economic theory to go beyond the traditional work-leisure dichothomy. His analysis extended the traditional decision on the supply of working hours and the demand of leisure to study the optimal distribution of time among the different activities that integrate the latter (composite) good. Taking advantage of this proposal, Gronau (1977) modified Beckers' framework to analyze the production of homework activities, including under this heading those tasks performed by the members of the family either to attend close relatives or to maintain the house – *e.g.* child rearing, house cleaning, etc. In his model, households' time could be devoted to three different uses: working in the market, homework production and leisure, and the household decided how to distribute its time endowment among these activities. Becker's paper, together with other works on the same topic by Gronau (1973a, b), raised the interest of economists in the study of the impact of household activities on overall economic activity (see Gronau, 1997).

Following Reid (1934), we define home production as "those unpaid activities with are carried on, by and for the members, which activities might be replaced by market goods, or paid services, if circumstances such as income, market conditions, and personal inclinations permit the service being delegated to someone outside the household group". Household production activities are not included in the economy activities, since they refer to activities not traded in the market, that is, they do not have market prices. Eisner (1988) estimates that home-produced output is about 20-50% of measured gross national output. However, they are included when individuals buy home work services in the market. As pointed out by Benhabid, Rogerson and Wright (1990), the household sector is large, whether measured in terms of input or output. They report than an average married couple spends 33% or its discretionary time working for paid compensation and 28% working in the home.

Ramey (2008) estimated the time spent in home production during the 20th century. She found that time spent in home production has remained approximately constant over the century but with important changes by gender. Mokyr (2000) calls the absence of a decline in housework during the era of appliance diffusion as the "Cowan Paradox". Cowan (1983) argued that while technological innovations may have greatly reduced the drudgery of housework, they did not decrease the time devoted to it. Greenwood, Seshadri and Yorukoglu (2005) argue that the diffusion of appliances led to a fall in time spent in home production. However, Jones, Manuelli and McGrattan (2003) show that the above result only occurs if the elasticity of substitution between labor and capital in the home production function is sufficiently high.

As shown by Benhabid *et al.* (1990a) and Ríos-Rull (1993), individuals employed in the goods market sector spend much less time working at home than do unemployed people. Additionally, they show that individuals employed with higher wages substitute out of home and into domestic services market production. As pointed out by Benhabid *et al.* (1991) this suggests a very high degree of substitutability between working in the market and doing activities at home and that home production could be an important element in explaining aggregate economic activity.

From a theoretical perspective, some authors have extended the basic framework proposed by Gronau to a macroeconomic context, studying the implications of household productive activities in a dynamic general equilibrium model. For example, Benhabid, Rogerson and Wright (1991), Greenwood and Hercowitz (1991) and McGrattan, Rogerson and Wright (1997) show that real business cycle models with explicit household production sectors perform better than the standard real business cycle model. However, as pointed out by McGrattan *et al.* (1997), the extent of the improvement depends critically on several parameters, including the elasticities of substitution between household and market variables in utility and production functions as well as the stochastic properties of the household and market technologies.

The literature contains a number of works that introduce the field of household goods on a DSGE model to analyze its implications for a variety of topics. Benhabid *et al.* (1991) were the first to develop a DSGE model in which domestic goods were included, comparing the results with the standard model and showing that the explanatory power of the model significantly enhanced. McGrattan *et al.* (1997) develop a DSGE with domestic production and taxes, finding that agents respond to changes in taxes by replacing domestic market activities with non-market activities. Schmitt-Grohé and Uribe (1997) use a model with production of domestic goods to study the effects of balanced-budget rules. Canova and Uribe (1998) develop a two-country version of the model to study the cyclical fluctuations internationally. Perli (1998) discusses in this context the effects of increasing returns on cyclical fluctuations. Finally, Baxter and Jermann (1999) use a model with home production to study the excess volatility of consumption to current income.

The model

This section develops a DSGE model in which discretionary time[1] is decomposed in three parts: working time, leisure and homework. These homeworks activities refer basically to meals, child care, laundry and cleaning, etc. Total consumption is a composite of market goods and services and home production. In this context, households must decide how much time to devote to home production.

Households

The economy is inhabited by a stand-in representative consumer with the following instantaneous utility function:

$$U(C_t, L_t) = \gamma \log(C_t) + (1-\gamma)\log(1 - L_t \qquad (11.1)$$

where C_t is total consumption, L_t is worked hours (either in the market or in home production), that is, non-leisure time, and the parameter γ $(0 < \gamma < 1)$ is the proportion of private consumption to total income.

Total available effective time endowment of the economy is normalized to 1, and is defined as non-sleeping hours of the working-age population. Each household can employ this endowment of time in two different activities (apart from leisure): good market production ($L_{m,t}$) and home work ($L_{h,t}$). Henceforth, leisure is defined as $1 - L_{m,t} - L_{h,t}$, whereas non-leisure time is given by:

$$L_t = L_{m,t} + L_{h,t} \qquad (11.2)$$

Total consumption is composed by consumption of market goods (denoted by the subindex m) and consumption of home work (denoted by the subindex h). It is assumed that total consumption is

[1] As is standard in the literature, discretionary time is defined as total time less sleeping and personal care time.

given by a CES type aggregation function such as:

$$C_t = \left[\omega C_{m,t}^{\eta} + (1-\omega) C_{h,t}^{\eta}\right]^{1/\eta} \tag{11.3}$$

where $C_{m,t}$ is the consumption of goods and services, $C_{hm,t}$ is the consumption of home production and where η is the parameter measuring the willingness of agents to substitute between the two goods, and ω is the proportion of each good in the total consumption.

The parameter η will be key for the relationship between home activities and working. The elasticity of substitution between consumption of market goods and services and consumption of home production is defined as $1/(1-\eta)$. If η is equal to 1, then both goods are perfect substitutes and total consumption is the same of each type of consumption. On the other hand, if $\eta = 0$, total consumption would be a Cobb-Douglas function of both types of goods and the elasticity of substitution would be unitary.

Therefore, the instantaneous utility function can be defined as:

$$U(C_{m,t}, C_{h,t}, L_{m,t}, L_{h,t}) = \gamma \log C_t + (1-\gamma)\log(1 - L_{m,t} - L_{h,t}) \tag{11.4}$$

Consumer's budged constraint states that consumption plus saving, S_t, cannot exceed the sum of labor and capital rental income:

$$C_{m,t} + S_t = W_t L_{m,t} + R_t K_t \tag{11.5}$$

where W_t is the wage, R_t is the rental price of capital and K_t is the physical capital stock.

Physical capital stock evolves as:

$$K_{t+1} = (1-\delta_K) K_t + I_t \tag{11.6}$$

where δ is the physical capital depreciation rate, I_t is gross investment. Assuming that $I_t = S_t$, and substituting in the budget constraint, we obtain:

$$C_{m,t} + K_{t+1} = W_t L_{m,t} + (R_t + 1 - \delta) K_t \tag{11.7}$$

The problem to be solved by households is to choose the sequences of $\{C_{m,t}, C_{h,t}, L_{m,t}, L_{h,t}, I_t\}$ so as to maximize:

$$\underset{\{C_t, L_{m,t}, L_{h,t}, I_t\}_t^{\infty}}{Max} \mathscr{L} = \sum_{t=0}^{\infty} \beta^t \left[\gamma \log C_t + (1-\gamma) \log(1 - L_{m,t} - L_{h,t})\right] \tag{11.8}$$

subject to the budget constraint and the technological constraint for home production to be defined later, given the initial capital stock K_0 and where $\beta \in (0,1)$, is the discount factor.

The goods market sector

As pointed out before, we consider a two-sector model: a final good sector and a household work services sector. The problem of the firm in the commodities market sector is to find optimal values for the utilization of labor and capital. The stand-in firm is represented by a standard Cobb-Douglas production function. The production of final output, Y requires labor services, $L_{m,t}$, and capital, K_t. Goods and factors markets are assumed to be perfectly competitive. The firm rents capital and hires labor to maximize period profits, taking public inputs and factor prices as given. The technology exhibits a constant returns to production factors and thus the profits are zero in equilibrium. The technology is given by:

$$Y_t - A_t K_t^{\alpha} {L_{m,t}}^{1-\alpha} \tag{11.9}$$

where A_t is a measure of total-factor productivity, α is the private capital share of output. We assume that A_t is the aggregate commodities market sector productivity shock which follows a stochastic log-linear autoregressive process with the disturbance term ε_t^A assumed to be normally distributed with mean zero and variance $\sigma_{\varepsilon_A}^2$.

$$\log A_t = (1-\rho_A)\overline{A} + \rho_A \log A_{t-1} + \varepsilon_t^A \tag{11.10}$$

The firms decision problem can be defined as a static maximization problem:

$$\max_{K_t, L_t} \left[A_t K_t^{\alpha} {L_{m,t}}^{1-\alpha} - R_t K_t - W_t L_{m,t}\right] \tag{11.11}$$

First order conditions are given by:

$$\frac{\partial \Pi_t}{\partial K_t} : R_t - \alpha A_t K_t^{\alpha-1} L_{m,t}^{1-\alpha} = 0 \tag{11.12}$$

$$\frac{\partial \Pi_t}{\partial L_t} : W_t - (1-\alpha) A_t K_t^{\alpha} L_{m,t}^{-\alpha} = 0 \tag{11.13}$$

From the above expressions, we obtain the following equilibrium conditions for the price of each input:

$$R_t K_t = \alpha Y_t$$

$$W_t L_{m,t} = (1-\alpha) Y_t$$

Notice that, using this description of the goods market sector, the measurement of the total output of the economy is the standard, where only market production is considered and home production is not included.

Home production sector

It is assumed that the production function for home activities is the following:

$$C_{h,t} = B_t L_{h,t}^{\theta} \tag{11.14}$$

where $0 < \theta < 1$, that is, assuming decreasing returns. We consider a labor intensive specification for the production of home work. Home production must be consumed by the households that produce them. McGrattan *et al.* (1997) use a CES function for the home production technology, where physical capital is an additional input to time. In this case, a fraction of total capital is used in the home production sector.

We additionally interpret B_t as a homework productivity shock. As in the case of the good market sector, we assume that it follows a stochastic log-linear autoregressive process with the disturbance term u_t^B assumed to be normally distributed with mean zero and variance $\sigma_{\varepsilon_B}^2$.

$$\log B_t = (1-\rho_B)\overline{B} + \rho_B \log B_{t-1} + u_t^B \tag{11.15}$$

Household's maximization problem

The Lagrangian function associated to the households' maximization problem is defined as:

$$\underset{\{C_t,L_{m,t},L_{h,t},I_t\}_t^\infty}{Max} \mathcal{L} = \sum_{t=0}^{\infty} \beta^t \left\{ \begin{array}{c} \gamma \log \left[\omega C_{m,t}^{\eta} + (1-\omega) C_{h,t}^{\eta} \right]^{1/\eta} \\ +(1-\gamma)\log(1 - L_{m,t} - L_{h,t}) \\ -\lambda_t \left[\begin{array}{c} C_{m,t} + K_{t+1} - W_t L_{m,t} \\ -(R_t + 1 - \delta) K_t \end{array} \right] \\ -\zeta \left[C_{h,t} - B_t L_{h,t}^{\theta} \right] \end{array} \right\}$$

Corresponding first order conditions are:

$$\frac{\partial \mathcal{L}}{\partial C_{m,t}} : \frac{\gamma \omega C_{m,t}^{\eta-1}}{\left[\omega C_{m,t}^{\eta} + (1-\omega) C_{h,t}^{\eta}\right]} - \lambda_t = 0 \tag{11.16}$$

$$\frac{\partial \mathcal{L}}{\partial C_{h,t}} : \frac{\gamma (1-\omega) C_{h,t}^{\eta-1}}{\left[\omega C_{m,t}^{\eta} + (1-\omega) C_{h,t}^{\eta}\right]} - \zeta_t = 0 \tag{11.17}$$

$$\frac{\partial \mathcal{L}}{\partial L_{m,t}} : \frac{(1-\gamma)}{\overline{H} - L_{m,t} - L_{h,t}} - \lambda_t W_t = 0 \tag{11.18}$$

$$\frac{\partial \mathcal{L}}{\partial L_{h,t}} : \frac{(1-\gamma)}{\overline{H} - L_{m,t} - L_{h,t}} - \zeta_t \theta B_t L_{h,t}^{\theta-1} = 0 \tag{11.19}$$

$$\frac{\partial \mathcal{L}}{\partial K_t} : \beta^t \left[\lambda_t (R_t + 1 - \delta))\right] - \lambda_{t-1} \beta^{t-1} = 0 \tag{11.20}$$

From the first FOC, expression (11.16), we find the shadow price for market goods:

$$\lambda_t = \frac{\gamma \omega C_{m,t}^{\eta-1}}{\left[\omega C_{m,t}^{\eta} + (1-\omega) C_{h,t}^{\eta}\right]}$$

The Lagrange parameters associated to home production (the shadow price of goods produced at home), can be derived from the second FOC, expression (11.17):

$$\zeta_t = \frac{\gamma (1-\omega) C_{h,t}^{\eta-1}}{\left[\omega C_{m,t}^{\eta} + (1-\omega) C_{h,t}^{\eta}\right]}$$

Combining expressions (11.16) and (11.18) we obtain the equilibrium condition for time devoted to working in the market:

$$\frac{(1-\gamma)}{\overline{H}-L_{m,t}-L_{h,t}} = \frac{\gamma\omega C_{m,t}^{\eta-1}}{\left[\omega C_{m,t}^{\eta}+(1-\omega)C_{h,t}^{\eta}\right]} W_t \tag{11.21}$$

Next, combining expressions (11.16) and (11.20), we find the equilibrium condition that equates the marginal rate of consumption to the rate of return of investment:

$$\beta \frac{\gamma\omega C_{m,t}^{\eta-1}}{\left[\omega C_{m,t}^{\eta}+(1-\omega)C_{h,t}^{\eta}\right]}(R_t+1-\delta) = \frac{\gamma\omega C_{m,t-1}^{\eta-1}}{\left[\omega C_{m,t-1}^{\eta}+(1-\omega)C_{h,t-1}^{\eta}\right]} \tag{11.22}$$

Finally, combining expressions (11.17) and (11.19) we find the equilibrium condition for time devoted to homework activities:

$$\frac{(1-\gamma)}{\overline{H}-L_{m,t}-L_{h,t}} = \frac{\gamma(1-\omega)C_{h,t}^{\eta-1}}{\left[\omega C_{m,t}^{\eta}+(1-\omega)C_{h,t}^{\eta}\right]} \theta B L_{h,t}^{\theta-1}$$

Equilibrium of the model

In this model households have to decide what proportion of their total time endowment is devoted to work in the market and how much of that time is devoted to home production. Both time decisions are interrelated and households can substitute home activities by working without affecting leisure. Given the first-order conditions for households and firms, the equilibrium of the model economy is given by the following static equation that determines the allocation of time:

$$\frac{\gamma(1-\omega)C_{h,t}^{\eta-1}}{\left[\omega C_{m,t}^{\eta}+(1-\omega)C_{h,t}^{\eta}\right]} \theta B L_{h,t}^{\theta-1} = \frac{\gamma\omega C_{m,t}^{\eta-1}}{\left[\omega C_{m,t}^{\eta}+(1-\omega)C_{h,t}^{\eta}\right]} (1-\alpha) A_t K_t^{\alpha} L_{m,t}^{-\alpha} \tag{11.23}$$

and one additional dynamic equation determining the optimal consumption path:

$$\beta(\alpha A_t K_t^{\alpha-1} L_{m,t}^{1-\alpha} + 1 - \delta) = \frac{C_{m,t-1}^{\eta-1}\left[\omega C_{m,t}^{\eta} + (1-\omega)C_{h,t}^{\eta}\right]}{C_{m,t}^{\eta-1}\left[\omega C_{m,t-1}^{\eta} + (1-\omega)C_{h,t-1}^{\eta}\right]} \tag{11.24}$$

Equations of the model and calibration

The competitive equilibrium for this economy is defined by a set of eleven equations, representing the sequences of the endogenous variables, Y_t, $C_{m,t}$, $C_{h,t}$, I_t, K_t, $L_{m,t}$, $L_{h,t}$, R_t, W_t and two technologies, A_t and B_t, which are assumed to be endogenous and to follow an autorregressive process of order 1. This set of equations is the following:

$$\frac{(1-\gamma)}{\overline{H} - L_{m,t} - L_{h,t}} = \frac{\gamma\omega C_{m,t}^{\eta-1}}{\left[\omega C_{m,t}^{\eta} + (1-\omega)C_{h,t}^{\eta}\right]} W_t \tag{11.25}$$

$$\beta \frac{\gamma\omega C_{m,t+1}^{\eta-1}}{\left[\omega C_{m,t+1}^{\eta} + (1-\omega)C_{h,t+1}^{\eta}\right]}(R_{t+1} + 1 - \delta) = \frac{\gamma\omega C_{m,t}^{\eta-1}}{\left[\omega C_{m,t}^{\eta} + (1-\omega)C_{h,t}^{\eta}\right]} \tag{11.26}$$

$$\frac{(1-\gamma)}{\overline{H} - L_{m,t} - L_{h,t}} = \frac{\gamma(1-\omega) C_{h,t}^{\eta-1}}{\left[\omega C_{m,t}^{\eta} + (1-\omega)C_{h,t}^{\eta}\right]} \theta B L_{h,t}^{\theta-1} \tag{11.27}$$

$$Y_t = C_t + I_t \tag{11.28}$$

$$Y_t = A_t K_t^{\alpha} L_{m,t}^{1-\alpha} \tag{11.29}$$

$$C_{h,t} = B_t L_{h,t}^{\theta} \tag{11.30}$$

$$K_{t+1} = (1-\delta)K_t + I_t \tag{11.31}$$

$$W_t = (1-\alpha) A_t K_t^{\alpha} L_{m,t}^{-\alpha} \tag{11.32}$$

$$R_t = \alpha A_t K_t^{\alpha-1} L_{m,t}^{1-\alpha} \tag{11.33}$$

$$\ln A_t = (1-\rho_A)\ln \overline{A} + \rho_A \ln A_{t-1} + \varepsilon_t^A \tag{11.34}$$

$$\ln B_t = (1-\rho_B)\ln \overline{B} + \rho_B \ln B_{t-1} + \varepsilon_t^B \tag{11.35}$$

Table 11.1: Calibrated parameters

Parameter	Definition	Value
α	Capital technological parameter	0.350
β	Discount factor	0.970
γ	Consumption-leisure preference parameter	0.400
δ	Capital depreciation rate	0.060
η	Goods substitution parameter	0.800
ω	Consumption of market goods proportion	0.450
θ	Home production productivity parameter	0.800
ρ_A	TFP autoregressive parameter	0.950
σ_A	TFP standard deviation	0.010
ρ_B	Home productivity autoregressive parameter	0.950
σ_B	Home productivity standard deviation	0.010

To calibrate the model, values must be assigned to the following set of parameters:

$$\Omega = \{\alpha, \beta, \gamma, \delta, \eta, \omega, \theta, \rho_A, \sigma_A, \rho_B, \sigma_B\}$$

The model contains 5 additional parameters to be calibrated. Table 11.1 shows the calibrated parameters to be used in the simulation of the model. In principle, there is no statistical information about the parameters of preferences and technological factors affecting the production and consumption of home produced goods. Rupert, Rogerson and Wright (1995) use micro data to try to determine these parameters.

Benhabid *et al.* (1991) used a value of $\eta = 0.8$. McGrattan *et al.* (1997) estimated values of $\omega = 0.414$ and $\eta = 0.429$. Here we assume that $\eta = 0.8$ following Benhabid *et al.* (1991) and $\omega = 0.45$, following McGrattan *et al.* (1997). More difficult is the calibration of the tech nological parameter associated to the house production function. McGrattan *et al.* (1997) used a house production function with two inputs: hours and capital, so that its parameters are not directly applicable to our model. We arbitrarily set $\theta = 0.8$, that is, decreasing returns. Finally, we assume that the parameters of the autoregressive process for productivity in the domestic sector are the same as the process of the overall productivity of the factors , that is, assume that $\rho_B = 0.95$ and $\sigma_B = 0.01$.

Table 11.2 shows the steady state values of the calibrated model

Table 11.2: Steady state values

Variable	Value	Ratio to $\overline{Y}$
$\overline{Y}$	0.64770	1.000
$\overline{C}_m$	0.49811	0.769
$\overline{C}_h$	0.31082	-
$\overline{I}$	0.14958	0.231
$\overline{K}$	2.49315	3.844
$\overline{L}_m$	0.31345	-
$\overline{L}_h$	0.23208	-
$\overline{R}$	0.09092	-
$\overline{W}$	1.34312	-
$\overline{A}$	1.00000	-
$\overline{B}$	1.00000	-

economy. Several aspects are highlighted. First, we find that the ratio of consumption of market goods on the market output is 77%, representing a saving rate at steady state of 23%, while the capital/output ratio is 3.8. These values are exactly the same as those that would result in the model without domestic sector, so its inclusion does not alter the steady state of the market sector of the economy.

Second, we can observe what is the distribution of time at steady state for market working activities and home production activities. With the calibrated parameters we find that the proportion of time devoted to market working is 0.31, while the proportion of time spent on housework is 0.23, with the remaining time (0.46) left for leisure. As expected time spent at home activities is less than the time spent working in the market, but still represents a significant proportion of total available time.

Total Factor Productivity shock

This section studies the dynamic effects on the economy of an aggregate productivity shock when homework activities are taken into account. The model developed above has two productivity shocks: a productivity shock in the production of good market sector and productivity shock in the home production sector.

We consider the case of a positive aggregate productivity shock in the goods sector. The summary of results are shown in Figure 11.1. A simple inspection of impulse-response function reveals that the impact of the shock on the economy is superior to that obtained in a context without home production sector.

The productivity shock causes an increase in output, as expected. However, the rise in output is greater than in the standard model without home production. The explanation of this effect can be found in the reaction of labor to the shock. The agents react to the shock by reducing time devoted to homework and increasing time devoted to working. In this setting, the substitution effects in the allocation of time are not restricted to labor-leisure but also to time devoted to homework. The rise in wages causes a rise in working hours just by reducing time devoted to homework activities while keeping leisure almost constant. This implies that the aggregate productivity shock has a negative impact on the consumption of goods and services produced at home.

In summary, the introduction of home production in the standard DSGE model amplifies the effects of a productivity shock on economic activity. This amplification will depend on the degree of substitution between working hours and time devoted to home activities, or equivalently, to the degree of substitution between market goods and household goods.

Conclusions

This chapter considers home production in a DSGE model. Available time is divided into three components: leisure, working time and time spent on houseworks. This leads to a two sectors model: a market sector and a home production sector. A differentiating characteristic between both sectors is that there is no market for the home production sector and home goods and services can only be consumed if produced by the households themselves.

Using this theoretical framework we have studied the effects of an aggregate productivity shock in the market sector. The main result derives from the substitution between time devoted to the production of home goods and services and working time in the market. In this setting, households can increase working time while keeping leisure constant, at the cost of reducing the consumption of home produced goods and services. A similar exercise can be done considering a productivity shock in the home production sector.

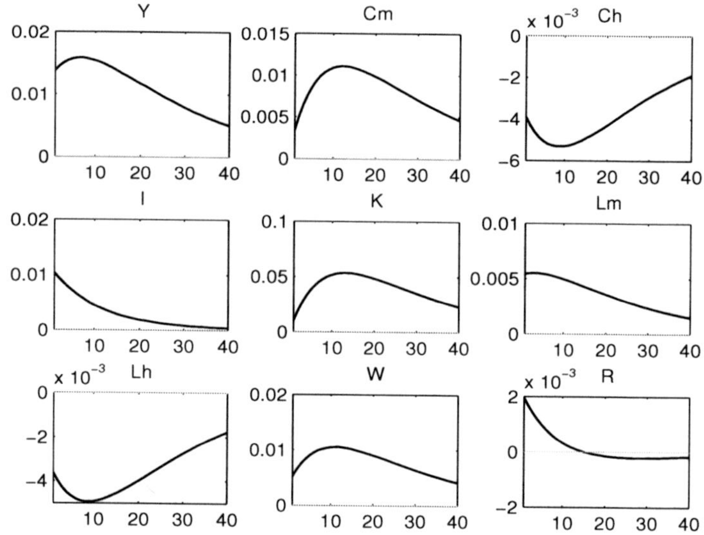

Figure 11.1: TFP in the goods market with home production

Additional interesting exercises can be done using this framework. For instance, we can study the effects of a productivity shock to the home production function. Another interesting exercise is to define a home production function with two inputs, time and capital, to study how ISTC shocks to the capital at home affects the dynamics of the variables.

Appendix A: Dynare code

The Dynare code for the model developed in this chapter, named *model11.mod*, is the following:

```
// Model 11.  Home production
// Dynare code
// File:  model10.mod
// José L. Torres.  University of Málaga (Spain)
// Endogenous variables
var Y, Cm, Ch, I, K, Lm, Lh, W, R, A, B;
// Exogenous variables
varexo e, u;
```

```
// Parameters
parameters alpha, beta, delta, gamma, omega, eta,
   theta, rho1, rho2;
// Calibration
alpha = 0.35;
beta  = 0.97;
delta = 0.06;
gamma = 0.40;
omega = 0.45;
eta   = 0.80;
thota = 0.80;
rho1  = 0.95;
rho2  = 0.95;
// Equations of the model economy
model;
gamma*omega*(Cm^(eta-1))/(omega*Cm^eta
   +(1-omega)*Ch^eta)=(1-gamma)/(W*(1-Lm-Lh));
gamma*(1-omega)*(Ch^(eta-1))/(omega*Cm^eta
   +(1-omega)*Ch^eta)=(1-gamma)/(B*(1-Lm-Lh));
((Cm^(eta-1))/(omega*Cm^eta+(1-omega)*Ch^eta))
   /((Cm(+1)^(eta-1))/(omega*Cm(+1)^eta
   +(1-omega)*Ch(+1)^eta))=beta*(R(+1)+1-delta);
Y = A*(K(-1)^alpha)*(Lm^(1-alpha));
Ch = B*Lh^theta;
K = (Y-Cm)+(1-delta)*K(-1);
I = Y-Cm;
W = (1-alpha)*A*(K(-1)^alpha)*(Lm^(-alpha));
R = alpha*A*(K(-1)^(alpha-1))*(Lm^(1-alpha));
log(A) = rho1*log(A(-1))+e;
log(B) = rho2*log(B(-1))+u;
end;
// Initial values
initval;
Y = 1;
Cm = 0.75;
Ch = 0.2;
Lm = 0.3;
Lh = 0.1;
K = 3.5;
I = 0.25;
W = (1-alpha)*Y/Lm;
```

```
R = alpha*Y/K;
A = 1;
B = 1;
e = 0;
u = 0;
end;
 // Steady state
steady;
// Blanchard-Kahn conditions
check;
// Disturbance analysis
shocks;
var e; stderr 0.01;
var u; stderr 0.01;
end;
 // Stochastic simulation
stoch_simul;
```

Bibliography

Baxter, M. and Jermann, U. (1999): Household production and the excess sensitivity of consumption to current income. *American Economic Review*, 89(4), 902-920.

Becker, G.S. (1965): A Theory of the Allocation of Time. *The Economic Journal*, 75(299), 493-517.

Benhabid, J., Rogerson, R. and Wright, R. (1990a): Homework in Macroeconomics I: Basic theory. *Working Paper n. 3344, NBER.*

Benhabid, J., Rogerson, R. and Wright, R. (1990b): Homework in Macroeconomics II: Aggregate fluctuations. *Working Paper n. 3344, NBER.*

Benhabid, J., Rogerson, R. and Wright, R. (1991): Homework in Macroeconomics: Household production and aggregate fluctuations. *Journal of Political Economy*, 99(6), 1166-1187.

Canova, F. and Uribe, A. (1908): International business cycles, financial markets and household production. *Journal of Economic Dynamics and Control*, 22(4), 545 572.

Campbell, J. and Sydney, L. (2001): Elasticities of substitution in real business cycle models with home production. *Journal of Money, Credit and Banking*, 33(4), 847-875.

Chiappori, P. (1988): Rational household labor supply. *Econometrica*, 56(1), 63-90.

Chiappori, P. (1992): Collective labor supply and welfare. *Journal of Political Economy*, 100, 437-467.

Cowan, R. (1983): *More work for mother: The ironies of household technology from the open hearth to the microwage.* New York: Basic Books.

Eichenbaum, M. and Hansen, L. (1990): Estimating models with intertemporal substitution using aggregate time series data. *Journal of Business and Economic Statistics*, 8(1), 53-69.

Eisner, R. (1988): Extended Accounts for National Income and Product. *Journal of Economic Literature*, 26(4), 1611-1684.

Greenwood, J., and Hercowitz, Z. (1991): The allocation of capital and time over the business cycle. *Journal of Political Economy*, 99(6), 1188-1214.

Greenwood, J., Seshadri, A. and Yorukoglu, M. (2005): Engines of liberation. *Review of Economic Studies*, 72(1), 109-133.

Greenwood, J., Seshadri, A. and Vandenbroucke, G. (2005): The baby boom and baby bust. *American Economic Review*, 95(1), 183-207.

Gronau, R. (1973a): The intrafamily allocation of time: The value of the housewives' time. *American Economic Review*, 63(4), 634-651

Gronau, R. (1973b): The effect of children on the housewife's value of time. *Journal of Political Economy*, 81(2), S168-99, Part II.

Gronau, R. (1977): Leisure, home production, and work-The theory of the allocation of time revisited. *Journal of Political Economy*, 85(6), 1099-1123.

Gronau, R. (1997): The theory of home production: The past ten years. *Journal of Labor Economics*, 15(2), 197-205.

Gronau, R. (2006): Home production and the macro economy: Some lessons from Pollak and Wachter and from transition Russia. *NBER Working Paper* No. W12287.

Hersch, J. and Stratton, L. (2994): Housework, wages, and the division of housework time for employed spouses. *American Economic Review*, 94(2), 120-125.

Jones, L., Manuelli, R. and McGrattan, E. (2003): Why are married women working so much? *Federal Reserve Bank of Minneapolis Staff Report* 317.

McGrattan, E., Rogerson, R. and Wright, R. (1997): An equilibrium model of the business cycle with household production and fiscal policy. *International Economic Review*, 38(2), 267-290.

Mokyr, J. (2000): Why was there more work for mother? Technological change and the household, 1880-1930. *Journal of Economic History*, 60(1), 1-40.

Perli, R. (1998): Indeterminacy, home production, and the business cycle: A calibrated analysis. Journal of Monetary Economics, 41, 105-125.

Ramey, V.A. (2008): Time spent in home production in the 20th century: New estimates from old data. *NBER Working Paper* n. 13985.

Reid, M. (1934): *Economics of household production.* New York: John Wiley & Sons.

Ríos-Rull, J. (1993): Working in the market, working at home, and the acquisition of skills: A general equilibrium approach. *American Economic Review*, 83(4), 893-907.

Schmitt-Grohé, S., and Uribe, M. (1997): Balanced-budget rules, distortionary taxes, and aggregate instability. *Journal of Political Economy*, 105(5), 976-1000.

Part VI

Imperfect competition

Chapter 12

Monopolistic Competition

Introduction

In the models developed in previous chapters we have assumed the existence of perfect competition in goods and input markets. This is a central assumption of the neoclassical approach. This resulted in market prices that are equal to the marginal cost of production, zero profits for firms and a price for the productive factors equal to their marginal productivity. This is a key assumption of the standard neoclassical model driving the economy to the so-called competitive general equilibrium. In this chapter we relax the perfect competition assumption, introducing imperfect competition in the DSGE model, which is a fundamental part of New Keynesian models.

Here we consider the existence of imperfect competition in the production sector (imperfect competition can also be introduced in the labor market). This change does not alter the structure of the model in relation to the behavior of households, but represents a major change to the structure of the production sector of the economy. Now the problem for the firms becomes more complex and it is necessary to introduce two types of goods: a final good and a differentiated intermediate good produced in a monopolistic competition market environment. Imperfect competition occurs in the intermediate goods sector. Differentiated intermediate goods are combined later into a final good, which is traded in an environment of perfect competition.

The final structure of the model is virtually identical to the standard DSGE model, except that now the prices of production factors depend on the elasticity of substitution between differentiated goods, reflecting the market power of firms to set prices. Thus, we find that both wages and the real interest rate would be lower compared to those obtained in the standard model. This is due to the existence of a mark-up in the price of goods relative to its marginal cost of production. A result of the lower price given to the factors of production, will also be their diminished use, which will result in a lower level of production. Indeed, in this framework we depart from the efficiency in the allocation of resources that results from a competitive environment.

The structure of the rest of the chapter is as follows. Section 2 briefly reviews the literature about monopolistic competition in DSGE models. Section 3 presents a simple DSGE model with monopolistic competition in the goods market. Section 4 shows the building block equations of the model, the calibration of the parameters and the steady state values. Section 5 studies the effects of an aggregate productivity shock. The chapter ends with some relevant conclusions.

Monopolistic Competition

In the basic DSGE model a very simple structure for the production sector of the economy is assumed: A technology with constant returns to scale and perfect competition in both final goods and factors markets. In this context, there is no market power affecting the determination of prices, which otherwise are perfectly flexible, so that the price of the final good is equal to its marginal cost of production. The result is a competitive equilibrium in the markets for goods, capital and labor, where the prices of the production factors are equal to their marginal productivity. In this setting, the resource allocation is efficient, since the marginal rate of substitution is equal to the marginal rate of transformation.

However, empirical evidence shows the existence of mark-ups in the goods and services markets, which means that the prices of these goods are higher than their production cost. In this sense, Basu and Fernald (1997) study the deviations from perfect competition and constant returns to scale in the U.S. economy using data for 34 industries, finding that deviations from the constant returns to scale hypothesis and differences between goods prices and their marginal cost are very small. Hall (1988) notes the existence of prices higher than marginal costs for the U.S. economy, derived from the fact that the observed variations in employment are smaller than the observed changes in production prices. This finding could also explain why productivity is pro-cyclical.

Imperfect competition is a central assumption in models with sticky prices. The introduction of imperfect competition in DSGE models is usually done by assuming an environment of monopolistic competition, although there are examples of oligopolistic structures as the model developed by Rotemberg and Woodford (1992). Most of these developments are based on the specification proposed by Dixit and Stiglitz (1977), in which there is a continuous (or a discrete number) of different goods. This results in an environment in which each firm has market power to set the price of the good it produces. These differentiated goods are then aggregated into a single final good, which is consumed by the households.

Imperfect competition is one of the pillars of the so-called New Keynesian economy. New Keynesian DSGE model considers the existence of market power in determining the price level, which allows the introduction of nominal rigidities. New Keynesian DSGE models were initially developed by Rotemberg (1982), Mankiw (1985), Svensson (1986) and Blanchard and Kiyotaki (1987), Rotemberg and Woodford (1997), among others. Another important feature of New Keynesian models is that labor can also be a differentiated product among households. This implies that households have some market power when setting wages, which in turn enables the introduction of rigidities in the wage determination process. Examples are Christiano and Eichenbaum (1992), and Canzoneri, Cumby and Diba (2005).

In general there are two alternative ways to introduce monopolistic competition in DSGE models. First, we can assume that firms sell directly each differentiated good to the households and they aggregate the intermediate goods in a final good through a CES function. The second option consists in assuming that each firm sells the differentiated good to a final good producer. In this case each firm produces an intermediate good that the final producer uses to produce the final good via a CES function. In each case, an additional assumption is that demand is given. The standard in the literature is to assume that the goods are intermediate and become a final good by only one firm. This is also the option chosen here.

If aggregation occurs in the productive sector, the existence of an aggregator firm is assumed, which determines the quantity produced of each differentiated good, using them to produce a final composite good to be sold to consumers, taking as given the prices for intermediate goods. This firm takes decisions on a competitive environment. The model is solved in two states. In the first stage firms determine the profit-maximizing price of the differentiated good they produce and therefore how much they will produce. In the second stage firms determine the quantity of inputs that will be used to produce the quantity determined in the first step to minimize costs. In the case we would like to suppose aggregation is done by the households and, the equivalent problem is also solved in two stages. In the first stage, the consumer chooses the optimum aggregate consumption as in a standard maximization problem. In the second stage, consumers choose the level of consumption of each differentiated good by solving a cost minimization problem.

The introduction of monopolistic competition will lead to the price of goods that exceeds their marginal cost of production, so there would be a mark-up that reflects the market power of firms. As a consequence, relative prices of production factors are lower than those obtained in a competitive environment, although in this setting factors of production are already traded in a competitive market. Therefore, monopolistic competition will create an inefficient situation with respect to the use of the factors of production, which in turn also lead to an inefficient situation in terms of total output of the economy. In fact, the mechanism through which imperfect competition affects the economy is the introduction of distortions on the price of production factors.

The model

The DSGE monopolistic competition model developed here keeps unchanged the households block, but incorporates a more complex analysis of the productive sector of the economy. The model structure is as follows. We assume that a single final good and a continuum of intermediate goods are produced, indexed by the subscript j, where j is distributed in the unit interval, $j \in [0,1]$. The final good is constructed from the aggregation of intermediate goods in a perfectly competitive environment and can be used by consumers either in consumption or investment. By contrast there is monopolistic competition in the intermediate goods market. Thus, each intermediate good is produced by a single monopolistic firm, which has market power to set the price of the good they produce.

Households

The economy is inhabited by an infinitely lived, representative household which has time-separable preferences, represented by the following instantaneous utility function:

$$U(C_t, 1 - L_t) = \gamma \log C_t + (1-\gamma)\log(1-L_t) \tag{12.1}$$

where C_t is consumption of goods and services and leisure is defined as $1 - L_t$, where the available discretionary time has been normalized to 1, that is, leisure is defined as the discretionary time less working time, L_t. The parameter γ $(0 < \gamma < 1)$ represents the proportion of consumption over total income.

The problem faced by the stand-in consumer is to maximize the value of her lifetime utility given by:

$$Max_{\{C_t, L_t\}_{t=0}^{\infty}} \sum_{t=0}^{\infty} \beta^t \left(\gamma \log C_t + (1-\gamma)\log(1-L_t)\right) \tag{12.2}$$

subject to the budget constraint:

$$C_t + S_t = W_t L_t + R_t K_t \tag{12.3}$$

where S_t is saving, W_t is the wage, R_t is the rental rate of capital and K_t is the physical capital stock.

Physical capital stock evolves according to:

$$K_{t+1} = (1-\delta) K_t + I_t \tag{12.4}$$

where δ is the depreciation rate and where I_t is gross investment. By assuming that $I_t = S_t$ and substituting the capital stock accumulation equation in the budget constraint, we find:

$$C_t + K_{t+1} = W_t L_t + (R_t + 1 - \delta) K_t \tag{12.5}$$

where K_0, is the initial capital stock which is assumed to be given and where $\beta \in (0,1)$ is the consumer's discount factor.

The Lagrangian problem to be solved by households is to choose C_t, L_t, and I_t so as to maximize:

$$\max_{(C_t, I_t, L_t)} \mathscr{L} = \sum_{t=0}^{\infty} \beta^t \left\{ \begin{array}{c} \gamma \log C_t + (1-\gamma)\log(1-L_t) \\ -\lambda_t \left[C_t + K_{t+1} - W_t L_t - (R_t + 1 - \delta) K_t\right] \end{array} \right\} \tag{12.6}$$

First order conditions for the household maximization problem

are:

$$\frac{\partial \mathcal{L}}{\partial C_t}: \gamma \frac{1}{C_t} - \lambda_t = 0 \tag{12.7}$$

$$\frac{\partial \mathcal{L}}{\partial L_t}: -(1-\gamma)\frac{1}{1-L_t} + \lambda_t W_t = 0 \tag{12.8}$$

$$\frac{\partial \mathcal{L}}{\partial K_t}: \beta^t \lambda_t [R_t + 1 - \delta] - \lambda_{t-1}\beta^{t-1} = 0 \tag{12.9}$$

where $\beta^t \lambda_t$ is the Lagrange multiplier assigned to the budget constraint at time t. Combining equations (12.7) and (12.8) we obtain the equilibrium condition that equal the marginal disutility of an additional hour working with the marginal utility of consumption generated by the additional working time:

$$\frac{1}{1-L_t} = \frac{\gamma}{(1-\gamma)} \frac{W_t}{C_t} \tag{12.10}$$

Combining expression (12.7) with expression (12.9) yields,

$$\frac{C_t}{C_{t-1}} = \beta [R_t + 1 - \delta] \tag{12.11}$$

the equilibrium condition that equates the marginal rate of consumption to the rate of return of investment.

The firms

What distinguishes between a DSGE model with perfect competition and a DSGE model with imperfect competition is the structure of the production sector of the economy. Let us assume the existence of imperfect competition. In this case, the productive sector of the economy will be divided into two parts: a sector that produces intermediate goods and a sector that produces the final good. The intermediate good sector would consist of a large number of firms, each producing a differentiated good (monopolistic competition). Firms now have to decide what amount of production factors will hire and the price of the goods they produce. In the final good sector we have a unique firm that aggregates intermediate goods into a single composite good that is to be consumed (or saved) by the agents (perfect competition). Moreover, we will assume that the market for production factors remains competitive.

Final good production sector

First, we describe the behaviour of the final good sector of the economy. Final good is produced by a representative firm in a competitive environment. This firm produces the final good by aggregating the continuing of intermediate goods using the following technology:

$$Y_t = \left[\int_0^1 Y_{j,t}^{\frac{\xi-1}{\xi}}\, dj\right]^{\frac{\xi}{\xi-1}} \tag{12.12}$$

where $\xi > 1$ is the elasticity of substitution across intermediate goods. This method of aggregation of intermediate goods is what is called the Dixit-Stiglitz aggregator. This parameter represents the mark-up in the goods market. We can assume either that this parameter is a constant or a stochastic component of the model. For instance, Smets and Wouters (2007) assume that the parameter representing the elasticity of substitution across intermediate goods is stochastic and reflects a shock on inflation, with the following process $\xi_t = \xi + v_t$, where $v_t \sim N(0, \sigma_v)$. Here we assume that this parameter is a constant.

The firm maximizes profits subject to the production function given by (12.12), and taking as given the prices of intermediate goods, $P_{j,t}$, and the price of the composite final good, P_t. Therefore, the maximization problem for the representative firm in the final good sector can be defined as:

$$\max_{Y_{j,t}} \Pi_t = P_t Y_t - \int_0^1 P_{j,t} Y_{j,t} dj \tag{12.13}$$

where profits are defined as the difference between total income by selling the final good and total cost by the use of the intermediate goods.

By substituting the technology of aggregation given by expression (12.12), yields:

$$\max_{Y_{j,t}} \Pi_t = P_t \left[\int_0^1 Y_{j,t}^{\frac{\xi-1}{\xi}}\, dj\right]^{\frac{\xi}{\xi-1}} - \int_0^1 P_{j,t} Y_{j,t} dj \tag{12.14}$$

First order conditions for each intermediate good j are given by:

$$\frac{\partial \Pi_t}{\partial Y_{j,t}} : P_t \frac{\xi}{\xi - 1} \left[\int_0^1 Y_{j,t}^{\frac{\xi-1}{\xi}} dj \right]^{\frac{\xi}{\xi-1}-1} \frac{\xi - 1}{\xi} Y_{j,t}^{\frac{\xi-1}{\xi}-1} - P_{j,t} = 0 \qquad \forall j$$

and solving results:

$$P_t \left[\int_0^1 Y_{j,t}^{\frac{\xi-1}{\xi}} dj \right]^{\frac{\xi}{\xi-1}-1} Y_{j,t}^{\frac{\xi-1}{\xi}-1} = P_{j,t} \qquad \forall j \tag{12.15}$$

Dividing the first order conditions for two types of intermediate goods j and i, and integrating over all intermediate goods, yields:

$$\int_0^1 P_{j,t} Y_{j,t} dj = P_{i,t} Y_{i,t}^{\frac{1}{\xi}} \int_0^1 Y_{j,t}^{\frac{\xi-1}{\xi}} dj = P_{i,t} Y_{i,t}^{\frac{1}{\xi}} Y_{j,t}^{\frac{\xi-1}{\xi}} \tag{12.16}$$

Given our assumption of perfect competition in the final good sector, profits are zero, $\Pi_t = 0$, and using (12.13), we arrive to:

$$P_t Y_t = \int_0^1 P_{j,t} Y_{j,t} dj \tag{12.17}$$

Solving the above expression we obtain that:

$$Y_t = \left(\frac{P_t}{P_{j,t}} \right)^{\xi} Y_{j,t} \qquad \forall j$$

The above expression implies that the demand of intermediate good j is a decreasing function of its relative price and an increasing function of the production of the final good. The assumption that there is perfect competition in the final goods market, allows us to derive the price of the final good. Integrating the above expression and imposing the production function of the final good, we obtain the relationship between the price of the final good and the intermediate good price as:

$$Y_t = P_t^{\xi} \int_0^1 P_{j,t}^{-\xi} Y_{j,t} dj$$

$$\left[\int_0^1 Y_{j,t}^{\frac{\xi-1}{\xi}} dj \right]^{\frac{\xi}{\xi-1}} = P_t^{\xi} \int_0^1 P_{j,t}^{-\xi} Y_{j,t} dj$$

where the price for the final good can be written as:

$$P_t = \left[\int_0^1 P_{j,t}^{1-\xi} dj\right]^{\frac{1}{1-\zeta}}$$

Intermediate goods production sector

Next, we describe the behaviour of intermediate goods sector producers. Each intermediate good j is produced by only one firm using the following production function:

$$Y_{j,t} = A_t K_{j,t}^{\alpha} L_{j,t}^{1-\alpha} - \Phi$$

where Φ are fixed costs, assumed to be a constant. The introduction of fixed costs in the production function implies that the technology shows increasing returns to scale. If we assume that $\Phi = 0$, then we would be in the case of constant returns to scale.

Intermediate goods producers solve a problem in two stages. In the first stage, firms determine the optimal price of the goods they produce and the quantity they produce. In the second stage, firms take as given the prices of production factors: wages, W_t, and the capital rental rate, R_t, and determine the amount of labor and capital to be hired in order to minimize costs.

For the behavior of monopolistic firms, we first solve the second stage to determine the amount of factors to be hired, and then solve the first stage to determine the price of the differentiated good.

Second Stage

The second step consists in solving:

$$\min_{L_{j,t},K_{j,t}} Cost = W_t L_{j,t} + R_t K_{j,t} \tag{12.18}$$

subject to the following technology:

$$Y_{j,t} = \left\{ \begin{array}{ccc} A_t K_{j,t}^{\alpha} L_{j,t}^{1-\alpha} - \Phi & if & A_t K_{j,t}^{\alpha} L_{j,t}^{1-\alpha} > \Phi \\ 0 & & Otherwise \end{array} \right\} \tag{12.19}$$

The auxiliary Lagrangian function corresponding to this problem is:

$$\min_{L_{j,t},K_{j,t}} Cost = W_t L_{j,t} + R_t K_{j,t} + \lambda_t \left[Y_{j,t} - A_t K_{j,t}^{\alpha} L_{j,t}^{1-\alpha} + \Phi \right]$$

First order conditions are given by:

$$\frac{\partial Cost}{\partial L_{j,t}} : W_t - \lambda_t (1-\alpha) K_{j,t}^{\alpha} L_{j,t}^{-\alpha} = 0 \tag{12.20}$$

$$\frac{\partial Cost}{\partial K_{j,t}} : R_t - \lambda_t \alpha K_{j,t}^{\alpha-1} L_{j,t}^{1-\alpha} = 0 \tag{12.21}$$

The Lagrange parameter associated to the technological restriction represents the shadow price of change in the ratio of use of capital and labor services. This means that the Lagrange parameter measures the nominal marginal cost, cm_t, and therefore, first order conditions for the minimization problem can be defined as:

$$W_t = cm_t (1-\alpha) K_{j,t}^{\alpha} L_{j,t}^{-\alpha} \tag{12.22}$$

$$R_t = cm_t \alpha K_{j,t}^{\alpha-1} L_{j,t}^{1-\alpha} \tag{12.23}$$

By solving for the amount of productive factors, we get:

$$L_{j,t} = cm_t (1-\alpha) \frac{Y_{j,t}}{W_t} \tag{12.24}$$

$$K_{j,t} = cm_t \alpha \frac{Y_{j,t}}{R_t} \tag{12.25}$$

By combining the above expressions we obtain the standard relationship between capital and labor:

$$W_t L_{j,t} = R_t K_{j,t} \frac{(1-\alpha)}{\alpha} \tag{12.26}$$

Finally, substituting both expressions in the production function, we arrive to:

$$Y_{j,t} = A_t \left(cm_t \alpha \frac{Y_{j,t}}{R_t} \right)^{\alpha} \left(cm_t (1-\alpha) \frac{Y_{j,t}}{W_t} \right)^{1-\alpha} \tag{12.27}$$

and rearranging terms results:

$$Y_{j,t} = A_t cm_t \alpha^{\alpha} (1-\alpha)^{1-\alpha} R_t^{-\alpha} W_t^{\alpha-1} Y_{j,t} \tag{12.28}$$

From that expression we can obtain the marginal cost for each firm producing the intermediate goods:

$$cm_t = \frac{1}{A_t}\left(\frac{1}{\alpha}\right)^{\alpha}\left(\frac{1}{1-\alpha}\right)^{1-\alpha} R_t^{\alpha} W_t^{1-\alpha} \tag{12.29}$$

As can be observed, the marginal cost does not depend on each firm, but it is the same for all monopolistic firms producing the intermediate goods. This is explained by the fact that they share the same technology, are subject to the same technological shocks and that the prices of the production factors are also the same.

The marginal cost represents the cost, relative to each production factor, of producing an additional unit of the intermediate goods. This means that the marginal cost can be calculated either in terms of labor services or in terms of capital services. Substituting the expression for the marginal cost in, for example, the first order condition for capital we obtain:

$$cm_t = \frac{1}{A_t}\left(\frac{1}{\alpha}\right)^{\alpha}\left(\frac{1}{1-\alpha}\right)^{1-\alpha}\left(\frac{\alpha}{1-\alpha}\frac{W_t L_{j,t}}{K_{j,t}}\right)^{\alpha} W_t^{1-\alpha}$$

and operating results:

$$W_t = cm_t (1-\alpha)\frac{Y_{j,t}}{L_{j,t}} \tag{12.30}$$

If we repeat the above operation, but now using the first order condition for labor, we find that:

$$cm_t = \frac{1}{A_t}\left(\frac{1}{\alpha}\right)^{\alpha}\left(\frac{1}{1-\alpha}\right)^{1-\alpha}\left(\frac{1-\alpha}{\alpha}\frac{R_t K_{j,t}}{L_{j,t}}\right)^{1-\alpha} R_t^{\alpha}$$

and operating results:

$$R_t = cm_t \alpha \frac{Y_{j,t}}{K_{j,t}} \tag{12.31}$$

First Stage

In the first stage, the monopolistic firm determines the optimal price for the intermediate good they produce. The profit maximization problem to be solved is the following:

$$\max_{P_{j,t}} \Pi_{j,t} = P_{j,t}Y_{j,t} - W_t L_{j,t} - R_t K_{j,t} \tag{12.32}$$

Substituting into the profit expression the demand function of the intermediate good obtained above from the maximization problem for the representative firm in the final good sector, the profit maximization problem can be written as:

$$\max_{P_{j,t}} \Pi_{j,t} = P_{j,t}P_{j,t}^{-\xi}Y_t - W_t L_{j,t} - R_t K_{j,t} \tag{12.33}$$

Moreover, given the price of the production factors solved in the second stage, expressions (12.30) and (12.31), we obtain that:

$$W_t L_{j,t} + R_t K_{j,t} = cm_t(1-\alpha)\frac{Y_{j,t}}{L_{j,t}}L_{j,t} + cm_t\alpha\frac{Y_{j,t}}{L_{j,t}}L_{j,t} \tag{12.34}$$

resulting in:

$$W_t L_{j,t} + R_t K_{j,t} = cm_t(1-\alpha)Y_{j,t} + cm_t\alpha Y_{j,t} = cm_t Y_{j,t} \tag{12.35}$$

Under the assumption of constant returns to scale (i.e., average cost is equal to marginal cost), the above maximization problem can be defined as:

$$\max_{P_{j,t}} \Pi_{j,t} = P_{j,t}P_{j,t}^{-\xi}Y_t - cm_t Y_{j,t} \tag{12.36}$$

or alternatively:

$$\max_{P_{j,t}} \Pi_{j,t} = P_{j,t}P_{j,t}^{-\xi}Y_t - cm_t P_{j,t}^{-\xi}Y_t \tag{12.37}$$

First order conditions are given by:

$$\frac{\partial \Pi_t}{\partial P_{j,t}} : (1-\xi)P_{j,t}^{-\xi} + \xi cm_t P_{j,t}^{-\xi-1} = 0 \tag{12.38}$$

Solving yields:

$$(1-\xi) = -\xi cm_t P_{j,t}^{-1} \tag{12.39}$$

and thus, the price of the intermediate goods is given by:

$$P_{j,t} = \frac{\xi}{\xi - 1} cm_t \tag{12.40}$$

where $\frac{\xi}{\xi-1}$ is the mark-up, representing the difference between the price and the marginal cost, which is assumed to be greater than 1. If $\xi = \infty$, the model converges to the standard case of perfect competition.

If we assume that all intermediate producer firms are identical and normalizing the price of the final good to 1, we obtain:

$$cm_t = \frac{\xi - 1}{\xi} \tag{12.41}$$

where marginal cost is below unity, given that $\xi > 1$.

Equilibrium of the model

The equilibrium of the model economy is given by the combination of first order conditions for the firms and first-order conditions for consumers. Combining expressions (12.30), (12.31) and (12.41), we arrive at the two fundamental equations that characterize this DSGE model with monopolistic competition, where the price of production factors is given by.

$$W_t = (1 - \alpha)\frac{\xi - 1}{\xi} A_t K_{j,t}^{\alpha} L_{j,t}^{-\alpha} \tag{12.42}$$

$$R_t = \alpha \frac{\xi - 1}{\xi} A_t K_{j,t}^{\alpha - 1} L_{j,t}^{1-\alpha} \tag{12.43}$$

Finally, given that all firms are identical and they hire the same amount of labor and capital by unit of output, we can just cancel the subscript j from the above expressions, arriving to the following two new equilibrium equations:

$$W_t = (1 - \alpha)\frac{\xi - 1}{\xi} A_t K_t^{\alpha} L_t^{-\alpha} \tag{12.44}$$

$$R_t = \alpha \frac{\xi - 1}{\xi} A_t K_t^{\alpha - 1} L_t^{1-\alpha} \tag{12.45}$$

In summary, the final structure of the model economy with monopolistic competition is similar to the standard neoclassical DSGE model, except for the equilibrium conditions for the wage and the capital rental rate. Once the price of the productive factors has been settled, equilibrium conditions for households are the following:

$$\frac{C_t}{1-L_t} = \frac{\gamma}{(1-\gamma)}(1-\alpha)\frac{\xi-1}{\xi}A_t K_t^{\alpha} L_t^{-\alpha} \tag{12.46}$$

$$\frac{C_t}{C_{t-1}} = \beta\left[\alpha\frac{\xi-1}{\xi}A_t K_t^{\alpha-1} L_t^{1-\alpha} + 1 - \delta\right] \tag{12.47}$$

This set of equations, together with the feasibility condition, defines the equilibrium of the economy.

Equations of the model and calibration

The equilibrium of the model economy is given by a set of eight equations, corresponding to the endogenous variables, Y_t, C_t, I_t, K_t, L_t, R_t, W_t and the variable representing total factor productivity, A_t, which is assumed to be endogenous by assuming that it follows an autoregressive process of order 1. This set of equations is the following:

$$\frac{1-\gamma}{\gamma}\frac{C_t}{1-L_t} = (1-\alpha)Y_t/L_t \tag{12.48}$$

$$\frac{C_t}{C_{t-1}} = \beta[\alpha Y_t/K_t + 1 - \delta] \tag{12.49}$$

$$Y_t = C_t + I_t \tag{12.50}$$

$$Y_t = A_t K_t^{\alpha} L_t^{1-\alpha} \tag{12.51}$$

$$K_{t+1} = (1-\delta)K_t + I_t \tag{12.52}$$

$$W_t = (1-\alpha)\frac{\xi-1}{\xi}\frac{Y_t}{L_t} \tag{12.53}$$

$$R_t = \alpha\frac{\xi-1}{\xi}\frac{Y_t}{K_t} \tag{12.54}$$

$$\ln A_t = (1-\rho_A)\ln\overline{A} + \rho_A \ln A_{t-1} + \varepsilon_t \tag{12.55}$$

Table 12.1: Calibrated parameters

Parameter	Definition	Value
α	Technological parameter	0.350
β	Discount factor	0.970
γ	Preferences parameter	0.400
δ	Physical capital depreciation rate	0.060
ξ	Elasticity of substitution between differentiated goods	5.000
ρ_A	TFP autorregressive parameter	0.950
σ_A	TFP standard deviation	0.001

The set of parameters to be calibrated are the following:

$$\Omega = \{\alpha, \beta, \delta, \gamma, \xi, \rho_A, \sigma_A\}$$

Table 12.1 shows the values of the calibrated parameters. The only additional parameter to be calibrated with respect to the basic model is ξ, i.e., the elasticity of substitution between differentiated goods, which reflects the market power of firms producing intermediate goods. This is equivalent to giving a value to the mark-up for the price of goods over the marginal cost of production. In the literature we find a number of works that aim to estimate this mark-up for the U.S. economy. For example, Hall (1988) estimated a mark-up value of 1.8, which implies an elasticity of substitution between differentiated goods of 2.25 ($\xi/(\xi-1) = 1.8$, $\xi = 1.8/0.8 = 2.25$). Rotemberg and Woodford (1992) use a mark-up value of 1.2 ($\xi = 6$). In general, we find values, either estimated or calibrated, for the mark-up between 1.1 and 1.8, corresponding to values of the elasticity of substitution between differentiated goods between 11 and 2.25. In our case we will use a value of 5 for the elasticity of substitution, equivalent to a mark-up of 1.25.

Table 12.2 shows the computed steady state values for the variables of the model. At the steady state, the level of consumption would be about 82% of total output, while saving would be the remaining 18%. We find now that production is 0.635, a lower value than that obtained in a competitive setting (see Table 2.2). This lower level of production in the steady state is a result of the inefficiencies generated by the monopolistic competition environment. The capital/output ratio is now around 3, so the accumulated capi-

Table 12.2: Steady State values

Variable	Value	Ratio to $\overline{Y}$
$\overline{Y}$	0.63595	1.000
$\overline{C}$	0.51845	0.816
$\overline{I}$	0.11750	0.184
$\overline{K}$	1.95834	3.079
$\overline{L}$	0.34706	-
$\overline{R}$	0.09092	-
$\overline{W}$	0.95384	-
$\overline{A}$	1.00000	-

tal is lower than that obtained in a perfect competition setting. This lower steady state value for physical capital is explained by the lower profitability of capital, which reduces savings. This applies also to the labor factor, as the wage is lower under monopolistic competition. As a consequence, hours worked are also lower than those obtained in the standard model.

Total Factor Productivity Shock

Finally, we study the effects of an aggregate productivity shock in a context of monopolistic competition. In qualitative terms, the effects are similar to those obtained in a competitive environment, although we observe important differences in quantitative terms. In general, we find that the effects over the variables of this technological shock are smaller on impact under monopolistic competition than under perfect competition, since inefficiencies produced by imperfect competition come into play, reducing the effects of the productivity shock.

The implications of monopolistic competition comes directly from the price of production factors. In this environment, the equilibrium prices for labor and capital are lower than their marginal productivity. The higher the market power of monopolistic firms, the higher the mark-up, and thus, the greater the difference between the marginal productivity of inputs and their prices. This is a direct consequence on the assumption that the elasticity of substitution between differentiated goods is strictly greater than unity. In this context, a shock to the marginal productivity of production factors

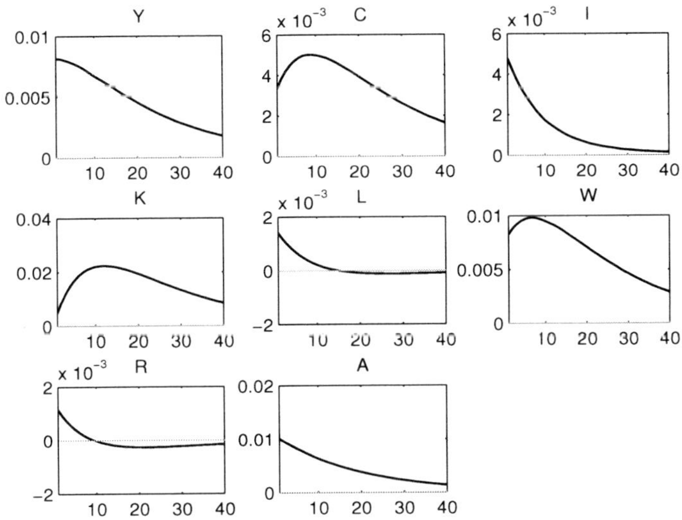

Figure 12.1: TFP shock with monopolistic competition

leads to a lower reaction of both wages and the rental rate of capital compared to a competitive environment. As a result, the owners of production factors will perceive a lower effect from the productivity shock.

Figure 12.1 shows the responses of the model variables to a positive productivity shock. It can be observed how both the wage and the real interest rate increase at a lower rate because they are not reflecting all of the increase occurring in the marginal productivity of labor and capital, as would be the case in a competitive environment. As a result, the impact of a productivity shock on investment, consumption and output, are quantitatively reduced

Conclusions

This chapter presents a prototype imperfect competition DSGE model. Imperfect competition is one of the key elements of New Keynesian DSGE models, in which a number of (nominal and real) rigidities and market failures are considered as fundamental ingredients to explain the dynamics of an economy. The usual way to introduce imperfect competition in DSGE modelling is to assume monopolistic competition in the production and/or input markets. Here we consider imperfect competition in the production sector.

The direct consequence of monopolistic competition is that the price of production factors is lower than its marginal productivity, due to the existence of a mark-up derived from monopolistic competition. The deviation from a competitive environment leads to an inefficient allocation of production factors, resulting in a lower equilibrium level of output for the economy, and lower effects from a productivity shock.

The key question here is how important are, at an aggregate level, the deviations from a perfect competitive environment for a particular economy.

Appendix A: Dynare code

The Dynare code corresponding to the model in this chapter, named *model12.mod*, is the following:

```
// Model 12:  Monopolistic Competition
// Dynare code
// File:  model12.mod
// José L. Torres.  University of Málaga (Spain)
// Endogenous variables
var Y, C, I, K, L, W, R, A;
// Exogenous variables
varexo e;
// Parameters
parameters alpha, beta, delta, gamma, zhi, rho;
// Calibration
alpha = 0.35;
beta = 0.97;
delta = 0.06;
gamma = 0.40;
zhi = 5.00;
rho = 0.95;
// Equations of the model economy
model;
C=(gamma/(1-gamma))*(1-L)*(1-alpha)*Y/L;
1 = beta*((C/C(+1))*(R(+1)+(1-delta)));
Y = A*(K(-1)^alpha)*(L^(1-alpha));
K = (Y-C)+(1-delta)*K(-1);
```

```
I = Y-C;
W = (1-alpha)*((zhi-1)/zhi)*A*(K(-1)^alpha)
    *(L^(-alpha));
R = alpha*((zhi-1)/zhi)*A*(K(-1)^(alpha-1))
    *(L^(1-alpha));
log(A) = rho*log(A(-1))+ e;
end;
// Initial values
initval;
Y = 1;
C = 0.8;
L = 0.3;
K = 3.5;
I = 0.2;
W = (1-alpha)*Y/L;
R = alpha*Y/K;
A = 1;
e = 0;
end;
 // Steady state
steady;
// Blanchard-Kahn conditions
check;
// Disturbance analysis
shocks;
var e; stderr 0.01;
end;
// Stochastic simulation
stoch_simul;
```

Bibliography

Blanchard, O. and Kiyotaki, N. (1987): Monopolistic competition and the effects of aggregate demand. *American Economic Review*, 77(4), 647-666.

Canzoneri, M., Cumby, R. and Diba, B. (2005): Price and wage inflation targeting: Variations on a theme by Erceg, Henderson and Levin. In Orphanides, A and Reifscheneider, D. (eds.), *Models and monetary policy: Research in the Tradition of Dale Henderson, Richard Porter and Peter Tinsley*. Washington, Board of Governors of the Federal Reserve System.

Christiano, L., Eichenbaum, M., and Evans, C. (2005): Nominal rigidities and the dynamic effects of a shock to monetary policy. *Journal of Political Economy*, 113(1), 1-45.

Dixit, A. and Stiglitz, J. (1977): Monopolistic Competition and Optimum Product Diversity. *American Economic Review*, 67(3), 297-308.

Hall, R. (1988): The relation between price and marginal cost in the U.S. industry. *Journal of Political Economy*, 96(5), 921-947.

Mankiw, N.G. (1985): Small menu costs and large business cycles: A macroeconomic model of monopoly. *Quarterly Journal of Economics*, 100, 529-539.

Rotemberg, J. (1982): Monopolistic price adjustment and aggregate output. *Review of Economic Studies*, 49(4), 517-531.

Rotemberg, J. and Woodford, M. (1992): Oligopolistic pricing and the effects of aggregate demand on economic activity. *Journal of Political Economy*, 100(6), 1153-1207.

Rotemberg, J. and Woodford, M. (1997): An optimization-based econometric framework for the evaluation of monetary policy. *NBER Macroeconomics Annual*, 12, 297-346.

Smets, F. and Wouters, R. (2007): Shocks and frictions in US business cycles: a Bayesian DSGE approach. *American Economic Review*, 97(3), 586-606.

Svensson, L. (1986): Sticky goods prices, flexible asset prices, monopolistic competition and monetary policy. *Review of Economic Studies*, 53(3), 385-405.

Index

CPSIA information can be obtained at www.ICGtesting.com
Printed in the USA
BVOW01s0834160816

459172BV00003B/42/P

9 781622 730247